S0-AHT-795

PN   Ogilvie, Mardel   FT. CROCKETT
4162   Communication Skills;
.035   Voice and Pronunciation.

PN   Ogilvie, Mardel   FT. CROCKETT
4162   Communication Skills:
.035   Voice and Pronunciation.

89011787

THE DAVID GLENN HUNT
MEMORIAL LIBRARY
WITHDRAWN
GALVESTON COMMUNITY COLLEGE
GALVESTON, TEXAS

COMMUNICATION SKILLS:
VOICE AND PRONUNCIATION

DAVID GLENN HUNT
MEMORIAL LIBRARY
GALVESTON COLLEGE

COMMUNICATION SKILLS: VOICE AND PRONUNCIATION

MARDEL OGILVIE
Herbert H. Lehman College
of the City University of New York

NORMA S. REES
Hunter College
of the City University of New York

McGraw-Hill Book Company
New York, St. Louis, San Francisco,
London, Sydney, Toronto,
Mexico, Panama

DAVID GLENN HUNT
MEMORIAL LIBRARY
GALVESTON COLLEGE

COMMUNICATION SKILLS: VOICE AND PRONUNCIATION

Copyright © 1969 by McGraw-Hill, Inc. All rights reserved. Printed in the United States of America. No part of this publication may be reproduced, stored in a retrieval system, or transmitted, in any form or by any means, electronic, mechanical, photocopying, recording, or otherwise, without the prior written permission of the publisher.

Library of Congress Catalog Card Number 74-84404

47626

1 2 3 4 5 6 7 8 9 0   MAMM   7 6 5 4 3 2 1 0 6 9

ACKNOWLEDGMENTS

Marchette Chute, "Spring Rain" © 1946 from AROUND AND ABOUT by Marchette Chute. Published 1957 by E. P. Dutton and Company, Inc. Reprinted with their permission.

Silvia Wright, selection from "Dear Fiduceary Trust Company" from "Dear Fiduceary Trust Company", *Harper's Magazine,* Vol. 215 (July, 1957) page 27. Reprinted by permission of *Harper's Magazine.*

Sara Teasdale, "Night" from COLLECTED POEMS by Sara Teasdale, © 1930 by Sara Teasdale Filsinger, renewed 1958 by the Guaranty Trust Company of New York. Reprinted with permission of The Macmillan Company.

Herbery Asbury, selection from "The Spectators Make Way for the Fireman" from THE GANGS OF NEW YORK: AN INFORMAL HISTORY OF THE UNDERWORLD by Herbert Asbury. © 1927. Reprinted with permission of Alfred A. Knopf, Inc.

Jules Henry, selection from "Learning in Schools" from "American Schoolrooms: Learning the Nightmare" by Jules Henry. Columbia University Forum, VI (Spring, 1963).

Don Marquis, "The Tom Cat" from THE AWAKENING AND OTHER POEMS by Don Marquis. © 1917 by Sun Printing and Publishing Association. Reprinted by permission of Doubleday and Company, Inc.

Robert Frost, "Dust of Snow" from COMPLETE POEMS OF ROBERT FROST. © 1923 by Holt, Rinehart and Winston, Inc. Copyright renewed 1951 by Robert Frost. Reprinted by permission of Holt, Rinehart and Winston, Inc.

Amy Lowel, "The City of Falling Leaves" from MEN, WOMEN AND GHOST, from COLLECTED POEMS OF AMY LOWELL. By permission of Houghton, Mifflin Company, Boston.

Charles K. Thomas, The Ten Major Regional Speech Areas (Map), Figure 4. From AN INTRODUCTION TO THE PHONETICS OF AMERICAN ENGLISH, 2/e. by Charles K. Thomas. © 1958. Reprinted with permission of The Ronald Press Company, New York.

J. S. Bigelow, "The Bat and The Scientist" from *The Atlantic Monthly,* Vol. 211, June 1963. By permission of J. S. Bigelow.

Edward Weeks, selection from "The Paripatetic Reviewer" from *Atlantic Monthly,* Vol. 212, June 1963. Reprinted with the permission of Edward Weeks.

J. B. Priestley, "The Right Accent!" from The *New York Times Magazine,* May 2, 1954. © by The New York Times Company. Reprinted by permission.

Peter Denes and Elliot N. Pinson, THE SPEECH CHAIN, Figure 3.11. Reprinted with permission of Bell Telephone Laboratories, Inc.

Ogden Nash, selection from "Curl Up and Diet" © 1935 by Ogden Nash. Originally appeared in *The New Yorker* in 1935. From VERSES FROM 1929 ON by Ogden Nash. Reprinted with permission of Little, Brown and Company.

Ogden Nash, "Song of the Open Road," from VERSES FROM 1929 ON by Ogden Nash. Reprinted with permission of Little, Brown and Company.

Rachel Carson, selection from UNDER THE SEA-WIND. Reprinted with permission of Oxford University Press.

Cornelia Otis Skinner, selection from "I Keep Hearing Voices" from BOTTOMS UP! By Cornelia Otis Skinner. Reprinted with permission of Dodd, Mead & Company.

Charles W. Morton, selection from "The Peanut Butter World". *The Atlantic Monthly,* April, 1963. Reprinted by permission of *The Atlantic Monthly.*

James Stephens, selection from "A Rhinoceros, Some Ladies, and a Horse," from JAMES, SEUMAS AND JACQUES: Unpublished Writings of James Stephens, edited by Lloyd Frankenburg. Reprinted with permission of The Macmillan Company.

Langston Hughes, "Buddy" from MONTAGE OF A DREAM DEFERRED by Langston Hughes. © 1951. Reprinted by permission of Harold Ober Associates, Inc.

Robert Frost, "Fire and Ice" and selection from "The Hardship of Accounting," from COMPLETE POEMS OF ROBERT FROST. © 1923 by Holt, Rinehart and Winston, Inc. © 1936 by Robert Frost. © renewed 1951 by Robert Frost. © renewed 1964 by Lesley Frost Ballantine. Reprinted by permission of Holt, Rinehart and Winston, Inc.

Wallace Stevens, selection from "Thirteen Ways of Looking at a Blackbird," from COLLECTED POEMS OF Wallace Stevens. © 1923. Reprinted with permission of Alfred A. Knoph, Inc.

Wallace Stevens, selection from THE POEMS OF OUR CLIMATE by Wallace Stevens. Reprinted with permission of Alfred A. Knoph, Inc.

Frank Sullivan, selection from SURPRISE! Reprinted with permission of Little, Brown and Company.

PREFACE

GALVESTON COMMUNITY COLLEGE LIBRARY

The purposes of this text are (1) to give you information and practice material which will help you to establish standards of voice and patterns of pronunciation, (2) to help you understand how to modify the use of your vocal mechanism to achieve the type of vocal attributes you desire, and (3) to aid you in articulating sounds and pronouncing words in a way satisfactory to you for even the most formal occasion.

As the authors have written this text, they have kept in mind that language is a living, constantly changing tool of communication. What is an acceptable pronunciation among the educated, socially advantaged today may not have been acceptable a few years ago. Furthermore, what are acceptable patterns of speech in one situation may not be acceptable in other situations: A pronunciation which attracts attention in one community may not even be noted in another. A particular vocal quality in one social set may indicate that you "belong"; in another, it may indicate that you are an outsider. The authors, therefore, assume that after you have learned more about this living language from these pages, after you have consulted with your instructor concerning the desirability of particular changes in your voice and pronunciation, and after you have trained yourself to listen carefully and accurately to the voices and pronunciations of the educated in your community, you will make value judgments of your own on the acceptability of certain vocal attributes and pronunciations. You will decide whether changes are necessary for the image you wish to portray to your listeners and whether you will make the changes in all or only in some situations. This text emphasizes a descriptive rather than a prescriptive approach to the study of spoken language.

The authors believe that you must learn to use your newly acquired voice and pronunciation patterns in everyday communication. The authors do not think that saying a sound in a list of words or even in a word in a sentence is enough. Consequently, you will find topics of conversation which emphasize particular sounds and readings which other students have enjoyed. The authors hope that you will maintain your new patterns even when your interest in what you are saying is intense. But above all, they hope that you will speak in a manner that enhances the image of yourself you wish to portray.

The authors have enjoyed teaching voice and pronunciation and believe that most students have found the courses interesting and profitable. They wish to share with you—teacher and students—some of the inherent excitement in this area.

We are indebted: to Dr. Arthur Bronstein and Dr. Beatrice Jacoby for sharing their knowledge of phonetics and voice science; to Dr. Harvey Halpern for his generous assistance in offering constructive criticism in the sections on voice; and to Dr. John Newman and Mr. Lawrence Raphael for their helpful guidance in the section on pronunciation.

We acknowledge obligation to Raymond Rees and Albert Abrams for preparing the illustrations and to Mrs. Alta Bogardus and Mrs. Frances Pine for their careful typing of the manuscript.

We are especially grateful to the late Dr. C. K. Thomas for his unusually careful, perceptive, and scholarly critique of the section on pronunciation.

We should also like to express appreciation to our students of many years who have helped us develop and refine our approaches and techniques for the improvement of voice and pronunciation.

Finally, we are indebted to the proprietors of the copyrighted materials which are reprinted with their permission in this book and to whom acknowledgment is made elsewhere.

MARDEL OGILVIE
NORMA S. REES

CONTENTS

PREFACE		v
PART ONE	Introduction	
CHAPTER ONE	The Speaker and the Listener	3
PART TWO	Producing an Effective Voice	
CHAPTER TWO	Analysis of Vocal Characteristics	19
CHAPTER THREE	Production of Voice	31
CHAPTER FOUR	Pitch and Pitch Variations in the Effective Voice	41
CHAPTER FIVE	Loudness Factors in the Effective Voice	55
CHAPTER SIX	Quality Factors in the Effective Voice	66
CHAPTER SEVEN	The Time Factor in Effective Speaking	88
PART THREE	Acquiring Effective Pronunciation	
CHAPTER EIGHT	Standards of Speech	105
CHAPTER NINE	Analysis of Sounds of American English	116
CHAPTER TEN	Stops	129
CHAPTER ELEVEN	Fricatives and Affricates	140
CHAPTER TWELVE	Nasals, Lateral, and Glides	163
CHAPTER THIRTEEN	Front Vowels	193
CHAPTER FOURTEEN	Central Vowels	207
CHAPTER FIFTEEN	Back Vowels	213
CHAPTER SIXTEEN	Diphthongs	224
PART FOUR	Using Effective Voice and Pronunciation in Communicative Situations	
CHAPTER SEVENTEEN	Pronunciation of Words	237
CHAPTER EIGHTEEN	Integrating the Factors of Voice and Pronunciation in Communication	243
INDEX		267

COMMUNICATION SKILLS:
VOICE AND PRONUNCIATION

PART ONE

Introduction

CHAPTER ONE

The Speaker and the Listener

In the classroom, you interact with a variety of instructors. You may hear but pay little heed to a professor whom you perceive as a "verbal lightweight," as a "turned-on," facile, unscrupulous propagandist, or as an egotistical self-proclaimed authority. On the other hand, you react vigorously to the Shavian scholar who during the term has become an important figure in your realm. You note that he is brilliant, intelligent, and exciting, that, humane, he has a fey sense of humor, that he is serious about developing an appreciation of Shaw's contributions to today's theater, and that he invites opposition but demands that you give a probing appraisal or reappraisal of your own viewpoints. In such instances you are being influenced by your perception of the speaker. In Aristotle's time, this perception was labeled *ethos*. Today you find it labeled *source credibility* or *source image*.

This example illustrates aspects of human communication involving interactions among speakers, messages, and listeners. Many proclaim that the message is *the influential* link in human communication. Again and again you hear, "It is *what* you say that is important, and not *how* you say it." Teachers of speech insist and have always insisted that the speaker have ideas of consequence to impart. Plato, Aristotle, and Cicero, among the earliest of all teachers of speech, stressed the need for a knowledge of arts and sciences.

Yet because of the reaction of that destination unit, the listener, *what* you say cannot be divorced from *how* you say it. Your listener must understand and appreciate your ideas. When he thinks you are angry, he may discount part of what you say. When he believes you are timid, he may question your motives. But when he perceives you as a confident, mature man or woman of good will, he will listen thoughtfully and appreciatively. The perception of the manner of your speaking by your listener affects his reception of your ideas. The listener's reaction provides feedback for you on the reception of your ideas. In summary, then, human communication involves a source unit, or speaker; a message; and a destination unit, or listener.

This text is primarily concerned with certain aspects of the interaction between the speaker and the listener. The speaker transmits his message over simultaneous channels of interpersonal communication: (1) speech, including the sounds produced by the vocal and articulatory mechanism; (2) gesture, posture, and facial expression, including all the nonspeech movements of the body of the speaker; and (3) manipulation of the environment outside the body, including the use of pictures or objects in a meaningful way.

The vocal signals the speaker uses and the listener hears make up the first of these simultaneous channels. These vocal signals possess two aspects: linguistic and nonlinguistic. The linguistic signals involve those vocal-auditory features which contribute to the formal message, such as the phonemic structure of the particular code which is the spoken language. For example, the phonemic contrast between the initial sounds in *pat* and *bat* is an instance of the phonemic structure of spoken English. The nonlinguistic features involve those vocal-auditory variables which convey information to the listener about the speaker. For instance, when William Buckley appears in a television interview, the listener may conclude that he is educated, superbly well controlled, somewhat condescending, an Easterner, and quite formal in a relaxed sort of way. The listener's evaluation of these factors helps to establish the *ethos,* or *source image,* of the speaker, which plays a major role in the *how* of the reception of the message.

FACTORS AFFECTING NONLINGUISTIC COMMUNICATION

In nonlinguistic communication, certain factors are relevant to the effective interaction of the speaker and listener. For educated listeners to interact effectively with a speaker—to attend wholeheartedly and to respond to his message—the speaker must be intelligible, must be perceived as having at least an adequate self-concept, must portray emotion acceptable to the listener's interpretation of the message, must appear cultured, and sometimes must even appear to belong to the "in" social group. Often region also influences the interaction, for some listeners look on one regional dialect with more favor than others. Lastly, the assessment of the formality of the speaking situation by the speaker has an impact on the listener. Do the speaker and the listener agree or disagree on this assessment?

INTELLIGIBILITY

For a listener to understand a spoken message readily, the degree of loudness of the speaker's voice must be related to the needs of the particular situation, his pronunciation must be clear and acceptable to the listener, and his intonation must be appropriate to the message.

The effective speaker, adjusting his volume to the situation, uses a loud voice in an auditorium or at an out-of-doors gathering (unless a public-address system is available) and a quiet voice in a library. Whereas teachers and pupils in a classroom facing a busy thoroughfare speak loudly, they speak softly in the school's broadcasting station. Sometimes speakers achieve special effects by modifying their volume in unexpected ways: A teacher gains the attention of a noisy group by using a quiet voice. A diminutive woman married to a large strapping husband and with four husky sons makes herself heard in her household of booming voices by "just whispering." When the speaker's voice, however, is too soft for the circumstances of his environment, his listener, missing some of the message, often stops attending to it.

The pronunciation factor involves the speaker's use of conventional speech sounds uttered in conventional combinations—words, phrases, and sentences. If the listener is to recognize the combinations readily and to approve them, the speaker's sounds must be similar to the listener's and must be articulated distinctly. When the speaker produces sounds carelessly, when he runs sounds together excessively, when he substitutes, omits, or reverses sounds, his listener may not understand him easily. Or when, because of his geographic origin, he says "dahg" /dɑg/ where the listener expects to hear "dawg" /dɔg/, the speaker's pattern may momentarily distract the listener. When, suffering from a severe cold, he distorts the nasal consonants /m/ and /n/ in "My name is Norman," producing "By dab is Dorbad," the listener is again distracted.

The speaker's conventional use of rate and intonation contributes greatly to his intelligibility. In situations where hearing is difficult, such as at a large and noisy party, listeners get cues from the speaker's rhythm which help them to distinguish between "Will you have another sandwich?" and "I haven't seen Mary all evening." The ambiguity of a sequence like "She is unhappily married" is resolved for the listener when the speaker uses the intonation appropriate to "She is unhappily married" or "She is, unhappily, married." Much of the difficulty in understanding the speaker from a foreign country comes from his use of unexpected patterns of intonation.

CONCEPT OF SELF

Effective interaction in terms of the speaker, the message, and the listener takes place between and among persons whose self-concepts are at least adequate or at best highly positive (those who perceive themselves as liked, wanted, acceptable, and able). These are people who have confidence in themselves, their ideas, and the products of their work. The voice that gives this impression is clearly audible, with a steady rhythm, with a rate slow enough for easy comprehension but varied so as to express enthusiasm and vigor, with an appropriate pitch and intonation pattern, and with a strong resonant quality.

One aspect of having a positive self-concept is the expression of warmth and friendliness to others, for the person with a positive self-concept feels at one with a large number of persons of all kinds and varieties. He works hard at making others understand him and at understanding others. The voice of this warm, friendly individual, flexible in pitch and loudness, indicates that the speaker has heard the previous comment, values its worth, and anticipates a reaction.

Ineffective communication occurs between and among persons with negative self-concepts. Various perceptions of the speaker result. Among them are three frequent ones: First, the effect of the speaker on the listener may be one of lack of self-confidence—of timidity, shyness, and insecurity. This effect is partly produced through a combination of vocal features. The pitch may be too high or may lack appropriate variations, so that the result is either monotonous or singsong; the rhythm may be unsteady or faltering; the rate may be too rapid or perhaps too slow; the quality may be thin or breathy or, on occasion, husky or nasal. Such vocal features have an overriding effect on the words of a particular message; they may qualify or even negate the words. Or they create an impression that the speaker would rather not talk or that he is talking to himself rather than to a listener. Second, the speaker may appear *too* self-confident. This kind of speaker seems to be overly aggressive, autocratic, bragging, or dogmatic. He appears to have so much confidence in his ideas that the listener rejects them, fearing that the confidence has no real basis. After all, nobody could be *that* good. Again, voice plays an important role: This speaker, typically using too loud a voice and aptly called a "loudmouth," seems to try to shout everyone else down. He may speak rapidly, with exaggerated variations in pitch; he may sound harsh or gruff; sometimes he may force his pitch too low in trying to sound authoritative. Third, the speaker may sound unfriendly to the listener. This speaker's voice is often monotonous, with a narrow pitch range. As a result, the listener believes the speaker is bored, tired, or perhaps distracted. His face and voice may be almost masklike. He does not respond to the ideas of others. Little or no effective interaction between speaker and listener takes place in any of these three instances.

Your concept of yourself at a particular time leaves its imprint not only on your voice but also on your pronunciation. When you perceive yourself as college-educated, well controlled, stable, and somewhat precise, you may well use the traditional acceptable speech of the community and, in addition, you may articulate your sounds very carefully. When you perceive yourself as college-educated, friendly, outgoing, and liberal in outlook, you may well use the acceptable speech of the community but you may not articulate your sounds as carefully as the somewhat precise person. Furthermore, you may use many of the variant pronunciations used less frequently by the educated and run together many more words than this somewhat precise person. When you perceive your-self as a scared rabbit, you may speak so rapidly that you slur over many of your sounds; your articulation may even sound slovenly to the listener. Your concept of yourself, reflected in your pronunciation pattern, affects the interaction be-tween you and your listener.

EMOTION

"Don't speak to me in that tone of voice" implies that the speaker is conveying an unmistakable impression of his feeling at the moment. *What* is said does not disturb the listener as much as *how* it is said. Although the listener may not be able to analyze the objectionable "tone of voice," he is sure of its meaning; he can even mimic the tone while relating the incident. Through his voice, the speaker is clearly revealing his emotional state. Just as the eyes are windows to the soul, the voice is the soul's loudspeaker. Starkweather emphasizes the reve-lation of emotion through voice:

> We hear angry argumentative voices from another room. We hear an edge of irritation in the voice of a salesclerk beset by too many demanding customers. We hear resignation in the voice of a bus driver who asks passengers to move to the rear. We hear excite-ment in the voice of the child at Christmas. Regardless of what a speaker conveys through his choice of words, his emotional state is often indicated by the way in which he speaks. The sounds of a speaker's voice, his vocal behavior, can carry information about his personality, his mood, and his present state of functioning. As listeners, we frequently interpret the same words differently when they are spoken in one or another tone of voice.[1]

Elsewhere Starkweather reports research showing that judges listening to speech which has been altered to eliminate the meaningful content are often able to identify the speaker's emotion or the strength of his feeling. He con-cluded that the listeners attended to aspects of pitch, rate, volume, and other features to make their judgments.[2]

Similarly, emotion affects pronunciation. A speaker becoming more and more dogmatic articulates his sounds with increased vigor. He stresses more of the vowels in syllables and separates more words and phrases with almost imper-ceptible pauses than he would if he were exchanging pleasantries with a neighbor. Or a speaker, becoming flustered and anxious, speaks faster and faster, articu-lates his sounds less and less clearly, so that the listener labels his speech "mumbling."

---

[1] John A. Starkweather, "Measurable Dimensions of Vocal Behavior," unpublished paper presented at a meeting of the American Association for the Advancement of Science, Denver, Colo., 1961.

[2] John A. Starkweather, "Variations in Vocal Behavior," in D. M. Rioch (ed.), *Disorders in Communication*, The Williams & Wilkins Company, Baltimore, 1964, pp. 424–429.

CULTURAL GROUP

Vocal and pronunciation characteristics exist on all kinds of local cultural and subcultural levels. The influence of the traditions of the social group on the speaking voice is always important. When a listener says, "She has a voice like a fishwife's," what does he mean? He means that the speaker does not belong to the "best people," that she is "not one of us." Bernard Shaw's Liza Doolittle took speech lessons from Professor Higgins because she believed she was doomed to be a flower girl forever unless she learned to speak like a lady; the before-and-after speech of the actress who plays Liza shows a marked change not only in articulation but also in voice—from a nasal, shrill quality to a gentle, ladylike tone of pleasing resonance and elegant intonation. Thus the voice reflects the social group to which the speaker belongs.

Similarly, the influence of the tradition of the social group on pronunciation is strong. If you have grown up among people who use cultivated pronunciation patterns, you are apt to use similar patterns. But if you have grown up where most of the inhabitants say "acrost," you are likely to possess the same pattern. Young men and women often change their social group by moving from a lower-class to an upper-class neighborhood, for Americans are noted for their upward mobility. To belong to the new group, these men and women sometimes adopt its pronunciation patterns. Vance Packard notes a difference in upper-class and middle-class vocabulary: The middle class sit on a davenport, wear a formal gown or tuxedo, and greet a newcomer with "Pleased to meet you," whereas the upper class sit on a sofa, wear a long dress or a dinner jacket, and greet a new friend with "Hello."[3] Similarly, pronunciation patterns often suggest different social classes.

Tom Wolfe[4] in two humorous articles comments satirically on the voices and pronunciations of certain groups on different cultural levels in New York City. He tells about New York's near but not quite elite who are "Pucci'd" and "Gucci'd" up to their temporal fossae, Pucci in the dress, Gucci in the shoes and handbags. These Pucci-Gucci girls are striving hard to pick up the key principles of voices heard at status luncheons: the nasality, the languor, the oiliness. He writes of the "dah-ling" voice, a "languid, weak baritone not a man's voice, you understand, but a woman's"[5] and of the pronunciation: dropping r's, as in dahling.

He contrasts this group with the truly elite who possess New York's wealth and position—the Bobby Kennedy's, Huntington Hartford, Averill Harriman, Nelson Rockefeller, John Lindsay, Henry Morgenthau. He mentions the nasality, the monotony, the delicacy, and the weakness of the voices of this group. He points to the difficulties some of them encounter as political orators, noting that Bobby Kennedy's voice turned shrill as he orated from a rostrum, that Rockefeller

[3] V. Packard, The Status Seekers, Pocket Books, Inc., New York, 1961, p. 124.

[4] Tom Wolfe, "Dah-ling! Your Honk Is Slipping," New York, vol. 1, p. 42, April 15, 1968. (Marshall Berger served as consultant for this article.)

[5] Ibid.

gradually coarsened his voice for public appearance. He calls Rockefeller's voice an "upper-class voice with a knish in it."[6]

Wolfe also considers other segments of the social continuum. He exemplifies with: "So I says to my brudd'n'law, 'Awriiiide, so whaddya wan me to do,' I says to him. . . ."[7] He also exemplifies the left of the middle of the continuum (the lower-middle-class girl) with: " 'Oh Mr. Steiiiiin, I had such a foiiiiin toiiiim,' pronouncing the *i* as if she has wrapped it around a Clorox bottle."[8]

Walter Loban, recognizing the influence of subcultures on speech, emphasizes the need for socially acceptable speech: "Even in an open society such as ours, however, where individual worth and aspiration are intended to count for more than fortunate or unfortunate birth, language still operates to preserve social class distinctions and remains one of the major barriers to crossing social lines."[9] He goes on to say that children need to perfect or acquire the prestige dialect— not because standard English is correct or superior in itself but because society exacts severe penalties from those who do not speak it.

REGION

Kenneth Goodman points out that the socially acceptable speech mentioned by Loban varies from region to region and that no dialect of American English has ever achieved the status of some imaginary standard which is correct everywhere and always. He writes:

> It is obvious that a teacher in Atlanta, Georgia, is foolish to try to get her children to speak like cultured people in Detroit or Chicago. . . . Cultured speech, socially preferred, is not the same in Boston, New York, Philadelphia, Miami, Baltimore, Atlanta, or Chicago. The problem, if any, comes when the Bostonian moves to Chicago, the New Yorker to Los Angeles, the Atlantan to Detroit. Americans are ethnocentric in regard to most cultural traits, but they are doubly so with regard to language. Anybody who doesn't speak the way I do is wrong. A green onion is not a scallion. I live in Detróit not Détroit. I can carry my books to work but not my friends. *Fear* ends with an *r* and *Cuba* does not. Such ethnocentrisms are unfortunate among the general public.[10]

You, too, may have personal prejudices about regional speech. If you have grown up in Cleveland, you may like the way Clevelanders speak. If you have grown up in Atlanta, you may be partial to the Atlanta brand of Southern speech.

---

[6] *Ibid.* p. 43.

[7] Tom Wolfe, "You and Your Big Mouth: How the Honks and Wonks Reveal the Phonetic Truth about Status," *New York*, vol. 1, p. 60, April 8, 1968.

[8] *Ibid.,* p. 61.

[9] Walter Loban, "Teaching Children Who Speak Social Class Dialects," *Elementary English*, vol. XLV, p. 593, May, 1968.

[10] Kenneth S. Goodman, "Dialect Barriers to Reading Comprehension," in Eldonna L. Evertts (ed.), *Dimensions of Dialect*, National Council of Teachers of English, Champaign, Ill. 1967, p. 41.

If you have grown up in New York City, you may enjoy the way John Lardner extols the virtues of New York City speech:

> I've noticed that out-of-town mothers make a certain amount of clamor about the danger that the children brought up in New York will acquire "New York accents." At its thickest the so-called New York accent is no worse than the flattened vowels of New England, the goitrous intonations of upstate New York and the near middle West, or the treacle of the South. (As regards New York idiosyncracies, I've known Tennesseans who said "goil" and "woild" as firmly as any Brooklyn native.)[11]

On the other hand, Labov reports a quite different attitude of most New Yorkers toward the speech of New York City:

> When most New Yorkers say that outsiders dislike New York City speech, they are describing an attitude which is entirely their own—New Yorkers show a general hostility toward New York City speech which emerges in countless ways.[12]

He goes on to say that the term *linguistic self-hatred* is not too extreme to apply to the situation which emerged from his interviews.

Attitudes today toward regional speech are more tolerant than formerly. J. B. Priestley, decrying the need for candidates for commissions in the Royal Navy to possess "Oxford" speech, says: "The great mistake and I cannot say if the Admiralty made it or not is to confuse a sensible, local accent with really bad slovenly speech. For the latter I hold no brief whatsoever."[13]

Priestley's point is well taken. Speech should serve the purpose of communication. When slovenly or unacceptable pronunciation interferes with effective communication, it should be eliminated. The man who says *t* and *d* for *th*, *dint* for *didn't*, *prespiration* for *perspiration*, and *drownded* for *drowned* appears uncultivated. Variant pronunciations, however, which reflect educated regional speech are acceptable. Although at one time in England a more or less single acceptable standard of speech existed, you now hear a variety of regional dialects in the House of Commons. Similarly, you hear a variety in the United States Congress. Thus our attitudes have changed toward regional speech. Both in England and in America, educated speech which does not arouse strong feeling in any class of society, which is clear and audible, and which serves the purpose of communication effectively is accepted speech, regardless of its regional variations.

Whatever your attitudes toward regional speech, the regions where you have lived make a difference both in your voice and in your pronunciations. The perceived rate of speaking, the particular vowels used, the rhythm and intonation

---

[11] John Lardner, "Debate: The Case for Living Here—And the Case for Just Visiting," *New York Times Magazine*, p. 45, April 29, 1956.

[12] William Labov, *The Social Stratification of English in New York City*, Center for Applied Linguistics, Washington, D.C., 1966, p. 488.

[13] J. B. Priestley, "The Right Accent," *New York Times Magazine*, p. 18, May 2, 1954.

patterns differentiate the voice of the educated person of Alabama from that of the educated person of Detroit. Raven McDavid writes:

> For stress and intonation, we are well aware of regional differences. Southerners have a wider interval than Midwesterners between highest and lowest pitch levels, and a greater difference in intensity between strongest and weakest stress. So the Midwesterner feels that Southern speech has a sing-song character, and Southerners feel that Midwestern speech is flat and monotonous. The "southern drawl" is much less a matter of absolute speed than of the prolongation of heavily stressed syllables, with a corresponding relaxation of the weakest stressed ones, so that there is an illusion of slowness even though the tempo may be fast.[14]

Admittedly, in educated speech few absolute differences in pronunciation exist. McDavid points out that conditional differences in the system do occur—noting that many New Yorkers do not distinguish *Hugh* and *you* and that Charlestonians do not distinguish *ear* and *air*. He goes on to note that even if there are no differences in the system of phonemes, there may be differences in the way individual phonemes are pronounced. Here he indicates that there are several varieties of the American /r/, especially after vowels, of the /l/, and of the /aɪ/ in *right* and the /aʊ/ in *out* and *loud*. Lastly, he emphasizes the variations in the incidence of phonemes, where regions differ in the vowel or consonant they choose in a particular word. He exemplifies with the variant pronunciations of *grease* and *greasy* (with an /s/ or a /z/) and with the distinction made by Chicago city people and suburbanites in their respective pronunciations of the name of their city (*aw* /ɔ/ in town, *ah* /ɑ/ outside).[15]

FORMALITY

The degree of formality influences your use of voice and pronunciation. In speaking formally to a large audience, you speak fairly loudly, slowly, and at a somewhat higher pitch. You articulate your sounds clearly. In a job interview, you usually monitor your voice, speaking softly and slowly to achieve an effect of seriousness on the interviewer. Similarly, you use pronunciation which you believe represents a cultured, educated individual. In speaking informally in the dormitory, students speak quickly and use less careful pronunciation and more colloquial vocabulary and construction.

Situations vary widely in their degree of formality. Labov[16] notes that when his subjects in his research answered questions formally recognized as part of an interview, their speech was careful. He explains that this situation was not as formal as a public address and was less formal than the speech which would be

---

[14] Raven I. McDavid, Jr., "Variations in Standard American English," *Elementary English*, vol. XLV, p. 562, May, 1968.

[15] *Ibid.*, pp. 562–563.

[16] Labov, *op. cit.*, p. 92.

used as a first interview for a job but was certainly more formal than casual conversation among friends or family members. The aspects of formality in terms of a continuum from substandard to formal are discussed in Chapter 8.

In summary, your voice and pronunciation, the vocal and articulatory nonlinguistic features of the spoken message, may enhance or detract from your communication of ideas. When your voice and pronunciation make for easy intelligibility, when they convey the impression that your self-image is positive, when they are consistent with the ideas and the feelings of the message you express, and when they do not offend, your listeners are better able to understand the ideas and to react positively to them. Your goal is to achieve habits of pitch, loudness, quality, intonation, stress, and sound production that contribute to your listener's comprehension and foster willingness on his part to accept your ideas.

RESISTANCE TO CHANGE

Because voice and pronunciation patterns are integrated with personality, you may hesitate to modify either. You may say, "Since I have been talking this way all my life, nothing can be done about it." Or when you first become aware of an unpleasant quality in your voice, you may be surprised or even indignant. Your response may be that this is *your* voice and always will be. And your friends and family often support this point of view. They may object to any noticeable change in the way you speak, making such comments as: "It doesn't sound like you. Why don't you be yourself?" "It's not natural." "You sound affected." Consequently, you may resist changing your voice and pronunciation patterns.

Admittedly, your voice and articulation are a fundamental part of your personality. You reveal yourself to others through them. You, perceiving your speech as *you* hear it, believe it makes the desired impression. Often you do not like to entertain the possibility that others' perception of your speech is different from your own. The possibility exists that as the voice and pronunciation patterns change, your listeners' perception of you will change in a way for which neither you nor they are prepared.

A subtler aspect of the resistance to change is that if one is going to change oneself in a basic way, the implication is that the old self was not good enough. You do not object as strongly to a change in appearance—even though you may initially protest against losing weight, adopting a new hair style, wearing contact lenses, or growing a moustache—as you do to changing your voice and speech patterns. When you change your appearance, you and your associates consider the changes as bringing out inherent potential. But when you change your voice and pronunciation patterns, both you and your associates usually consider the change a fundamental one and resist it.

Why, then, overcome this resistance? The improved voice and pronunciation patterns will help you to interact with others effectively. The perception of your speech by others will be positive. When you meet a stranger, your voice and speech patterns will be an asset and not a liability.

PROGRAM OF IMPROVEMENT

You are about to begin a program, under the guidance of your instructor, of evaluating and perhaps changing your voice and pronunciation patterns. What does such a program include? First, it involves your hearing yourself as others hear you. You listen to your voice objectively to evaluate its strengths and weaknesss. Admittedly, your reaction is that of a layman, but it results from your feeling toward your voice. Listening to recordings of your voice as a conversationalist helps you in this first step. Listening to the voices of others is also of some assistance, for you may hear in them what you like or dislike in yourself. This listening makes use of feedback in monitoring your own voice.

To help you listen to the positive and negative effects of voice on communication, the authors have devised the following exercises:

1   While visiting a local supermarket, listen to the conversations around you. Pick out and describe the voices of persons you would prefer not to know. Try not to be unduly influenced by content of speech, manners, or dress.
2   Listen to a conversation when you cannot hear the words spoken but when you can hear the voices, such as when people are talking in the next room. Decide on the emotional tone. Can you determine whether the speakers are calm, angry, enthusiastic, tired? How?
3   Go to the department store in your community which sells the most expensive merchandise, and then go to the store which sells "bargain" merchandise. Compare the voices of the salesclerks and the customers in the two situations. Could you determine which store you were in by listening to voices alone? How?

Second, you will listen carefully to how you and others utter sounds and how you combine them into words and phrases. Again, the speaker uses feedback in listening to his product. In this process, basic to understanding the nature of acceptable speech and to evaluating your own pronunciation patterns, you listen to the sound forms of a word or phrase and forget the spelling forms. You believe that you know how to "sound out" words, for in oral reading you have been "sounding out" words for a long time. But you have been listening for the meanings of words and phrases. You must now listen for the sounds that they contain. For example, you find out how *status, research,* or *intelligentsia* is pronounced. You learn that context influences the pronunciation of sounds. Compare the pronunciation of *but* in each of the following sentences:

But is spelled b-u-t.
I'll go, but I don't think I'll participate.

Usually you will hear different pronunciations of the vowel in *but* in the two sentences.

Thus, you break down the word or phrase into sounds. You must not only be aware that you have difficulty in pronouncing a certain word, but you must also know exactly which sound is inaccurate. You must, therefore, be able to isolate single sounds. To help you listen to sounds, the authors have devised the following exercises:

1   Pick out the word where the vowel in the accented syllable has a different pronunciation from the other three:
   a.   team, believe, inn, ski
   b.   imp, women, strip, yield
   c.   any, says, led, rays
   d.   cook, should, wood, cup
2   Pick out the words in the following list which contain the /s/ sound: aisle, slip, caps, women's, shirt, face. Pick out the words in the following list which contain the /f/ sound: enough, cough, though, fan, finish, fore. Select the words in the following list which contain the /z/ sound: zoo, pads, bids, zone, maize, azure. Pick out the words in the following list which contain the /t/ sound: tease, capped, cracked, then, bottle, Thomas.
3   Indicate how many sounds exist in these words: ring, salmon, laugh, half, lesson. Make each of the sounds of these words separately.
4   List ten words with the sound /o/ as in *coat*, with /i/ as in *tree*, and with /e/ as in *tray*.
5   Utter the following words individually: go, to, the, store. Notice the changes in pronunciation when you speak these words as a sentence. Do the same with:
   a.   Five and six are eleven.
   b.   I have to be there at eight.
   c.   Let us get a coke.
6   First isolate the vowel in each of the italicized words. Then find a word that possesses the same vowel.
   a.   The *length* does not *vary very* much.
   b.   The *wrong room.*
   c.   The *fifth psalm.*

Third, with your instructor's help, you will listen to find out specifically what in your own voice and pronunciation patterns adds and detracts from your communication. Furthermore, as the instructor criticizes unacceptable sounds of other members of the class, you often can identify them in yourself. At this point you may discover that many of your favorite friends, idols, and even members of your own family do not have as effective a voice or as acceptable pronunciation patterns as you previously believed. You may tend to become overly critical of the voice and pronunciation of all speakers. But you will be providing yourself with voice and pronunciation patterns against which you can match your own.

Fourth, you will proceed from a body of knowledge which you will study. To know how voice is produced helps you to correct vocal difficulties. To know how a sound is made assists you in making the sound accurately. To know about facets of pronunciation aids you in learning to pronounce words acceptably. You sometimes have to decide which voice, which articulation of a sound, or which pronunciation of a word or phrase you prefer. You base these decisions more wisely on current information about the processes of oral language than on unsubstantiated opinion.

Fifth, you will learn with the help of your instructor to use your voice or to make certain sounds or combinations of sounds differently. You will practice this work faithfully—first in designated exercises, then in readings, and finally in conversation. Sometimes the breakdown may be even finer. For example, you may have to learn to make /s/ in isolation, then in nonsense syllables, then in words, then in phrases, then in reading selections, and finally in conversation. Your degree of awareness must be somewhat consistent, for you must continue to monitor your voice and pronunciation and to incorporate the changes you deem advisable in everyday conversation. At first, your speech may be overly careful as a result of the acquisition of new patterns, but these patterns will quickly become assimilated into new habits.

You cannot improve your speech all at once. Your instructor will suggest which aspect to attack first. Sometimes you attack voice; sometimes you attack the sound easiest to change; sometimes, that which makes the most difference in your communication; sometimes, that which brings multiple results. Consistently, however, you must continue to monitor both voice and pronunciation to make sure that you are incorporating the improved voice and pronunciation patterns in your everyday speech.

PART TWO

Producing an Effective Voice

CHAPTER TWO

Analysis of Vocal Characteristics

In your efforts to achieve a more effective voice, you must be able to identify vocal characteristics and to recognize their acceptable and unacceptable limits. What vocal characteristics are appropriate to the age, sex, and physical makeup of the speaker? What vocal variables give the impression of friendliness or unfriendliness and of self-confidence or lack of it? How does your own voice fall short of effectiveness?

The human voice is but one instance of the phenomenon of sound. An understanding of how sound is produced, transmitted, and perceived provides a framework for the study of voice.

THE NATURE OF SOUND

Sound may be defined in two ways:

1   Sound is the sensation perceived by the ear.
2   Sound is the propagation through air of waves set up by a vibrating body.

Thus far, the authors have been considering vocal sound in terms of the first definition, that is, from the standpoint of the listener and his perceptions. The second definition emphasizes the physical event that results in sound. Consider the old philosophical dilemma: If a tree falls in the forest where there is no one to hear it, does it make a noise? According to the first definition, the answer is *no*; according to the second, *yes*.

Throughout this chapter and those that follow, both definitions of sound apply. Useful and accurate analysis of voice rests on an understanding of the characteristics of the physical event resulting in voice as well as on its perception by the human ear. The following material on the characteristics of sound begins with an explanation of the physical aspects and proceeds to a discussion of how listeners perceive these physical aspects.

ONSET AND TRANSMISSION OF SOUND

The change from silence to sound is based on a change in the physical environment from rest to motion. A force applied to a body sets that body in motion. Although various motions are capable of producing sound, the kind of sound most pertinent to this discussion is that produced by the regular, periodic movement known as *vibration*.

Vibration occurs when the equilibrium of an elastic body is disturbed so that it oscillates regularly and alternately in opposing directions. The body's *elasticity* is its property of tending to spring back to its resting position after the force which sets it in motion has been removed. This elasticity, or resilience, is one of two essential characteristics of any medium producing or transmitting vibrations. The other essential characteristic of a vibrating body is *inertia*. Inertia is the tendency of a body to remain in its condition of rest or motion unless and until some opposing force acts to change that condition.

Figure 1 shows the effects of elasticity and inertia on the motion of a taut string. The string, when plucked, is displaced from its resting position to position *A*. The string springs back to its resting position because of its elasticity but continues to move to position *B* because of its inertia. At this point the string's elasticity opposes further motion away from the resting position and the movement of the string is reversed. The process continues as the string again overshoots the resting position in the direction in which it is traveling. The alternating oscillation around the resting position illustrated by the taut string is periodic vibration, the basis of sound. Other familiar examples of vibrating bodies at the source of sound are tuning forks, violin strings, and the tightly stretched skins of drums.

When some energy or force disturbs the equilibrium of a potential sound source, periodic vibration begins. Striking a tuning fork against a hard surface sets the prongs into vibration; pulling a bow across a violin string or plucking it with a finger activates the string; hitting a drum skin with a drumstick sets the drum skin in motion. In these instances energy is applied to the vibrating body, setting the body in motion but allowing it to maintain its natural period and rate of oscillation. This vibration is known as *free vibration*. But when the energy

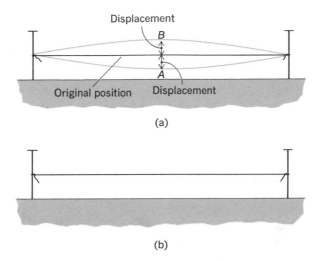

FIGURE 1.   A taut string (a) in vibration and (b) at rest.

applied is itself an oscillating motion, the vibrating body takes on the rhythm of that motion; this vibration is known as *forced vibration*. An example of forced vibration occurs when the hilt of a vibrating tuning fork is placed against a flat board to increase the tone's audibility. The board then vibrates with the same rhythm as that of the tuning fork.

In addition to the vibrating body and the energy applied to set it in motion, a third element is essential to sound production: a medium for the transmission of vibration. This medium must itself consist of matter capable of vibration. The most familiar example of such a medium is air.

The vibratory movements of air particles form alternating changes of pressure composed of successive *compressions* and *rarefactions*. As the elastic particles of air are displaced by a disturbance among them, they tend to return to their original positions. When, through displacement, some of the air particles are closer together (more dense), *compression* occurs. When the displacement has reached the limit determined by the medium's elasticity, the particles revert toward their resting positions but move beyond those points because of their inertia. At this stage some of the particles are more distant from each other (less dense) than usual, creating an instance of rarefaction.

Transmission of vibration results from such a disturbance of air particles because the motion travels outward from the point where the disturbance first occurs. Note that the motion travels, and not the individual particles comprising the medium. The alternating compressions and rarefactions set up by the particle motion, however, travel outward as displaced particles act to displace still other particles. This motion of air particles is found in a *sound wave*.

The motion of beads on a string stretched between two fixed points illustrates wave movement. If the first bead is pushed so that it strikes the bead next to it,

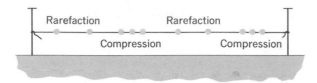

FIGURE 2.   Alternate points of compression and rarefaction at a stage of wave motion of beads on a string.

the second bead will start moving and then strike the third bead. Each bead in turn pushes its neighbor, and if the original force is great enough, the motion will continue to the end of the string although each bead has moved only a fraction of the distance. As the impact of striking causes the first bead to recoil, the first bead reverses its direction and moves back toward its original position on the string. Figure 2 shows alternate points of compression, where some beads are closer together than they were, and of rarefaction, where other beads are further apart than they were. Although air particles do not actually touch one another as do the beads on the illustrative string, the analogy roughly depicts the motion of air particles in a sound wave.

A sound wave may be considered in terms of space, or the distance between one point of compression and the next point of compression (or between one point of rarefaction and the next point of rarefaction) along a plane outward from the original disturbance. This distance is the *wavelength*. A sound wave may also be considered in terms of time, or the number of compressions and rarefactions occurring within a given unit of time. The latter approach provides the basis for the concept of *frequency,* discussed below.

When the study of sound is viewed as a physical event, onset and transmission of sound take place as a force sets in motion a body capable of vibration, which in turn creates waves of alternating pressure in the medium surrounding it. The vibrator, energy for vibration, and medium for transmission of vibration are three essential factors in sound production (see definition 2 on page 19). On the other hand, when the study of sound takes into account how sound is received and interpreted (see definition 1), a fourth factor is added: the listener. The listener determines whether sound is heard at all and, if heard, how it is evaluated and utilized. The listener's hearing acuity permits him to hear or not, depending on the loudness of sound and the environmental listening circumstances. The listener also makes judgments about sounds, such as whether they are pleasant or unpleasant, soothing or frightening, meaningful or unintelligible. When the sound in question is the human voice, the listener's perceptions determine whether the voice contributes to or detracts from the speaker's message.

FREQUENCY AND PITCH
You have already learned that sound waves may be analyzed in terms of spatial relationships, or the distance between one point on a wave and a corresponding

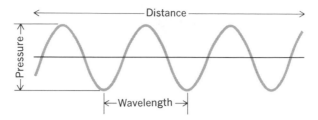

FIGURE 3.   A sine wave expressed in terms of space. The horizontal axis is *distance,* the vertical axis is *degree of pressure.* The latter could also be degree of displacement of the particles from the resting position.

point on the next wave. A diagram of the simplest kind of wave, a sine wave, illustrates the concept of wavelength. Figure 3 shows how a sine wave is made up of periodic alternations of pressure. The crest of the curve corresponds to the compression part of the wave, while the trough corresponds to the rarefaction part of the wave.

Sound waves may be analyzed in terms of time as well as in terms of space. If the horizontal axis in Figure 3 were labeled *time* instead of *distance,* the diagram would illustrate how the sine waves repeat themselves exactly in time. The number of complete waves, or cycles, repeated within a given unit of time is the *frequency* of that vibration. A cycle is a complete vibration, from resting position to maximum displacement in one direction, to maximum displacement in the opposite direction, and back again to resting position. The unit of measurement of time ordinarily is the second. Frequency is thus expressed in terms of cycles per second, or hertz (Hz). This aspect of vibration is illustrated in Figure 4.

The sine waves in Figures 3 and 4 are graphic presentations of the simplest of all sounds having periodicity, known in music and physics as a *pure tone.* The way the wave repeats itself regularly shows its periodicity. Although uncommon in nature, the properties of pure tones are more obvious than those of more complex sounds. Furthermore, complex musical sounds such as those heard in the human voice can be analyzed into the pure tones comprising them.

Since the horizontal axis of a sine wave corresponding to a pure tone may represent either distance or time, it follows that wavelength and frequency are

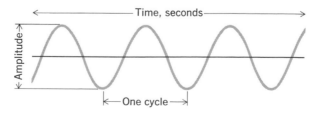

FIGURE 4.   A sine wave expressed in terms of time.

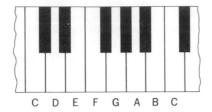

FIGURE 5.   A C scale on a piano keyboard (played on white keys only).

related. The relationship is an inverse one; sound waves of shorter length are higher in frequency. This distance-time relationship permits sound waves to travel through the medium at the same rate regardless of their frequency.

Many investigators have studied how human ears perceive frequency. Researchers have determined that listeners with normal hearing do not perceive frequencies below 16 Hz as tones and do not hear frequencies above 20,000 Hz at all. The perceptual, or psychological, correlate of frequency is *pitch*. The listener's perception of pitch as high or low[1] depends largely on frequency of vibration, although factors of distance, intensity, and resonance also influence perceived pitch. Other things being equal, the faster the frequency of vibration, the higher the pitch of the perceived sound.

Knowing something about the relation of frequency to the musical scale will be helpful when you evaluate the pitch of your own and others' voices. Divisions called *octaves* make up the musical scale. Each octave consists of eight units of this scale. When you sing *do, re, mi, fa, so, la, ti, do*, you are producing an octave segment of the most familiar of all scales, the diatonic major scale. The interval from one step to another in this scale is a whole tone, except between the third and fourth steps (from *mi* to *fa*) and between the seventh and eighth steps (from *ti* to *do*), where the intervals are halftones, or semitones. By convention, the letters A to G name the steps of the scale. The octave scale always begins and ends on the same step letter. Thus, a C octave begins on C and ends on C one octave above. A section of a piano keyboard, shown in Figure 5, illustrates this arrangement.

To the listener, two octave points, such as one C and the next C or *do* at the beginning and *do* at the end of the octave scale, seem alike or corresponding. The mathematical relationship between two octave points is simple to express: The frequency of the vibration at any step of the musical scale is double the frequency of the step one octave below and half the frequency of the step one octave above. To illustrate, if middle C has a frequency of 256 Hz, the C below middle C is at 128 Hz and the C above is at 512 Hz.

The tones on the musical scale correspond to a conventional frequency standard; for example, orchestral instruments are ordinarily tuned so that their A

---

[1]Do not confuse *low* with *soft*; here *low* will always refer to pitch, never to degree of loudness.

above middle C corresponds to 440 Hz. In this system, then, A is always at some integral multiple or division of 440 Hz. The frequencies of the other tones have fixed values on the equally tempered scale used by musicians; their values derive from that point of reference in which A = 440 Hz. On the other hand, the scale from *do* to *do* has only relative values, in that the starting point of *do* may be anywhere on the letter scale of fixed values.

The foregoing discussion has treated tones of the musical scale as if they were pure tones having energy at only a single frequency of vibration. Musical sounds, however, including voice, are not pure tones but complex tones. A complex musical tone consists of a number of component frequencies. The component of lowest frequency, the *fundamental frequency,* ordinarily gives the musical sound its tonal character, interpreted as pitch. The sound waves of complex tones, like those of pure tones, may be represented graphically, as in Figure 6.

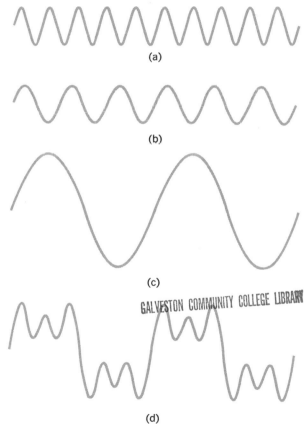

(a)

(b)

(c)

GALVESTON COMMUNITY COLLEGE LIBRARY

(d)

FIGURE 6.   The wave form of a complex musical tone; (*a*), (*b*), and (*c*) are the wave forms of pure-tone components of complex tone (*d*). (Reprinted from Denes and Pinson, *The Speech Chain,* Bell Telephone Laboratories, New York, 1963.)

INTENSITY AND LOUDNESS

Sound waves vary not only in frequency but also in *intensity,* or the magnitude of energy being transmitted. Sound waves are instances of motion; the energy expended in this motion is known as intensity. The intensity of a given sound is based on two aspects of the sound wave. The first, already considered, is the frequency of vibration. The second is the amplitude of vibration, or the maximum displacement of the vibrating particles. Examine Figures 3 and 4 to see how frequency and amplitude are represented on the wave form of a pure tone. Frequency and amplitude together determine intensity because the rate of energy being expended in any activity is made up of the amount of work done and the time taken to do it.

Power is the term familiar to students of physics for work done per unit of time. The intensity of a sound may be expressed in terms of the amount of power transmitted over an area of 1 square centimeter (1 cm^2) at any point along the sound wave. As the distance from the original sound increases, the power of the sound wave decreases. The unit of power is the watt; the number of watts per square centimeter is the intensity of the sound at that point. The power of audible sounds extends over a wide range, with the strongest sound the ear can tolerate being billions of times more powerful than the faintest sound the ear can perceive. To measure such a range in absolute units of power, i.e., watts (or microwatts, since the actual amounts involved are extremely small), would require the use of lengthy figures with many decimal places. It is customary to express sound energy in terms of intensity relative to some other reference intensity. The unit of relative intensity in common use is the *decibel.*

The decibel, then, is a ratio unit rather than a fixed or absolute unit. An example of an absolute unit is an *inch;* the magnitude of an inch does not vary whether you are measuring the height of a heel or the height of a wall. The decibel is a concept more like a *half.* In order to know how much half of something is, you must know its size. A *half* has no fixed value but is relative to the magnitude of the substance under consideration.

One decibel expresses the ratio 1.259 to 1. If the intensity of sound A is 1 decibel (1 dB) greater than the intensity of sound B, sound A is 1.259 more intense than sound B. If we knew the intensity of sound B in watts per square centimeter, to compute the absolute intensity of sound A would be possible. Therefore, to express the intensity of a given sound in decibels relative to a known intensity is convenient. The most commonly used reference intensity is 10^{-16} watt/cm^2. This point, which is roughly the intensity of the faintest sounds human ears can hear, is 0 dB. The intensity of any sound can then be expressed in decibels relative to the known zero reference point. For example, the loudest sound the ear can tolerate is 130 dB.

In practice, sound energy is frequently measured in terms of sound pressure rather than in units of power. The moving particles of sound waves produce measurable pressure variations. The unit of pressure is the *dyne;* measurement of sound pressure is in dynes per square centimeter. Zero decibels relative to sound-pressure level (instead of power) is equivalent to 0.0002 dyne/cm^2.

Another way of showing the relative nature of the decibel is to consider how increases of sound pressure correspond to increases in decibels. If a sound-pressure level of 0.0002 dyne/cm^2 is equivalent to 0 dB of intensity, 0.002 dyne/cm^2 (a tenfold increase in sound pressure) is equivalent to 20 dB and 0.02 dyne/cm^2 (a hundredfold increase in sound pressure) is equivalent to 40 dB.

While intensity, measured in decibels, is the magnitude of sound energy, the magnitude of the sensation perceived at the ear is *loudness*. Although the sensation of loudness depends largely on intensity, the human ear is not equally sensitive to all audible sounds. For example, when a listener with normal hearing compares a 1,000-Hz tone and a 125-Hz tone of equal intensities, the 1,000-Hz tone appears louder. For a given frequency, however, increased intensity produces increased loudness. Although workers in auditory research have used a scale to indicate degrees of loudness, no loudness scale as useful as the one for pitch is available. Subjective factors in listening, then, determine the listener's judgment of loudness level and of adequate and inadequate uses of loudness.

HARMONICS, RESONANCE, AND QUALITY

The kind of motion which produces a pure tone is the simplest form of oscillation: sinusoidal or simple harmonic motion. That the complex tones of voice or music are made up of vibrations at more than one frequency and that the component vibrations may all be sinusoidal in character has already been noted. Musical tones normally are composed largely of vibrations at frequencies which bear a simple mathematical relationship to one another. The components above the fundamental, or lowest, frequency are integral multiples of the fundamental frequency. Such multiples of the fundamental frequency are known as *harmonics*.[2] If a complex tone has a fundamental frequency of 100 Hz, the first harmonic will be at 200 Hz and the second harmonic at 400 Hz. Vibrations at other frequencies above the fundamental may also be present; these vibrations, together with the harmonics, are called *upper partials*. Any complex tone, then, is made up of a fundamental frequency and upper partials. When the tone is musical, there are strong harmonic components. When the tone is a noise, there are strong inharmonic partials.

Complex tones are common because most vibrating bodies exhibit more than one vibration at the same time. (See Figure 6.) A vibrating string, for example, moves as a whole, with segments of the same string simultaneously vibrating independent of the over-all movement. The vibration of the whole string is the slowest and usually also the strongest. The partial, or segmental, vibrations are higher in frequency. If you have ever seen two children turning a jump rope, you may have noticed that the over-all movement from one "ender" to the other is

---

[2] The term *harmonics* is sometimes used interchangeably with the terms *overtones* and *partials*, although in physics and music these words have separate meanings. For further discussion, see I. J. Hirsh, *The Measurement of Hearing*, McGraw-Hill Book Company, New York, 1952.

the largest and slowest movement observable, while smaller portions of the rope may also be in motion. These smaller movements are both weaker and faster than the motion of the rope as a whole.

The complexity of vibrations at the original vibrating body determines in part the composition of a given sound. But another factor affecting the sound is the action of resonating surfaces or chambers modifying the vibrations before they reach the medium of transmission. *Resonance* occurs when a body capable of vibration responds with its own vibration to that of the original source. When the resonator's natural frequency of vibration is the same as that of the vibrator, the resonance is greatest. In many musical instruments, for example, the vibrations from the original source, such as string or reed, must travel through chambers and past other surfaces before being emitted to the air. The resonating surfaces or chambers are set into motion (forced vibration) by the action of the vibrator. Columns of air and flat surfaces are common resonators in musical instruments.

Since the vibrator is expending energy at more than one frequency and since resonators have natural frequencies to which they respond most strongly, the makeup of a particular sound-producing mechanism determines which original vibrations are resonated and which are not. Thus the final sound varies from the vibration at the source. These variations result in the characteristic tones of musical instruments, called *timbre,* and of the human voice, called *quality.*

The various sounds of speech range from the complex, relatively musical sounds of vowels to the somewhat noisy sounds of voiceless consonants. Each conventional sound of the language is readily identifiable because of its characteristic pattern of components. Each vowel, for example, exhibits a predictable pattern of fundamental frequency and emphasized partials. Acoustic analysis shows that concentrated energy is present at frequency levels above the fundamental in patterns typical of each vowel of the language. These levels of frequency prominence, known as *formants,* may be displayed graphically by instrumentation capable of spectrographic analysis. Figure 7 is an example of the spectrogram of the word *see.*

To the listener, the combined factors of harmonics and resonance result in the attribute of sound *quality.* When a violin and an oboe produce tones alike in pitch, loudness, and duration, the differing qualities permit the listener to distinguish easily between the sounds. Similarly, listeners can often identify their acquaintances by voice quality alone.

TIME

Sounds alike in other respects may vary from one another in time. Although this attribute of sound is obvious, students learning to analyze sound sometimes overlook it. From the standpoint of the physical event, the time factor of a sound is its *duration,* or length of vibration.

Auditory research shows that duration of sound affects its perception. Sounds

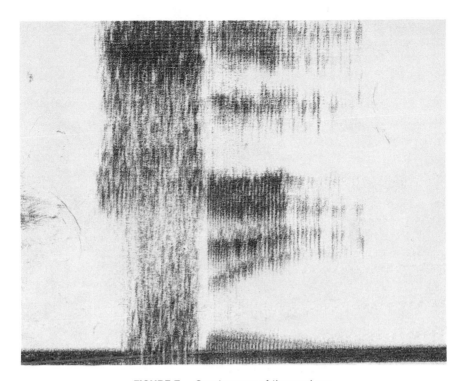

FIGURE 7.   Spectrogram of the word *see*.

must have at least minimal duration in order to be perceived properly. The listener may not hear a sound at all if it is of less than this minimal duration, or he may perceive it as a click even though the vibration has all the properties of a musical sound.

Since sounds ordinarily occur not singly but in series, the listener distinguishes patterns of time allotments as well as the duration of individual sounds. The arrangement of units of sound in a series along the dimension of time is the *rate* and *rhythm* of that series. Rate is measured in number of sound units per given period of time, such as words or syllables spoken per minute. Perception of rate and rhythm depends largely on how these factors interact with other factors of sound production. If the listener is attending to sounds communicating meaning, such as speech or Morse code, time patterns have a crucial effect on intelligibility.

APPLICATIONS TO ANALYSIS OF VOICE

Earlier in this chapter, voice was described as one instance of sound. Voice, therefore, can be analyzed in terms of the variables of frequency, intensity, harmonics, resonance, and time. Listeners perceive voices as different from one another in the corresponding attributes of pitch, loudness, quality, rate, and rhythm. These factors determine whether a voice is an effective instrument for communication or whether it calls attention to itself and inhibits communication of meaning and emotion.

Voices in need of improvement may be deficient in one or more of the perceived vocal attributes. Detailed discussions of each factor and procedures for developing skill in its use follow in the next four chapters.

CHAPTER THREE

Production of Voice

Improving your voice requires at first a conscious awareness of how you use your vocal mechanism based on two factors: your ability to perceive voice objectively and accurately, and your ability to control the vocal mechanism to produce the desired result. These two abilities depend on an automatic control system whereby you adjust your vocal product to match your plans for communication. In such a system, feedback of the product permits you to evaluate and correct your output. Training in perception, or listening, will improve your ability to evaluate the auditory and kinesthetic feedback you receive when producing voice, while a knowledge of the vocal mechanism and how it operates will enable you to make adjustments to achieve the desired product.

MECHANISM FOR PRODUCING VOICE

The physical essentials of sound production, as noted earlier, are a vibrating body, energy for vibration, amplification, and a medium for transmission. In the human sound-producing mechanism, the vocal bands are the vibrating body and the respiratory system provides the energy for vibration.

Air, inhaled through either the mouth or the nose, passes through a chamber common to both mouth and nose, the pharynx. From the pharynx, at a level just below the base of the tongue, the inhaled air passes through a rather firm but elastic tube, the larger upper part of which is the *larynx* ("Adam's apple") and the narrower lower portion, the *trachea* (windpipe). The cartilage tissue of larynx and trachea provides a firmness which permits the airway to remain open under normal circumstances. If you wish to know the texture and behavior of cartilage tissue, bend your outer ear forward and observe how it springs back when you take your hand away.

The trachea divides into two branches: the right and left bronchi. Each of these tubes further subdivides many times, ending in the tiny air sacs of the lungs. Lung tissue is supplied with numerous small capillaries, providing for the interchange between inhaled and exhaled air. (See Figure 8b.)

The cartilages of the larynx form a firm but flexible housing for the vocal bands, which consist of elastic connective tissue stretching across the larynx from front to back and attached to the walls of the larynx by muscle tissue. The vocal bands form a valve midway in the respiratory passageway. When the vocal bands are held in a closed position, the air pressure may be maintained, as in holding the breath, or food may be prevented from getting into the lungs during swallowing. Further, in the closed position, the force of the dammed-up air beneath the bands can be released slowly. In this way, the elastic edges of the bands are set into vibration much as the musician's breath sets the reed of a wind instrument into vibration. If the vibration is fast enough, vocal tone results. (See Figures 3 and 4.)

BREATHING

The human infant begins its breathing career with the birth cry and does not interrupt it until death. Although quiet breathing is automatic and not usually under conscious control, the breathing rhythm is modified consciously for speaking.

THE RESPIRATORY MECHANISM

Inhalation takes place when the previously inhaled oxygen has been consumed to the point where the oxygen level of the blood falls below that necessary for maintaining life. This automatic regulating system, or servomechanism, begins with expansion of the structures surrounding the lungs to allow for expansion of the lungs themselves.

The chamber housing the lungs is the thorax, or thoracic cavity, which comprises most of the upper part of the trunk. It is open above to the upper respiratory passageway. Its walls are the ribs, sternum, and vertebrae of the spinal column; its floor is the diaphragm; the clavicle (collarbone) lies across the top. For the thorax to expand in its capacity requires that the walls move outward and upward and the floor down. Muscle fibers running between and over the ribs contract to lift the entire rib cage. Since the rib cage is widest at the base, the lifting motion also tends to increase the side-to-side dimension of the thoracic cavity. The diaphragm, itself muscle tissue, is capable of contraction. When at rest, the diaphragm is an irregularly dome-shaped structure forming both the floor of the thoracic cavity and the roof of the abdominal cavity. As the diaphragm contracts during inhalation, the dome shape becomes somewhat flattened, with a resulting increase in the area of the thoracic cavity at its base.

This enlargement of thorax allows for the passive expansion of the lungs within. As the area of the lungs increases, the pressure within the body becomes less than that of the external atmosphere. Air then flows by way of mouth or nose through the passageway leading to the lungs until the pressure is equalized. At this point, the inhalation phase is complete.

Exhalation begins with downward and inward movement of the rib cage and relaxation of the diaphragm, which returns to its domelike shape. Since the lungs then must occupy a smaller area, air is forced through the upper respiratory passageway and out through the nose or mouth. The cycle then recurs. (See Figures 8a and 8b.)

The respiratory procedure is modified within the limitations of bodily needs to make phonation, articulation, and the onflowing rhythm of speech possible. The speaker inhales through the mouth as quickly as possible, avoiding an awkwardly long pause each time he needs to replenish his oxygen supply. On the other hand, the exhalation phase is lengthened to suit the speaker's phrasing.

INADEQUATE PATTERNS OF BREATHING FOR SPEECH
Problems of voice related to breathing are usually the result of inadequate control of exhalation rather than a failure to take in sufficient breath. Good breath support for phonation implies not only that the exhaled breath last as long as necessary for meaningful phrasing but also that it remain steady. Poor control of the breath results in breath being wasted before or during speech, insufficient breath being available to complete the phrase, and/or the breath being exhaled in a jerky, irregular fashion.

Breathiness, the audible exhalation of air not used for phonation, results when the speaker emits air from the lungs in greater quantity than necessary for phonation and articulation. This voice quality appears to consist of a kind of whisper combined with a weak vocal tone. In addition, it usually lacks sufficient loudness, because while a relatively large quantity of air is emitted, much of it is wasted. The breathy voice is often labeled childish or immature or is associated with a superfeminine, clinging-vine sort of personality.

When the speaker who expels breath wastefully chooses to speak in long phrases, he finds himself out of breath with several syllables left to say. One resulting pattern is that the speaker utters the last few syllables by "squeezing out" the breath that ordinarily remains in the lungs even after exhalation (residual air), causing the voice to become noticeably strained at the ends of phrases. Sometimes the speaker, anticipating being out of breath before a logical pause, tries to keep ahead of his need for additional breath by speeding up

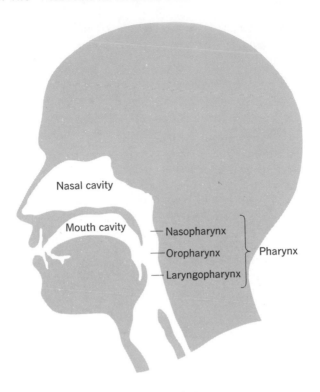

Nasal cavity

Mouth cavity

— Nasopharynx

—Oropharynx   } Pharynx

— Laryngopharynx

FIGURE 8a.   The upper respiratory passageways.

his utterances. This speaker may speak the ends of the phrases so rapidly and softly that he becomes unintelligible; he may even omit the last few words or syllables. He then hurriedly gasps for a new breath, begins the next phrase, and proceeds to race through his remaining words. He appears breathless because of the audible gasps. If you have been described as a breathless or breathy speaker, you should learn to control your breath by using it more sparingly. Some listeners associate breathiness with superficial vivacity; others associate it with nervousness and irritability.

Some speakers emit breath in spurts rather than with smooth control. The resulting voice may be uneven or jerky, with bursts of loudness. Or the speaker may begin every phrase with sudden release of air pressure and concomitant loudness, while his breath and voice fade away rapidly after the first syllable or two. Because of the inconsistent breath support, this speaker's loudness and quality vary unexpectedly and interfere with intelligibility.

IMPROVING BREATH SUPPORT

To develop smooth control of the outgoing breath, you must become consciously aware of the mechanisms involved. One efficient type of breathing emphasizes the use of the large muscles covering the abdominal and visceral area in the

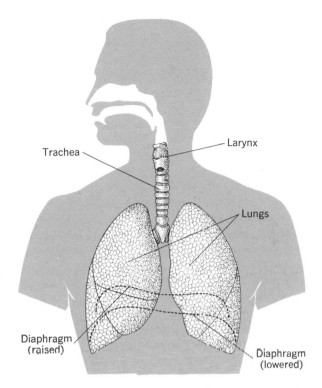

Trachea

Larynx

Lungs

Diaphragm
(raised)

Diaphragm
(lowered)

FIGURE 8b. Respiratory passageways; the larynx, trachea, and lungs.

front of the lower trunk. You can locate this musculature by thinking of how you look when you stand with your best posture. The muscles that you contract when you "pull your stomach in" are the abdominal muscles used in exhalation.

The relationship between the abdominal musculature and the respiratory mechanism described earlier lies in the smooth control of the outgoing breath. You have seen that during inhalation the diaphragm flattens. Since the diaphragm forms the roof of the abdominal cavity, the visceral organs within receive pressure from the lowered diaphragm. These soft organs respond to the pressure by moving against the abdominal wall, causing it to bulge forward and its muscles to relax. On the other hand, the relaxation of the diaphragm to its rounded dome shape during exhalation is essentially a passive movement. This upward movement can be aided indirectly by contraction of the abdominal muscles, pushing the viscera inward and upward to exert pressure on the diaphragm. The diaphragm itself is not under conscious control, so that the layman's expression "breathe from your diaphragm" has little logic. You can, however, exert conscious control to contract the abdominal muscles as gradually and slowly as you wish, thus regulating the rate of flow of breath during exhalation.

Some students accomplish good results by controlling the movements of the lower rib cage. But while there is no conclusive evidence to show that breathing emphasizing movements of the abdominal wall is clearly superior to all other types of breathing, such as those involving the greater activity in the thoracic area, experience shows that abdominal breathing is generally easy to learn and that it brings satisfactory results in terms of improved voice production. Consequently, a procedure for learning abdominal control of breathing for speech follows.

DEVELOPING ABDOMINAL CONTROL OF EXHALATION

1   Breathing exercises are best practiced in a standing, rather than sitting, position. Maintain good posture, with the ears in a vertical line with the shoulders and the heels; try to keep the shoulders down and relaxed, not held back or hunched. Inhale slowly, relaxing the abdominal wall so that it bulges somewhat. If you are unable at first to relax the abdominal muscles during inhalation, you will find it more natural to do so while lying on your back. When you have acquired the feel of the desired movement, return to the standing position. Place your hands against your abdomen; note its pressure on your hands as you inhale. (Tight clothing and belts will hinder this exercise.)

2   With a full supply of inhaled air and the abdomen in its most relaxed and forward position, exhale slowly through the mouth while contracting the abdominal muscles. Use your hands to push in on the abdomen until you are sure of the proper movement. Repeat the inhalation and exhalation slowly, noting that the bodily movement may be the opposite of what you had previously thought correct.

3   Extend the duration and increase the smoothness of the exhaled breath. As you repeat the above exercises, gradually shorten the inhalation phase and lengthen the exhalation phase without changing the direction of the muscular movements.

4   Exhale the breath slowly on a prolonged /s/ sound. If you make the sound so soft that it is barely audible, it will last longer. Time the exhalation using a clock equipped with a second hand; try to increase the number of seconds you can keep /s/ going. If you hear sudden changes in the sound, your exhalation is not smooth. Keep the sound steady by contracting the abdominal muscles smoothly and gradually. Practice until you can sustain an /s/ which is steady but barely loud enough to be heard.

APPLYING CONTROLLED EXHALATION TO VOICE PRODUCTION

1   Repeat exercise 4 above, substituting a comfortably pitched *ah* /ɑ/ for the /s/ sound. Maintain your mouth position and pitch throughout the duration of the sound. Do the same for *mah* /mɑ/. Be sure to use the same abdominal movement as in the previous exercises.

2   Substitute a chant of *mah, mah, mah* for the steady sound. Maintain the smoothness of the abdominal contraction during exhalation. Find out how

many *mah* syllables you can say before you are out of breath, but be sure to stop *as soon as* you feel you are out of breath. Inhale quickly and repeat, trying to increase the number of syllables uttered.

3   Substitute *bah, bah, bah,* then *pah, pah, pah* in the last exercise. Be sure not to waste air on the /p/; say /p/ gently in each syllable.
4   Substitute counting in the same exercise, maintaining a steady pitch, like a chant. Find out how far you can count without running out of breath. Check to make sure you are using abdominal breathing correctly.

The application of good breathing support to the use of your voice does not, of course, end with the mastery of these exercises. Further activities for learning to apply good breathing techniques to speech are in the material to follow in this chapter and in the chapters on pitch, quality, and time.

INITIATION OF TONE

The foregoing procedures are aimed at helping you to develop control over exhalation. You know that the pressure of the exhaled breath against closed vocal bands is the force responsible for the vibration resulting in voice. The moment of change from silence to voice often presents difficulties affecting vocal patterns (refer to Chapter 6). For smooth initiation of tone, there must be sufficient energy to bring about and maintain the closure of the vocal bands, but not more than the task requires. The breath pressure should build up smoothly and coordinate with the closing of the vocal bands. If the vocal bands are closed with more force than necessary, the pressure will be released with a sudden burst. Smooth release of pressure occurs more easily when the speaker has in mind the tone he wishes to produce as he begins to phonate. The voice which results is then planned rather than accidental.

INITIATING TONE SMOOTHLY

1   Be careful to use good breathing techniques and maintain a comfortable pitch throughout these exercises. Phonate on *ah* /ɑ/, listening closely as voice begins. Is there a smooth onset, an almost inconspicuous change from silence to sound? If not, you may hear the glottal attack—a noisy, sharp laryngeal click. Voices which are hoarse or strained or harsh often have conspicuous glottal attacks to initial vowel sounds in speech. Try to eliminate the glottal attack by:
a.   Sighing into the tone.
b.   Yawning into the tone.
c.   Inserting an /h/ before the vowel sound. As you repeat this exercise, try to shorten and weaken the /h/ so that it becomes inaudible. Exercises for applying these techniques for smooth initiation of tone to reading and speaking are found in Chapter 6.

2   In a breathy or weak voice, the tone at its onset may be noticeably breathy due to poor timing of the vocal-band closure. The closure should be made just before the first release of breath. You can learn to feel the tension necessary for closure by sitting on a chair and attempting to lift your body up by pressing your hands down on the sides of the seat. The vocal bands will close to maintain the air pressure in the lungs needed for the lifting activity. Or you can accomplish the same result in a standing position by facing a wall and pushing yourself away vigorously with your hands. When you have the feel of vocal-band closure, repeat the lifting or pushing activity while simultaneously producing the ah /ɑ/ sound. Repeat the exercise without the associated physical activity of lifting or pushing, making sure that closure precedes phonation. This exercise may produce an exaggeratedly strong closure at first.

3   Learn to "think" the tone before you produce it. Using the sustained ah /ɑ/ again, choose a comfortable pitch mentally and attempt to produce it accurately. Avoid trial-and-error phonation, in which you slide up or down to the pitch desired. Repeat the exercise several times, changing the pitch slightly each time but not attempting any very low or very high pitch. If your sense of pitch is unreliable, ask your instructor or another student for help.

RELAXATION AND TENSION

The problems associated with initiation of tone are closely related to the comparative tension or relaxation of the vocal mechanism. The balance between relaxation and tension of any bodily function under conscious control is a delicate one. You may think of relaxation as desirable and of tension as undesirable. Yet if you were completely relaxed, you could not sit, stand, or even hold your head up.

To achieve balance between tension and relaxation in bodily posture, the muscles needed to keep the body erect and in motion should be in use while all other muscles are relatively relaxed. When too much muscular tension characterizes posture, the body seems constantly poised for movement; when too much relaxation characterizes posture, the body seems limp and unresisting to the pull of gravity. The student of voice production must discover the necessary amount and kind of muscular tension of the vocal mechanism while at the same time eliminating any superfluous tensions that complicate and distort voice production.

The overly tense speaker is more common in our society than the overly relaxed speaker. Hypertension is apparent in tight, hunched posture, rapid and abrupt movements, immobile jaw and lips, rapid or staccato speech, and harsh, strident, nasal, or hoarse voice. Insufficient tension is apparent in flabby, slouched posture, lethargic movements, slow rate of speech, and weak, breathy, or denasal voice.

ACHIEVING A BALANCE BETWEEN RELAXATION AND TENSION

1   Review the section on abdominal breathing and assume the proper posture. Stand erect, with shoulders comfortably *down*. The head should be in the same line as the body, with the chin neither thrust forward nor tucked in forcibly against the neck. The strong muscles at the back of the neck, not the muscles running from the face down through the throat, should be used to hold the head up. You can check on the relaxation of throat muscles by observing yourself in a mirror and feeling the muscles with your fingers. Remember that tense muscles feel hard to the touch and bulge visibly; relaxed muscles feel soft and are not conspicuously visible through the skin. Learn to sit with the same erect but relaxed posture. Pay special attention to the way you hold your head in a sitting position.

   The wrong clothing may handicap good posture as well as good breathing habits. Tight, uncomfortable clothing and even ill-fitting or high-heeled shoes inhibit relaxation. Dress comfortably when doing these exercises.

2   Breathing for speech implies its own pattern of necessary muscular tensions. The abdominal breathing technique outlined earlier brings the focus of muscular tension down to the large, strong muscles of the abdomen and away from the upper chest, throat, and face. The overly tense speaker finds that the combination of good posture and abdominal breathing helps to relax hypertense musculature around the throat. The limp speaker achieves greater strength in speaking by using the same procedures. Review the section on abdominal breathing to remind yourself of the desirable pattern of tension and relaxation of the abdominal wall. The relaxed shoulders and upper chest should remain *down* during both inhalation and exhalation.

3   The lips, tongue, and jaw should also be relatively relaxed during phonation. Control of lips and tongue is discussed later in the chapters on voice quality and pronunciation.

   a.   Observe whether your lower jaw is sufficiently relaxed by opening your mouth for *ah* /ɑ/ and then wiggling the jaw from side to side. Place your thumb under your chin to see whether you can feel a hard, bulging muscle. If so, try to relax that area consciously. Chewing gum, or even pretending to chew, often achieves quick results in relaxing tense jaw muscles.

   b.   Having achieved a relaxed jaw in the open position, phonate on *ah* /ɑ/ and sustain the tone to see whether you can maintain the muscle relaxation under the jaw. Keeping your tongue flat on the bottom of the mouth will help.

   c.   Phonate on *ah* /ɑ/ and sigh slowly down from a high to a low pitch within your own range. Keep the jaw relaxed; hold your thumb under your chin to observe any quick tightening of the muscles.

   d.   Gently say, "Oh, my!", using a wide pitch variation from high to low. Observe whether your jaw is still relaxed.

   e.   Repeat with "Oh, well", "Oh, no!", "Why not?".

4   Combine the techniques of relaxation with good posture and effective breathing while reading aloud the following sentences and passages:

   a.   I've been feeling sleepy all day.
   b.   A long, soaking bath will make you feel better.
   c.   I think I'll just curl up with a good book.
   d.   The weary traveler trudged slowly home.
   e.   Where never is heard a disparaging word
        And the skies are not cloudy all day.
   f.   He was despised and rejected,
        A man of sorrows and acquainted with grief.

New Testament

   g.   Come unto him, all ye who labor,
        Come unto him, ye who are heavy laden,
        And he will give you rest.

New Testament

LISTENING AND OBSERVING

1   Investigate the types of breathing used by your friends and members of your family. Do you notice any differences in breathing when you compare men, women, and children?

2   Wriggle into your tightest piece of clothing. Notice how you can fasten buttons or zippers more easily after you have exhaled fully, not after taking a breath. Relate this observation to abdominal breathing.

3   Watch the breathing movements of an operatic singer. The special needs for breath support will make the bodily movements conspicuous.

4   Compare the number of syllables you can say when speaking the same words loudly and then softly.

5   Listen to your voice in tense states such as anger and fear. Say: "Stop that this minute!" "If you don't leave, I'll call the police!" "Get out of the way of the truck!" "Did I really deserve an F on that paper?"

6   Tighten the fist of your right hand. Notice how the left hand becomes tense also. Pound your fist on the table. Note how your jaw tightens and how you tend to clench your teeth. These examples show how muscular tension spreads from one part of the body to another.

CHAPTER FOUR

Pitch and Pitch Variations
in the Effective Voice

The attribute of sound known as *frequency* to the physical scientist and inter-preted as *pitch* by the listener contributes conspicuously to the variations among voices. As a listener, you often make rapid and confident assumptions about the speaker based on his use of pitch. For example, when you hear a relatively high-pitched voice at the other end of the telephone, you may say, "Is your mother at home?" Or when you talk at length about your skin-diving hobby, your date's low-pitched, monotonous "How fascinating!" suggests her boredom.

Effective use of pitch level and pitch variation is one of the speaker's tools for conveying meaning and feeling accurately and for obtaining the desired response. To learn to control your use of pitch, you need to know how the physiological mechanism for pitch operates and how to identify appropriate and inappropriate uses of pitch.

THE MECHANISM FOR PITCH

Vocal pitch is the perceived result of the rate of vibration of the vocal bands. When the vocal bands vibrate faster, the fundamental frequency increases and the perceived pitch of the tone is correspondingly higher. Conversely, when they vibrate more slowly, the fundamental frequency decreases and the perceived pitch is correspondingly lower. Two factors combine to determine the rate of vibration of the vocal bands: (1) the elasticity of the vocal bands, and (2) the force of air pressure below the vocal bands. Increasing either the tension of the vocal bands or the air pressure results in higher frequencies of vibration.

Although laryngeal structure varies somewhat from person to person, the individual speaker can, within limits, modify the rate of vibration of his vocal bands. The positions of laryngeal cartilages in relation to one another are highly variable because of the complexity of their muscular attachments. By adjusting muscular contractions, the speaker produces changes in elasticity of the vocal bands which permit them to vibrate over a wide range of frequencies. At the same time, the speaker can vary the degree of force of air pressure against the vocal bands. Increasing the air pressure beneath the vocal bands causes them to vibrate faster and the pitch to rise.

Thus, an individual can vary his vocal pitch. Among speakers, however, obvious differences in pitch exist that correspond in part to individual differences in laryngeal structure. Vocal bands vary in the degrees of elasticity they can achieve. The thinner vocal bands of smaller larynges, being more elastic, can vibrate more rapidly than the more massive and less elastic vocal bands usually found in large larynges. Since the larynges of men are, on the average, considerably larger than those of women and children, men's voices characteristically have lower pitch levels. The voice "change" of adolescent boys is a more or less abrupt lowering of pitch brought about by the pubertal growth of the male larynx. In addition to differences in laryngeal size, other factors such as age affect vocal-band vibration.

USES OF PITCH IN NORMAL VOICES

The study of variation of pitch within and among different voices includes (1) habitual pitch level of the speaking voices, (2) pitch ranges of speakers and singers, and (3) pitch variables in the expression of meaning and feeling.

HABITUAL AND OPTIMUM PITCH

Habitual pitch is a name given to a concept—a reference point, or level, around which the pitch variations of speaking center. It is probably the pitch most frequently heard in any speaking. When you judge one woman's voice as higher than that of another, you are comparing the two habitual pitch levels.

The habitual pitch of a given voice may not, however, be the pitch that produces the best possible results from that speaker's vocal mechanism. A time-honored principle in voice improvement is that each voice has a pitch level at which it functions most efficiently. *Optimum pitch* is the term for this hypothetical level. Eisenson and Ogilvie define optimum pitch as that level or range where the speaker can produce voice of good quality and adequate loudness with the greatest ease.[1] The optimum pitch, then, lies within a narrow range of pitch rather than at a single level. Optimum pitch level or range is found within the lowest segment of the total singing range but not at the very bottom of that range.[2]

The relationship between the concepts of habitual and optimum pitch is that while the optimum pitch level is a theoretical point in the pitch range of each voice, the habitual pitch is the pitch actually used in the speaking voice. The most effective use of pitch level occurs when the habitual pitch and the optimum pitch are the same.

PITCH LEVELS OF MEN'S AND WOMEN'S VOICES

Research studies have provided some pertinent data about the pitch levels of male and female voices. Investigations have shown that while the pitch levels of male and female children are about the same, the average male voice, during adolescence, drops about one octave and the average female voice drops about two tones. The investigations of Hanley[3] and Philhour[4] show that the average pitch levels of American male speakers are close to C_3 (C below middle C), while Snidecor[5] found that the pitch level of superior female speakers was $G\#_3$ ($G\#$ below middle C). Additional research on the voices of young adults, however, is needed to describe more completely the ranges of habitual pitch levels and their relationship to the speaker's sex.

You have no doubt heard voices where the pitch level alone did not help to identify the speaker's sex. A columnist, writing about television actresses, describes the voice of one Western heroine as lower than that of the man she loved! Men's and women's voices, then, each cover a range of habitual pitch level, and the pitches of the highest male voices overlap the pitches of the lowest female voices.

PITCH RANGES OF NORMAL VOICES

The total range of pitch over which the voice can extend is the individual's *singing range*. The range of trained singers may cover more than three octaves.

[1] J. Eisenson and M. Ogilvie, *Speech Correction in the Schools*, The Macmillan Company, New York, 1963, p. 283.

[2] C. Van Riper and J. V. Irwin, *Voice and Articulation*, Prentice-Hall, Inc., Englewood Cliffs, N.J., 1958, p. 451.

[3] T. D. Hanley, "An Analysis of Vocal Frequency and Duration Characteristics of Selected Samples of Speech from Three American Dialect Regions," *Speech Monographs*, vol. XVIII, pp. 78–93, 1951.

[4] W. Philhour, Jr., *An Experimental Study of the Relationships between Perception of Vocal Pitch in Connected Speech and Certain Measures of Vocal Frequency*, Ph.D. dissertation, University of Iowa, Iowa City, Iowa, 1948.

[5] J. C. Snidecor, "The Pitch and Duration Characteristics of Superior Female Speakers during Oral Reading," *Journal of Speech and Hearing Disorders*, vol. 16, pp. 44–52, 1951.

Speaking range, however, ordinarily covers about one and one-half octaves, within which an even smaller range accounts for the pitch variation of most speaking. The speaking range is usually within the lower segment of the individual's total singing range.

Voice teachers have traditionally considered wide pitch range an important element in the effective voice. Although superior speaking voices *appear* to possess wider pitch changes than untrained or average voices, the evidence is limited. The authors have observed, however, that students with severely narrow speaking-pitch ranges frequently have singing ranges as wide as three octaves. Such observations imply that the extent of the total singing range does not necessarily affect habits of pitch variation in speaking.

FACTORS INFLUENCING PITCH USE

The speaker's habitual pitch does not remain at a static level but tends to change with varying circumstances. Pitch and loudness often vary together. That increased air pressure beneath the vocal bands produces higher pitch has already been noted; the same increase also produces greater loudness. Consequently, when a speaker uses a louder voice than usual to reach the ear of a distant listener in a large audience or to talk over the competition of a noisy environment, his habitual pitch level tends to rise.

As noted in Chapter 1, states of emotion influence the range used in speaking. The speaker in good spirits is likely to use a higher pitch and a wider pitch range than one suffering the effects of illness or fatigue. Generally, the circumstances that tend to raise the habitual pitch concomitantly produce wider pitch ranges, and conversely, those that tend to lower the habitual pitch produce narrower pitch ranges. You may have observed how actors make use of these vocal variations of pitch to communicate aspects of emotion.

Within the limits of their pitch ranges, speakers vary pitch to express meaning and feeling. Early in the study of speech as a science, Bloomfield pointed out that "we use features of pitch very largely in the manner of gestures, as when we talk harshly, sneeringly, petulantly, caressingly, cheerfully, and so on."[6] As you listen to a speaker whose words you cannot hear distinctly, you are able to tell from his voice, with its rise-and-fall patterns of pitch, whether he is asking a question or declaring his opinions and, in addition, how he feels about the topic of his conversation. The pitch-variation factor helps the distracted listener who is not following the speaker's ideas to utter such noncommittal remarks as "Oh, is that so?" and "Certainly, dear." On the other hand, the simulated voice of a mechanical robot in science-fiction films, typically lacking in pitch variation, contributes to the effect of a machine devoid of human emotion. Recent investigators into linguistic science have analyzed in considerable detail the patterns of pitch changes in the spoken language. Some of their findings are discussed in Chapter 18.

[6]L. Bloomfield, *Language,* Holt, Rinehart and Winston, Inc., New York, 1933, p. 114.

LISTENING AND OBSERVING: THE EFFECT OF VOCAL PITCH
ON THE REACTION OF THE LISTENER

1   When watching a play or television drama, observe how the characters suit
the pitch of the voice to the role. If it is a family drama, shut your eyes and
listen to see whether you can identify each member of the family by voice
alone. Note that generally the younger the character, the higher the pitch
level. If you are watching a serious drama, see whether the pitch level of the
actor's voice is one of the clues for judging the personality of the character.
Would you have cast the play using persons with similarly pitched voices? If
so, why? If not, why not?

2   During rush hours, listen to the pitch of a bus driver's voice exhorting his
passengers to move to the rear. Can you tell whether the driver is irritated
and impatient or tolerant and resigned to the hardships of his job? Which
feeling is reflected by a relatively low pitch level with few variations? Which
by higher pitch with greater variations?

3   Listen to some mothers of young children in the neighborhood playground.
As they talk to their children, can you predict which mothers are likely to be
obeyed promptly? What are the pitch levels of the voices associated with
firmness? What are those associated with uncertainty and indecision? What
pitch level do you hear in the voice of the mother who seems overanxious?

4   Visit some elementary school classrooms and listen to the pitch of teachers'
voices. Observe whether the pitch level and range of pitch variation help you
pick out the teacher who is tired, the one who fears her control of class dis-
cipline is slipping, the one who is conducting and enjoying a successful lesson.

IMPROVING THE USE OF PITCH

Although uses of pitch vary among individual speakers, some voices are characterized by pitch levels and patterns outside the expected limits. Such voices
present problems in usage of habitual pitch level, of pitch variation, or of both.

PROBLEMS OF PITCH LEVEL

In some cases of excessively high or excessively low habitual pitch levels, these
levels are the result of organic changes or conditions in laryngeal structure and
functioning. Pathological processes that load one or both vocal bands with superfluous tissue, such as vocal nodules, cause slower and less regular vibrations
than normal vocal bands produce. Thickened vocal bands resulting from chronic
abuse may be incapable of the rapid vibrations associated with high pitches.
Glandular disorders occasionally hasten the growth of laryngeal size and the
consequent lowering of pitch, while in other cases they delay or prevent the
change of voice. Among students of voice improvement in college classrooms,
however, such disorders are relatively infrequent.

More commonly, problems of appropriate pitch placement appear to be
related, consciously or unconsciously, to the speaker's self-concept. For example,

speakers may imitate the pitch levels of a member of the family, a film or television personality, or another admired hero. The young woman who emulates the voice of Marlene Dietrich or the young man that of Sean Connery in the role of James Bond may well be using pitch levels too low for their own mechanisms to produce efficiently. Or a daughter who imitates her mother's girlish, high-pitched voice may be using a level that is inappropriate outside the family group.

Listeners make subtle judgments based on their reactions to the speaker's pitch level. While most listeners tend to associate higher pitch levels with immaturity and lower levels with maturity, other reactions may be more complex. Some male ears find the relatively high-pitched voice of a kittenish young girl attractive; others do not. Although low pitch sounds assertive in one voice, in another, the low pitch sounds forced and appears to be inadequately masking feelings of insecurity. When a young woman says "What a wonderful idea!" with high pitch, she may sound enthusiastic; when she uses the same pitch with "I just adore the theater!", she may sound flighty. Similarly, a low-pitched voice may give the impression of seriousness in one context and of indifference in another. The speaker's pitch level, as one aspect of his delivery, therefore suggests much about himself and his feelings.

USING AN EFFECTIVE PITCH LEVEL

If critical listeners have described your voice as *too high* or *too low,* you may need to learn to use a new pitch level. Compare your habitual and optimum pitch levels to discover whether your listeners' impression of pitch is correct. Be sure to investigate these two pitch levels carefully with the help of your instructor before making any decision regarding changing the pitch of your voice.

Be sure that you do not change your pitch needlessly, thereby creating new difficulties. A voice with insufficient loudness and defective quality is not always the result of using the wrong pitch. Although raising or lowering the habitual pitch has been a favorite technique in voice improvement, the authors' experience indicates that many speakers with conspicuously poor voices have habitual pitch levels at or near their optimum. On the other hand, the severely defective voice resulting from laryngeal pathology may be so limited in pitch range that the concept of optimum pitch does not apply. Since optimum pitch is supposed to result from the most effective use of the vocal mechanism, it follows that an abused or diseased vocal mechanism can have no optimum pitch because it cannot function effectively at any pitch level.

Furthermore, listeners' judgments about pitch are not always valid. Even judges with trained ears find it difficult to isolate pitch from factors of loudness and voice quality.[7] The influence of other vocal variables on pitch judgments helps explain why some voices seem "higher" or "lower" than other voices with

---

[7] N. Schneiderman, *An Investigation of Selected Factors Affecting the Judgment of Pitch Placement of Defective Voices,* unpublished doctoral dissertation, New York University, New York, 1959.

comparable fundamental frequency. Some students who believe their problem to be one of pitch find that improvement in vocal quality is also perceived as a change in pitch level.

Regardless of whether or not you think you may profit from altering your habitual pitch, follow the recommended procedures for locating your habitual and optimum pitch levels. When you have established these levels, you will know whether you need to change your habitual pitch level. If no change in pitch level is indicated, avoid shifting your pitch to a level at which you cannot develop adequate loudness and quality. Change your pitch level *only* if a clearly demonstrated discrepancy between your habitual pitch and optimum pitch exists. *Once having determined your best pitch, use it in all subsequent vocal exercises except where otherwise indicated.*

LOCATING YOUR HABITUAL PITCH

To find your habitual pitch, try to match the reference level around which your pitch varies with a note on the piano. If your use of pitch is characterized by monotony, you will easily find a note corresponding to the pitch recurring most often in your voice. If, however, your use of pitch is characterized by wide variations, you may have more difficulty choosing a reference level. To produce a relatively stable pitch, count aloud or recite a series such as the days of the week. Match this pitch level with a note on the piano. Repeat this procedure on several occasions to verify your original findings.

FINDING YOUR OPTIMUM PITCH

Many techniques ranging from the elaborate to the simple have been suggested for locating optimum pitch level. For most students, a relatively simple procedure is satisfactory:

1   Compare your habitual level against your total singing range. If your habitual pitch is only one or two tones higher (using the piano as your guide) than the lowest note of your singing range, it is too low. The habitual pitch should be at least four or five tones higher than the lowest note available to allow for sufficient variation and ability to drop the pitch when needed. Some experts have suggested that if the total singing range, including falsetto, is divided into four equal quarters, the point one-quarter up from the lowest tone can reliably be selected as the optimum pitch.[8] Apply these measurements to select an approximate level that is at or near your optimum pitch.

2   Chant *mah, mah, mah* or recite or count on the pitch level selected by the above procedure and at the pitch levels two or three tones above and below that point. Use the same degree of loudness and the same speech sample

[8]G. Fairbanks, *Voice and Articulation Drillbook*, rev. ed., Harper & Row, Publishers, Incorporated, New York, 1959, pp. 122–123.

for each trial. For example, if your singing range extends from E below middle C (E_4) to E two octaves higher, your optimum level is probably near A below middle C. Chant or recite on the A and on each of the levels three or four half-steps above and below. The point or range where the voice reveals its best quality can then be confirmed as the optimum level. If that pitch also yields the greatest loudness and the least strain, so much the better. Many experts find this informal method useful.[9]

3   If your voice is severely disordered, so that it possesses only a narrow pitch range, the above procedure will probably not be applicable. For a very tense, strained, and high-pitched voice, phonating on *ah* while moving the jaws and tongue vigorously in a chewing fashion may yield a much lower-pitched sound of improved quality. This tone may provide the starting point for practicing and for extending the pitch range below its usual limit. If your voice is weak, breathy, or low-pitched as well as limited in pitch range, a higher and stronger tone may result when you phonate while attempting to raise yourself from your chair or while using some other exercise involving energetic pushing or lifting. (You may recall that a similar technique was suggested in the last chapter as a procedure to help eliminate breathy onset of vocal tone.) Use this tone to help extend your upper pitch range, but be careful to avoid strain. Follow your instructor's recommendations in applying either of the foregoing techniques.

When you have learned to use a wider and more flexible pitch range, you may be able to proceed with conventional methods of determining your pitch level. In other words, the optimum pitch may change as other aspects of the voice change. If you think of the pitch level derived from any of the suggested procedures as a *practice pitch*, you will not be surprised if at a later time you and your instructor find it profitable for you to alter your pitch level.

USING YOUR OPTIMUM PITCH

In all exercises, match your voice to the tone of a piano or other guide until your use of the new pitch level has become habitual. If your ear for pitch is uncertain, you may find it easier in the beginning to match the pitch of a tone produced by your instructor rather than one from a piano.

1   Limit the first exercises to vocalizing or chanting on the selected pitch without varying from that level.
   a.   Sustain *ah* on your optimum pitch level so long as your breath supply lasts.[10]

[9]W. Johnson, F. L. Darley, and D. C. Spriestersbach, *Diagnostic Methods in Speech Pathology,* Harper & Row, Publishers, Incorporated, New York, 1963, pp. 135–136; C. Van Riper and J. V. Irwin, *op. cit.,* p. 298.

[10]Remember to apply what you have learned about breathing for speech. Review page 36.

b. Do the same for *mah, mah, mah; mo, mo, mo; may, may, may;* etc. Do not hurry; say four or five such syllables and then prolong the last one as long as the breath lasts. This exercise gives you an opportunity to practice the new pitch level with a variety of vowels combined with an easy consonant.

c. Maintaining your optimum pitch level on a chant, count as far as your breath allows.

d. Recite the days of the week.

e. Recite the months of the year, taking a new breath as needed.

f. Chant a nursery rhyme such as "Mary Had a Little Lamb."

2   *After establishing the pitch firmly by chanting the first few syllables,* repeat exercises 1c through *f,* allowing yourself to vary the pitch slightly according to your natural inclinations.

3   Linguistic analysis shows that most American English sentences follow a 2-3-1 pitch pattern, with 2 corresponding to average pitch, 3 higher than average, and 1 lower than average. (See Chapter 18.) When you read the following sentences representative of this pattern, you should start at your optimum pitch, then rise above this pitch on stressed words, and finally fall below your optimum level at the end of the utterance. You need not, however, stray far from the reference level of your optimum pitch for these sentences. Play the note on the piano corresponding to your optimum pitch before reading each sentence to be sure that you begin on that level.

a. He's my brother.

b. Come sit next to me.

c. Where's my English Lit book?

d. It's half-past seven.

e. I overslept this morning.

4   When you can use appropriate pitch variations around your optimum pitch level in the foregoing exercises, read aloud the selections that follow. The selection of verse, with its pattern of parallel sentences, allows you to practice returning to your optimum pitch level at the beginning of each line. The prose selection, descriptive in style, gives you the opportunity to read more complex rhythms without having to vary your pitch too far from the optimum level.

a. Over the mountain
         And over the graves,
     Under the fountains
         And under the waves,
     Over floods that are deepest
         Which Neptune obeys,
     Over roads that are steepest,
         Love will find out the way.

     When there is no place
         For the glow-worm to lie,

When there is no space
        For receipt of a fly;
Where the midge dare not venture
        Lest herself fast she lay,
If love come, he will enter,
        And will find out the way.

English Ballad

b.   The island lay in shadows only a little deeper than those that were
     swiftly stealing across the sound from the east. On its western shore the
     wet sand of the narrow beach caught the same reflection of palely
     gleaming sky that laid a bright path across the water from island beach
     to horizon. Both water and sand were the color of steel overlaid with the
     sheen of silver, so that it was hard to say where water ended and land
     began.[11]

RACHEL CARSON, from *Under the Sea-wind*

5   Give your name and address, using your optimum pitch level.
6   Describe aloud the appearance and the contents of the room you are work-
    ing in, while maintaining your optimum pitch level.
7   For further practice in using your optimum pitch level, repeat some of the
    exercises on page 40, checking your pitch against the piano periodically.

MISUSE OF PITCH VARIATION: THE MONOTONOUS VOICE

Effective use of pitch involves not only the habitual use of the voice at its best
pitch level but also appropriate changes in pitch. Although factors such as stress
and rhythm may also contribute to monotony of voice, this section is primarily
concerned with pitch. Monotonous voices are commonly of two types: the voice
where the habitual pitch never varies with changing circumstances and the voice
where the range of pitch variation around the habitual reference level is excessively
narrow. Sometimes both aspects of monotonous use of pitch appear in the same
voice, such as where the total pitch range is limited to four or five tones.

Excessively narrow pitch ranges result from a variety of causes. When the
habitual pitch of the voice is too low, the functional pitch range of the voice is
small. For example, if the lowest step of the speaker's singing range is F below
middle C and her habitual pitch lies at G below middle C, she can lower her pitch by
only one whole step. If, however, the speaker's habitual pitch is near the top of
the total pitch range, the speaking range may be narrow because the voice
operates inefficiently at that level. The young man whose voice does not drop to
a lower pitch during adolescence typically speaks with a pitch that is not only too
high but also constricted within a small range of variations. In these voices, the
reference level of habitual pitch tends to remain fixed instead of shifting to a
higher or lower level under the influence of changing circumstances.

[11] By special permission of Rachel Carson, *Under the Sea-wind*, Oxford University Press, Fairlawn, N.J.

LISTENING AND OBSERVING: VARIATIONS IN PITCH

1   Listen to the voices of your instructors. How much pitch variation do you hear in the voice of the instructor who seems to be wearily repeating a lecture he has given many times? How much in the voice of the instructor who seems to be stimulated anew by the material of his lecture?

2   Read aloud a story such as *The Three Bears*. First, read it as if to an audience of adults; then read it again as if to an audience of children. In which reading did you use wider pitch variations? Why?

ACHIEVING GREATER USE OF PITCH VARIATION

Check your use of pitch variations to learn whether you need to increase them. Consider both (1) whether your habitual pitch changes appropriately to the circumstances, and (2) whether your pitch varies sufficiently around the habitual level.

The earlier directions for locating optimum pitch included finding your total singing range. If you followed that procedure, you now know whether your available pitch range is smaller than the one and one-half octaves typical of normal speaking voices. If so, your use of pitch variation in speaking may be too limited. If, on the other hand, your singing range is as wide as two octaves or more, observe whether your customary range of pitch variation for speaking makes use of most of the available range.

First, to discover whether your habitual pitch level changes according to the emotional significance of your words, read aloud the sentences that follow. (Tape-record your efforts, if possible.) Try consciously to express the underlying feelings. Locate the varying pitch levels of your voice while reading *each sentence*. Your instructor or a skilled classmate can assist you if you are unsure of your accuracy at this task.

1   Pass the salt, please.
2   I could sleep for a week.
3   I could eat a bear!
4   Watch out for that truck!
5   I'm not myself today.
6   I've never laughed so much in my life.
7   What a peaceful scene.
8   What did she say then?
9   Do you really think I could win?
10   I don't care to discuss it any further.

If your habitual pitch does not shift from sentence to sentence, your use of pitch may tend toward monotony. For example, if your reference pitch levels in reading sentences 2 and 3 are the same or within one or two tones of each other, your pitch variation is not sufficient to reflect changes in emotional content.

Second, to discover whether your use of pitch variation around the habitual level is sufficiently wide, examine your reading of the above sentences again.

Those sentences suggesting lower pitch levels should be read with narrower pitch changes; those suggesting higher pitch level, with greater pitch changes. Match the highest and lowest pitches used in reading each sentence with the corresponding piano note to measure the pitch range actually covered. Again, when your pitch range does not extend beyond four or five tones in any of these sentences, your use of pitch is restricted.

INCREASING YOUR PITCH VARIATION

The exercises that follow are based on exaggeration of pitch changes. When your voice is monotonous, the pitch movements you do use are likely to be in the appropriate direction. You can practice to achieve wider use of pitch variation by attempting to express the intellectual and emotional content of speech more vigorously.

1   You sometimes speak in single words, shifting the pitch within the word according to the desired message. Each of the single words that follow can be spoken in a manner to convey several different meanings. Read aloud the words on the left, using a rising or falling pitch movement or combination of movements that will express each sentence in turn.

    a.   oh   (1) You living doll, you!
                  (2) Now I get it.
                  (3) I don't believe it for a minute.
                  (4) Are you quite sure?
                  (5) What a surprise!
    b.   you   (1) Step over here.
                  (2) *You* won the beauty contest?
                  (3) I've finally reached your name.
                  (4) Yes, I mean you.
                  (5) Don't tell me you're here again.

2   Read aloud the following phrases in a manner expressive of the feelings in the parentheses following each phrase. Remember to exaggerate pitch movements.

    a. Who, me?   (disbelief)
    b. I did not!   (indignation)
    c. Ah ha!   (righteousness)
    d. Certainly not.   (conviction)
    e. Oh, shut up.   (irritation)
    f. Who did you say?   (astonishment)
    g. Not for a minute.   (anger)
    h. In a minute!   (annoyance)
    i. Oh, dear.   (disappointment)
    j. Leave me alone!   (fear)

3   Find a word that describes the emotional content of each sentence that follows. Then read the sentences aloud, selecting and using a pitch level that will communicate the indicated feeling.

    a.   I'm all worn out today.

    b.   Oh, no, not again.

    c.   I said, forget it.

    d.   Did you see that?

    e.   Come here this minute!

    f.   I just saw a six-car collision.

    g.   Congratulations! I'm delighted that you were elected.

    h.   Won't you join us for lunch?

    i.   Pass it, you idiot.

    j.   This has been the saddest day of my life.

4   Read the following passages, using appropriate pitch levels and wide pitch variations. Try to exaggerate pitch movements to express the feeling of each one. If possible, tape-record your attempts at exaggeration and observe whether your use of pitch is as extreme as it seemed while you were recording.

    a.   He watches chess games in silence. What a superior man!

    b.   Seeking fish? Don't dive in the pond—go home and get a net.

                                         Chinese Proverbs

    c.   In Paris they simply opened their eyes and stared when we spoke to them in French! We never did succeed in making those idiots understand their own language.

                                         MARK TWAIN

    d.   How do I feel today? I feel as unfit as an unfiddle,
        And it is the result of a certain turbulence in the mind and a certain burbulence in the middle.

                                         OGDEN NASH

5   Read the following prose and verse selections, continuing to practice the use of wide pitch variations to express meaning and feeling.

    a.   In the morning they asked her, "Did you sleep well?" "Oh, terribly badly!" said the princess. "I hardly closed my eyes the whole night. Heaven knows what was in the bed. I seemed to be lying on something very hard, and my whole body is black and blue this morning. It was terrible!" They saw at once that she must be a real princess when she had felt the pea through twenty mattresses and twenty featherbeds. Nobody but a real princess could have such a delicate skin.

               HANS CHRISTIAN ANDERSEN, from *The Princess and the Pea*

    b.   And all who heard should see them there,
        And all should cry, Beware! Beware!
        His flashing eyes, his floating hair!
        Weave a circle round him thrice,
        And close your eyes with holy dread,
        For he on honey-dew hath fed,
        And drunk the milk of Paradise.

    SAMUEL TAYLOR COLERIDGE, from *Kubla Khan*

6   Read aloud the following passages of varying emotional content. Use a pitch level and a pitch range appropriate to each. Where for a particular passage you choose a lower pitch level, remember that the pitch range may be relatively narrow, while for another calling for higher pitch level, remember that the pitch range will be wider.

a.   Ask not that events should happen as you will, but let your will be that events should happen as they do, and you will have peace.

EPICTETUS, from The Manual

b.   If thou didst ever hold me in thy heart,
Absent thyself from felicity awhile,
And in this harsh world draw thy breath in pain,
To tell my story.

WILLIAM SHAKESPEARE, from Hamlet

c.   The Emperor lay pale and cold in his gorgeous bed. . . . Cloth had been laid down in all the rooms and corridors so as to deaden the sounds of footsteps, so it was very, very quiet. But the Emperor was not dead yet. He lay stiff and pale in the gorgeous bed with velvet hangings and heavy golden tassels. There was an open window high above him, and the moon streamed in upon the Emperor and the artificial bird beside him.

HANS CHRISTIAN ANDERSEN, from The Nightingale

d.   Once upon a time there was a girl more
beautiful and witty and charming
than tongue can tell,
And she is now a dangerous raving maniac
in a padded cell,
And the first indication her friends and
relatives had that she was mentally
overwrought
Was one day when she said, I weigh a hundred
and twenty-seven, which is exactly what
I ought.[12]

OGDEN NASH, from Curl Up and Diet

7   Practice using improved patterns of pitch variation in conversation. Make two-minute impromptu talks on one or more of the following topics:

a.   The time I was absolutely speechless.
b.   The effect of malicious gossip.
c.   The time I felt loneliest.
d.   A close shave.
e.   My favorite daydream.
f.   A sure way to lose a friend.

---

[12] By special permission from Little, Brown and Company, Boston. Copyright 1935 by Ogden Nash; originally appeared in the *New Yorker* in 1935.

CHAPTER FIVE

Loudness Factors in the Effective Voice

Of the several attributes of sound, you are most aware of loudness, which, you will recall, is the listener's interpretation of the measurable attribute of intensity. The concept of loudness is comparatively familiar because of the crucial importance of loudness to audibility. When a sound is not loud enough to be audible to the listener, for him the sound does not occur. If a speaker is not fully audible, the listener strains to hear him and loses part of the message.

Factors of loudness not only determine whether the listener can receive the speaker's message but also help the listener to understand the meaning and feeling of the speaker's words. When a speaker says, "I want to talk to you" in a voice of moderate loudness, the listener expects him to discuss a routine matter; when he whispers the same sentence, the listener anticipates a subject of some intimacy; when he shouts the sentence, the listener infers that the matter is urgent. Variations in loudness also contribute to patterns of stress and emphasis in spoken language.

In this chapter, you will learn how the physiological mechanism for voice produces variations in loudness. In addition, you will study some of the factors that affect loudness in speaking voices and some approaches to evaluating the loudness of your own voice. Finally, you will find techniques to apply in improving your own use of loudness.

THE MECHANISM FOR LOUDNESS

Modifications in the loudness of the voice result from interplay among breathing, pressure at the glottis, and resonance. Studies of vocal-band activity show that as the intensity of the laryngeal sound increases, the vocal bands open and close more vigorously and rapidly during each cycle of vibration and that they remain closed during a greater part of the cycle. These more vigorous movements of the vocal bands appear to be related to increased air pressure in the trachea. The greater buildup of air pressure beneath the closed vocal bands forces the elastic bands apart more energetically, with the result that they return to the closed position more rapidly. Increased air pressure may also be responsible in part for raising vocal pitch, since more rapid vibrations produce higher frequencies. Changes in pitch and loudness, then, frequently occur together.

The total amount of air exhaled during each vibratory cycle is not necessarily greater when the voice is louder. Rather, with increased vocal intensity, the longer, closed portion of the cycle permits a greater buildup of air pressure below and a more rapid release of that pressure during the shorter, open portion of the cycle. Persons with effective voices, therefore, do not necessarily utilize more breath to increase loudness. On the other hand, since those with breathy and hoarse voices waste outgoing breath, they tend to use even more air when attempting to speak louder.

In addition, the resonating chambers of the upper respiratory passageway through which the vocal sound travels affect the final intensity and perceived loudness of the voice. Resonance modifies, reinforces, and amplifies the laryngeal tone. That the resonating cavities and surfaces reinforce some frequencies more than others suggests that the maximal effect of resonance on intensity may occur when the voice is used at optimum pitch level.

Still another factor affecting vocal intensity is the size of the opening through which the voice reaches the outside air. When the mouth opening is wide, more sound energy escapes. When the mouth opening is narrow at the lips or teeth, less sound energy escapes and more is absorbed within the vocal mechanism. Consequently, a relationship exists between the speaker's loudness and his habits of articulation.

PERCEPTION OF VOCAL LOUDNESS

Although the sensation of loudness is intimately related to the strength of the signal, knowing the intensity of a given sound is not sufficient for determining how loud it appears to the hearer. For this purpose, to consider the signal strength at the listener's ear is more correct than to consider it at the original source. How much of the vibratory energy is lost between the speaker's lips and the listener's ear depends on the distance between them and on the acoustic environment. Many examples of the effect of acoustic environment exist: In a poorly designed auditorium, the speaker on the stage may sound comfortably loud to some members of the audience but may be almost inaudible to others at the same distance from the stage. In a gymnasium with hard-surfaced floor and walls, sound energy carries better than in an acoustically treated dining hall. Out of doors, the intensity of sound dissipates rapidly in all directions, and consequently, the listener may find it quite difficult to hear a speaker even at a moderate distance.

Whether a given sound is audible to the listener depends also on the amount and kind of competing noise concurrently present. A sound of given intensity may be audible to a listener in quiet surroundings but may fall below his threshold of hearing when there is competing background noise. The listener may judge a voice to be comfortably loud at a noisy cocktail party but may judge the same voice at the same intensity to be excessively loud at a small, intimate dinner party.

When the signal is speech, however, the listener wants not only to detect it but also to understand it. Since speech sounds are of unequal strength, sometimes a listener can hear certain speech sounds but not others. Consequently, he fails to understand the speaker. Whereas the speaker's loudness depends largely on the loudness of his vowel sounds, his intelligibility depends on the audibility of his consonants and their similarity to those of the listener's dialect. Listeners confuse loudness with intelligibility when they say "I can't hear you" rather than "I can't understand you" to a chronic mumbler. While watching a television film with a poor sound track, you may have vainly tried to improve your comprehension by turning the volume knob. The listener's judgment about the loudness of speech therefore results partly from the speaker's clarity of diction.

Still another influence on the listener's perception of loudness is the speaker's vocal quality. When the listener finds the speaker's vocal quality pleasant, he is willing to accept more intensity than when he finds it conspicuously unpleasant. Many listeners, reacting to a shrill, harsh, or nasal voice quality, describe the voice as too loud.

DETERMINANTS OF ADEQUATE LOUDNESS

You have discovered that loudness affects the speaker's audibility, intelligibility, and communication of ideas and emotion. You also need to learn what factors determine whether loudness is adequate and how speakers modify their loudness to adapt to varying circumstances.

ENVIRONMENTAL DETERMINANTS OF LOUDNESS

As already indicated, a voice is comfortably loud when the listener can hear it well and understand it easily. In quiet listening circumstances, a listener with normal hearing can discriminate speech sounds accurately when the intensity of the speech signal is about 60 dB above the reference level of 0.0002 dyne/cm^2 measured at the ear. Research shows further that the average level of voice in quiet surroundings is about 65 dB. Maximum intelligibility is possible at this 65-dB level when the speaker and listener are in a quiet room and when the speaker articulates his consonants clearly and conventionally.

But in a noisy environment, the 65-dB level may not be loud enough for full intelligibility. The factor determining intelligibility of speech in the presence of noise is the signal-to-noise ratio, or the relationship between the intensity of the speech signal and that of the competing noise. As long as speech is at least 10 dB more intense than the background noise, the noise does not interfere with the spoken message. The speaker ordinarily maintains a favorable signal-to-noise ratio through his auditory monitoring. Listening to the loudness of his voice against the background of environmental noise, he modifies his level accordingly. When the background noise increases, the speaker automatically raises the intensity of his voice. You have spoken at times against the competition of loud construction noises or low-flying airplanes; when the noise stopped unexpectedly, you found yourself shouting.

Speakers usually attempt to modify the intensity of their voices to suit the size of the audience and the acoustic properties of the room. For instance, you speak with moderate intensity when you have a conference with your instructor but with greater intensity when you make an announcement in a large lecture hall. Speakers with little experience in addressing groups of listeners sometimes find it difficult to judge whether the people in the back of the room can hear them. Acoustic characteristics vary so widely from room to room that speakers cannot rely solely on their own ears to know whether their voices are loud enough for all listeners.

EFFECTS OF MEANING AND FEELING ON LOUDNESS

The useful range of vocal intensity extends between the minimum level required for audibility and the maximum level the speaker's vocal mechanism can achieve or the listener's ear can tolerate. The speaker uses his range of loudness to communicate some aspects of meaning and feeling not conveyed by words alone. When you wish to share a confidence, you speak softly even though there is no one around to overhear. When you scold a naughty child, you use a loud voice to convince him of your annoyance and of the importance of the matter. When you pay a condolence call, you speak quietly to indicate your feelings of sympathy and sorrow.

Variations in loudness, together with variations in pitch and time, also produce effects of syllable stress and word stress that are conventional in the spoken language. Specific uses of loudness for stress in pronunciation and for the communication of meaning appear in Chapter 18.

CULTURAL DETERMINANTS OF LOUDNESS

A speaker's customary uses of vocal intensity may reflect the cultural preferences of the segment of society with which he identifies himself. Probably you expect to hear softer voices from representatives of the upper classes than from members of the working classes. Cultural expectations of vocal loudness extend to occupational categories, so that you accept relatively loud voices from entertainers, businessmen, or lawyers but not from research scientists, psychoanalysts, or writers. The influence of cultural expectations on habits of vocal intensity is both subtle and powerful.

LISTENING AND OBSERVING: FACTORS AFFECTING VOCAL LOUDNESS

1   Use an instrument capable of presenting noise through earphones, such as an audiometer, to demonstrate the effect of competing noise on the loudness of a speaker's voice. Have one of your classmates attempt to read aloud at a steady level of loudness while wearing the earphones. Introduce a masking noise to both earphones and gradually increase the intensity by turning the attenuator dial. As you do so, you will hear the reader's voice grow correspondingly louder. When you take your turn as the subject in this demonstration, you will probably be unaware of the increasing intensity of your reading until the operator of the audiometer suddenly cuts off the masking noise. What accounts for the speaker's unconscious increase in vocal intensity?
2   Listen to the voices of participants in a bridge-club meeting. How does a player manage to make himself heard over the sound of everyone talking at once? How do the voices sound when an argument arises over a player's particular play?
3   The term "loud" is often applied to matters other than sound. There are loud colors; there are loud kinds of behavior. Charles Dickens described a character as "stout, loud, red, bluff, and free from any drawback of delicacy." What is the relationship between excessive loudness of voice and loud colors, dress, or manners?

IMPROVING THE USE OF LOUDNESS
INAPPROPRIATE LOUDNESS LEVELS

You have heard voices that are too loud for comfortable listening as well as some that are too soft for easy intelligibility. That these habits sometimes develop from cultural or environmental influences has already been noted. Certainly the speaker's personality also affects his use of loudness. An aggressive or belligerent person may tend to "shout down" his hearers with an overly loud voice, whereas the timid or insecure speaker who has little confidence in his ideas speaks too softly to be heard. Because children often use very loud voices, adults with habits of excessive loudness may seem immature and lacking in self-control. Conversely, the narrow, restricted person may speak with a quiet voice and few vari-ations in loudness—or, for that matter, in any other vocal attribute.

Habits of insufficient or excessive loudness occasionally result from a hear-ing loss. Some types of hearing loss cause the speaker to hear his own voice louder than the voices of others. Such a speaker reduces his vocal intensity in an attempt to match the loudness of his voice with that of other speakers. In other instances of hearing impairment, the speaker speaks too loudly because he raises his voice in order to be able to hear it better himself.

Habitual excessive loudness can abuse the vocal mechanism, producing irri-tation and swelling of delicate tissues. A vicious circle begins, with swollen vocal bands requiring still greater force for vibration and with more irritation and swelling occurring. Since vocal bands thus affected cannot vibrate smoothly or at high frequencies, the voice changes in pitch and quality. Thus, a chronically loud voice often eventually becomes lower-pitched as well as strained or hoarse.

On the other hand, insufficient loudness, a more common problem than excessive loudness, may result from more fundamental problems of quality, pitch, or articulation. When the speaker's voice is breathy or severely hoarse, he may not be able to achieve much loudness. When his habitual pitch is far too high or far too low, he is using his voice in so inefficient a manner that his range of loudness is probably very limited. When he habitually speaks with his mouth barely open and with little movement of articulators, both his audibility and his intelligibility suffer.

LISTENING AND OBSERVING: INEFFECTIVE LOUDNESS LEVELS

1   A 1966 article on the women's page of the *New York Times* described the custom of New York's fashionable women to lunch together at expensive restaurants in town several times weekly. The owners of one such restaurant said that "When women make up as much as 60 per cent of the luncheon crowd, . . . the place begins to sound like a parrot cage."[1] Does this state-ment imply that groups of women talk louder than groups of men and women? Listen to the voices of women talking together and compare their loudness levels with those of other groups. Why did the men quoted in this article use an unflattering simile to describe the sound of women talking together?

2   You may know someone who customarily speaks so softly that you must strain to hear him and who, when asked to repeat something you failed to understand, suddenly increases his loudness startlingly. What impression do you get of the speaker with such a pattern? Why does he seem to want his listeners to attend carefully to his words? Is there an underlying implication that he must shout to get through to you? Listen to some of your acquaint-ances to see whether you can identify any other unusual habits of vocal loudness; consider their effects on listeners.

[1] *New York Times*, p. 24, Feb. 14, 1966.

EVALUATING YOUR USE OF LOUDNESS

Feedback from your listeners may have already indicated that your loudness deviates from comfortable levels. If your voice tends to be too loud, they may have suggested that you stop shouting or advised you to get a soapbox. If your voice is too soft, listeners may frequently ask you to repeat or show that they are straining to hear by leaning toward you or frowning.

To help you and other members of your class learn to evaluate your own loudness more accurately, tape-record a brief group discussion with speakers seated equally distant from the microphone. When you play back the recording, compare the loudness of your voice with that of other speakers in spontaneous conversation. This exercise gives you an opportunity to hear yourself as others hear you and to match the loudness of the recording against your perception of your vocal intensity.

Students have also found it useful to supplement their auditory judgment of loudness with visual aids. Compare the intensity of your own voice with that of another speaker on an instrument designed to show the intensity changes of an acoustic signal. One such instrument is the loudness indicator found on tape recorders. When you speak into the microphone, two bars at the sides of a round light approach each other. Set the volume control of the tape recorder so that the bars just touch when a speaker using a moderately loud voice utters his loudest syllables. Then record your own speech, maintaining the same volume setting and holding the microphone the same distance from your mouth as did the previous speaker. Observe the movements of the loudness indicator. If the bars meet rapidly and vigorously, separating seldom, your voice is too loud and is overloading the mechanism. If the bars move little and seldom or never meet, your voice is too soft.

You may "see" the intensity of your voice on other, more sophisticated instruments, such as a VU meter or oscilloscope. On the VU meter, a volume-indicator meter such as is found on speech audiometers, you can observe the fluctuations of the needle corresponding to the intensity levels of your voice at the microphone. On an oscilloscope you can see the relative intensity levels of your voice in the varying heights of the sound waves displayed on the screen. Again, you may evaluate the levels of your own voice by comparing the visual patterns with those of a speaker with effective habits of loudness.

ACHIEVING APPROPRIATE LOUDNESS

REDUCING EXCESSIVE LOUDNESS

1   Using one of the visual means for measuring loudness described above, speak into the microphone using various loudness levels. When you achieve a level that causes visual patterns similar to those of the speaker with adequate loudness, practice speaking and reading aloud to maintain those patterns. At first, use simple materials such as counting or reciting nursery rhymes. When you can maintain your loudness at the desired level without

watching the visual display constantly, proceed to read aloud some of the passages from subsequent exercises in this chapter. Continue this practice until you can judge your loudness with some degree of accuracy with only an occasional glance at the volume display to confirm your judgment.

2   Excessive loudness may be related to overly forceful release of breath. The exercises on page 37 help you to reduce the amount of breath you use in attacking speech sounds and initiating voice. If you habitually use a strong glottal attack on vowel sounds, do the exercises on page 82. You will dis-cover that developing a smooth initiation of vowel sounds is easier when you use your voice at softer levels than may be habitual for you.

3   Students are frequently successful in reducing excessive loudness when they pay particular attention to the intellectual and emotional content of reading material. The following passages imply the use of a soft voice.

a.   Read the sentences below with less than your normal loudness, but be sure, in reducing your degree of loudness, that you do not resort to a tight-lipped pattern with little movement of the articulators. Use a mirror to help you maintain your usual oral activity. Avoid whispering or breathiness. Try to suit your loudness to the content.

(1)   Don't breathe this to a soul.

(2)   The Jones family is in mourning.

(3)   This is a quiet, sleepy little town.

(4)   Betty's grandmother is becoming quite old and frail.

(5)   Still waters run deep.

(6)   If a little tree grows in the shade of a larger tree, it will die small.

[*African Proverb*]

b.   Read the following selections, using a suitably soft voice.

(1)   Oh, love is handsome and love is fair,
      And like a jewel while it is new;
      But when it is old, it waxes cold,
      And fades away like morning dew.

Irish Ballad

(2)   The wolf also shall dwell with the lamb,
      And the leopard shall lie down with the kid;
      And the calf and the young lion and the fatling together;
      And a little child shall lead them.

Old Testament

(3)   A great sorrow is a great repose, and you will come out of your grief stronger than when you entered it.   A. DUMAS

(4)   The austere serenity of Shangri-La. Its forsaken courts and pale pavilions shimmered in repose from which all the fret of existence had ebbed away, leaving a hush as if moments hardly dared to pass.

JAMES HILTON

INCREASING LOUDNESS

1   Since adequate breath support is essential to achieving the necessary loud-ness, review the techniques for controlling exhaled breath. Practice again the exercises on posture and breathing in Chapter 3. For some speakers, achieving smooth release of air for phonation results in considerable increase in perceived loudness.

2   Similarly, when your voice lacks loudness because of deviations of pitch or quality, you should work to improve these factors first. As a speaker with a hoarse voice develops better quality, his voice often grows stronger and more flexible without special attention to achieving additional loudness. When a student whose pitch is far too high or far too low for his range learns to use a more effective pitch level, he frequently finds that he can speak louder without additional effort. See Chapter 6 for suggestions for improving vocal quality and Chapter 4 for suggestions for improving pitch. After you have worked successfully to improve pitch or quality, you may need to give some concentrated attention to maintaining the improved voice at louder than conversational levels. Keeping in mind any techniques you have mastered for quality or pitch, do exercises 4 through 7 below.

3   Another cause of insufficient loudness is the habit of inadequate movement of the articulators. While insufficient loudness is only one aspect of this problem, it is possible to attack the whole pattern successfully with a unified approach. Relaxation procedures are in order, as is the practice of techniques to widen the oral aperture and to increase articulatory activity. Review the exercises on pages 39 and 72. Your voice may become surprisingly louder when you open your mouth wider.

4   You can begin to increase your control of loudness variation by this exer-cise: Using a comfortable pitch level, say *ah* and sustain it as long as you can before running out of breath. Make sure to use adequate breath sup-port and to open your mouth wide. Repeat the sustained tone five times, beginning with a barely audible level and increasing the intensity on each successive tone until the fifth tone is as loud as you can make it. Maintain the same pitch level throughout. When you do this exercise using a VU meter or other sound-level indicator, you can observe visually the increasing power of your voice. Repeat this procedure several times, aiming to make the fifth *ah* louder than before.

5   Some students whose loudness is sufficient for conversation seldom increase their loudness beyond that level. Read aloud a paragraph such as the one that follows, trying to make your voice audible to segments of your class-room audience in the following order:

a.   To classmates standing directly beside you (but no one else)
b.   To those in the first row only
c.   To those in the first and second rows
d.   To the entire class
e.   To anyone who happens to be in the corridor

The weather forecast for this evening is clear and cold with a chance of showers. The temperature will be in the low twenties. Tomorrow will be fair and continued cold, with temperature in the thirties. Winds will be from 5 to 10 miles an hour.

6   Practice using your voice over competing noise at levels loud enough for your listeners to hear. Seat yourself and one of your classmates in front of the classroom but with your backs to the others. While your classmate reads a paragraph aloud, you read another. The other members of the class are to take notes on the material *you* are reading. Try to read louder than your partner so that the listeners can understand everything you read.

7   Again, you may find it considerably easier to increase your loudness when you attempt to convey the intellectual and emotional significance of selected reading material. The following passages for reading aloud imply greater than usual loudness.

   a.   Read these sentences, suiting your loudness to the content.

   (1)   Never darken my door again!
         Don't you see that car coming toward you?
         Open up—it's the police!
         Come and get it!
         The king is dead, long live the king!

   (2)   Justice is the crowning glory of the virtues.   [CICERO]

   (3)   I'm as mad as a wet hen.   [P. G. WODEHOUSE]

   (4)   An individual is as superb as a nation when he has the qualities which make a superb nation.

WALT WHITMAN, from *Leaves of Grass*

   (5)   There's certainly too much pepper in that soup!   [LEWIS CARROLL]

   b.   Read the following verses, increasing your loudness to a level appropriate to the content.

   (1)   How beauteous mankind is! O brave new world,
         That has such people in it!

WILLIAM SHAKESPEARE, from *The Tempest*

   (2)   Now Landsmen all, whoever you may be,
         If you want to rise to the top of the tree,
         If your soul isn't fettered to an office stool,
         Be careful to be guided by this golden rule:
         Stick close to your desks and never go to sea,
         And you all may be Rulers of the Queen's Navee!

W. S. GILBERT

   (3)   Thy right hand, O Lord, is become glorious in power:
         Thy right hand, O Lord, hath dashed in pieces the enemy.
         And in the greatness of thine excellency
         Thou hast overthrown them that rose up against thee:

Thou sentest forth thy wrath, which consumed them as stubble.
And with the blast of thy nostrils the waters were gathered together,
The flood stood upright as an heap,
And the depths were congealed in the heart of the sea.

Old Testament, The Song of Moses

c.   The prose passages which follow encourage you to use increased loudness:

(1)   Justice travels with a leaden heel, but strikes with an iron hand.

[JUDGE JEREMIAH S. BLACK]

(2)   Who shall enumerate the many ways in which that costly piece of fixed capital, a human being, may be employed! More of him is wanted everywhere! Hunt, then, for some situation in which your humanity may be used.

ALBERT SCHWEITZER

(3)   He's not the finest character that ever lived. But he's a human being, and a terrible thing is happening to him. So attention must be paid. He's not to be allowed to fall into his grave like an old dog.

ARTHUR MILLER, from *Death of a Salesman*

(4)   The battle, sir, is not to the strong alone; it is to the vigilant, the active, the brave. Besides, sir, we have no election. If we were base enough to desire it, it is now too late to retire from the contest. There is no retreat, but in submission and slavery! Our chains are forged! Their clanking may be heard on the plains of Boston! The war is inevitable—and let it come! I repeat, sir, let it come.

PATRICK HENRY, from *Give Me Liberty or Give Me Death*

CHAPTER SIX

Quality Factors
in the Effective Voice

Definitions of *quality* frequently include such terms as the *color* or *texture* of sound. The use of terms borrowed from sensory experiences of vision and touch confirms the quality of sound as a perceptual phenomenon. The listener's perception of quality corresponds generally to the combinations of frequency and intensity in the sound waves he hears. When the sound is voice, the complexities of the wave form result from how the tone is produced at the larynx and how it is amplified and modified as it passes through the cavities of the upper respiratory system. The listener's interpretation of this attribute as quality is for him one of the unique features distinguishing the speaker. When a cold alters the speaker's voice quality, his acquaintances comment, "You don't sound like yourself today."

THE MECHANISMS RESPONSIBLE FOR VOCAL QUALITY
Chapter 3 covers the sound-producing mechanisms of the larynx and vocal bands and gives a brief account of the resonating mechanism. Since the functioning of the resonating mechanism is fundamental to the quality of voice, this chapter includes a more detailed discussion.

The mechanism for resonance consists of chambers of the upper respiratory tract above the larynx. The outgoing air, having been set into vibration at the vocal bands, passes through a series of resonating chambers before it leaves the body through mouth or nose. Immediately above the larynx lies the first resonator, the *pharynx*. The pharynx is an irregularly cylindrical structure extending upward behind the mouth and nose. Membranes and muscle tissue comprise the pharyngeal walls.

The mouth is a second resonator and, during the production of almost all speech sounds, the last section of the passageway through which the breath travels. The roof of the mouth, the palate, has two parts: the hard palate and the soft palate. As you run the tip of your tongue along the palate, moving back from the upper teeth, you feel a thin membrane covering a bumpy bony structure. At about the point where the tongue can reach no further back, the hard bone ends and soft tissue begins. The hard palate, then, is the front part of the palate extending backward from the curved bony ridge housing the teeth. The soft palate, or *velum,* directly behind the hard palate, consists largely of muscle tissue. It ends in the *uvula,* an appendage of the soft palate that, when relaxed, hangs downward toward the base of the tongue. (See Figure 8a.)

The walls of the mouth are the teeth, lips, and cheeks. The rear of the mouth is open to the oropharynx. The tongue, which covers the floor of the mouth and fills the oral cavity when the jaws are closed, is a highly flexible, muscular organ capable of varied movement and delicate shaping. The attachments of the tongue are the lower jaw and the *hyoid bone,* a horseshoe-shaped bone lying above the larynx.

The nasal passages comprise the third set of resonators. The nasal septum, a partition of cartilage and bone tissue, divides the nasal passages. During the production of nasal speech sounds and under most conditions of quiet breathing, the nasal passages are the final portion of the respiratory mechanism through which the breath passes. Both hard and soft tissue make up these irregularly shaped cavities.

The major resonators of pharynx, mouth, and nose account for the modification and amplification of the vibrated air after it leaves the larynx. The complicated linking, or coupling, of these sections of the resonating system partly explains the great variability of vocal quality available to the speaker. Changes in vocal quality also result from the numerous ways in which each chamber can vary in size and in texture and tension of the resonating surfaces.

The size and shape of the pharynx vary with changes brought about by muscular contractions of the pharyngeal walls and the velum. When pharyngeal muscles contract, the circumference of the tube tends to narrow and the resonating properties of the chamber change. When, through complex muscular action, the soft palate moves up and back toward the rear wall of the pharynx, the upper pharynx, or nasopharynx, is closed off and the resonating pharynx is limited to the lower sections. The nasal port is closed or almost closed during the production of all speech sounds except the nasal consonants *m, n,* and *ng* (/m/, /n/, and /ŋ/). For these nasal sounds, the velopharyngeal closure does not take place and the nasal port is open, permitting the vocal sound to resonate in the nasal passages. (See Chapter 12.)

Changes in texture of the walls of the pharynx also contribute to variations in its resonating function. Harder surfaces result from muscular contraction; softer, spongy surfaces, from inflammation of pharyngeal tissue under conditions of respiratory infection or irritation. The relative hardness or softness of the tissue determines in large part how effectively the surfaces act as resonators. Hard surfaces reflect vibration. Spongy, soft tissue, tending to absorb vibration, may muffle the vocal tone.

The nasal passages are the least variable of the resonators in size and shape. As is the case with the pharynx, infections and irritations bring about changes in the texture of the tissues lining the nasal passages. These conditions cause swelling and accumulation of fluid which may even result in the complete blockage of one or both nasal passageways. Under such circumstances, since the speaker cannot produce nasal consonants adequately, his voice quality alters.

The mouth is the most complex resonator. Its size and shape can be greatly modified by combined actions of lips, jaw, and tongue. The entire oral cavity can be opened or closed to the outer air by opening or closing the lips; the aperture at the lips can vary from a broad smile or wide yawn to a narrow pursing. Raising and lowering the lower jaw, or *mandible,* alter the height of the oral cavity. The tongue, exceptionally mobile, can move forward or back, high or low; it can decrease the dimension of the mouth cavity by pressing against the hard palate; it can cut the mouth off from the remainder of the resonating system by pressing against the velum. When raised somewhat toward, but not touching, the velum, the back of the tongue decreases greatly the size of the aperture between mouth and pharynx, thus affecting the coupling between these cavities. As the center of the tongue approaches the palate, the mouth becomes divided into two resonating chambers.

IMPROVING VOCAL QUALITY

In this section the types of ineffective vocal quality will be discussed and a program will be suggested for dealing with each. The student who attempts to improve his voice quality frequently achieves his goal best by working both on habits of initiation of tone and on those of resonance. Some voices, such as those that are thin in quality, appear to be caused by inadequacies of both laryngeal tone and oral resonance. Furthermore, vocal quality is affected by changes in pitch placement, breathing, and articulation. The material that follows is intended to help the student to locate and apply the most useful procedures for improvement of his voice quality. The order of presentation of the common problems of vocal quality reflects both their frequency of incidence and the general applicability of the techniques offered for improvement.

NASALITY

Nasality is probably the most common voice disorder. Admittedly, nasal resonance is necessary and acceptable when uttering the nasal consonants *m*, *n*, and
ng (/m/, /n/, and /ŋ/). In addition, some spillover of nasal resonance to vowel
sounds that precede and follow the nasal consonants is characteristic of spoken
English. The acceptable degree of nasality on vowels is somewhat dependent on
the region of the country where the speaker lives. Furthermore, a recognizable
component of nasality, adding brilliance, is present in the superior voice. When,
however, the nasality sounds conspicuous and excessive to the listener, the
effect is decidedly unpleasant. Severe nasality can affect not only vowel sounds
but also consonants. To distinguish between acceptable and unacceptable types
or degrees of nasality, the unpleasant quality is termed *excessive nasality* or
hypernasality.

The layman says that the excessively nasal speaker talks "through his nose."
Although the nose is certainly involved, other factors also account for hypernasality. In fact, it is possible to distinguish between two varieties of hypernasality.
First, there is the nasality that results from inadequate velopharyngeal closure.
When the velum fails to move up and back far enough to cause the vibrated air
to be deflected into the oral cavity, much of the air escapes into the nasopharynx
and through the nasal passages. As a result, the voice takes on the characteristics of excessive nasal resonance. Sluggish use of the other parts of the speech
mechanism commonly accompanies inadequate velar movement, producing not
only nasal vowels but also weakly articulated and sometimes nasally emitted
consonants. Concomitantly, such a speaker tends to use insufficient loudness
and little pitch variation. This kind of hypernasality, which can result from a cleft
or paralyzed palate, may also occur in speakers with intact speech mechanisms.

A second and distinctly different type of hypernasality takes place when the
air vibrates strongly in the pharynx instead of escaping passively through the
nasal passages. The speaker with this vocal quality uses the mechanism, not
with the sluggishness typical of the first kind of nasality, but rather with excessive
tension. Although the velum may be in the proper raised position rather than
hanging down relaxed, the back of the tongue is characteristically so high as to
almost block the opening between the mouth and the oropharynx. The vibrated
air is thus trapped in the oropharynx or may be forced into the nasopharynx
through an incomplete velopharyngeal seal. Muscular tension of pharyngeal
resonating surfaces accompanying these movements contributes to the production of a "brassy" or "twanging" kind of nasality. This voice seems to become
more nasal as the pitch rises. Often the speaker's jaw is severely tense and his
jaw and mouth movement limited.

To the listener, excessive nasality is not only unpleasant but also one of the
most conspicuous of the various common distortions of vocal quality. The sluggish-
nasal speaker may seem to be whining and self-pitying or at best lacking in
energy. Since this speaker's articulation tends to be weak and his voice soft and
unvaried, the listener may conclude that he has little motivation for making him-

self understood. The brassy-nasal voice gives a rather different impression. Listeners often judge such speakers to be domineering and driving; some listeners consider that the brassy-nasal voice sounds ill-bred.

REDUCING EXCESSIVE NASALITY

1   If your vocal quality is a sluggish nasality combined with general lack of energy and weak tone, begin with the pushing exercise on page 38. Vocalize, while pushing, on *ah*, trying to sustain the tone with steady strength. Relax the pushing movements as soon as the tone is well begun, but sustain the energy with the same loudness and quality until your breath is depleted. Maintain a comfortable pitch and adequate breath support throughout these exercises. Maintain the same mouth opening for the duration of the tone. Once you have established a strong tone free of excessive nasality, proceed to exercise 4 below.

2   If your problem is the brassy nasality resulting from excessive tension of tongue and jaw, practice the following exercise: Select a pitch level comfortably within your range. Phonate on *ah*, watching yourself in a mirror. Open the jaw as wide as possible. Maintain the opening without change, as if frozen, *so long as you sustain the tone*. Now watch the movement of your tongue during this procedure. Does the tongue tip retract from the lower teeth and the entire tongue rise in the back of the mouth, blocking the opening into the pharynx? If so, repeat the exercise with your tongue tip pressed behind the lower teeth to keep it forward and down. Raise and lower your jaw several times without vocalizing, letting the tongue follow the movement of the lower jaw passively. Do not rely on your kinesthetic awareness alone to judge whether your tongue moves as planned; continue to use a mirror. Sustain the *ah* as before, with tongue as flat as possible and jaw down. Distinguish between the quality of *ah* when the tongue is humped and tense and when it is flat and relaxed.

3   Repeat exercise 3 for relaxed vocal tone on page 39 in Chapter 3, applying also the techniques in exercise 2 above.

4   Using the technique (exercise 1 or 2 above) which best reduces your nasality, sustain a tone fairly free of nasality on the following vowel sounds: *oh* /o/, *ow* /au/, *oo* /u/, *ay* /e/, *ee* /i/. Allow your pitch to shift slowly from a high to a low level without increasing nasality. The tongue tip should remain forward and the entire tongue should be as low in the mouth as possible during this exercise. Since, however, all the other vowels require that the tongue be higher than for *ah*, you will need to experiment until you find the precise adjustment which yields the quality you want without distorting the vowel. Try to find the most open-mouthed position for each vowel. Check with your instructor to evaluate the results.

5   When you are able to produce each of the vowels in the preceding exercise without excessive nasality, read aloud the following words containing these vowels:

pa	go	law	zoo
father	stove	ought	choose
rah-rah	loaf	caught	rude
say	see	take	speech

6   In the following words, nasal consonants adjacent to the practice vowels make it more difficult to keep the vowels free from unpleasant nasality. If you cannot easily maintain good oral resonance free of excessive nasality on the vowels, slow down each word by prolonging the vowel until you have made the necessary adjustment as in exercises 4 and 5. Then gradually speak the words at normal speed.

palm	name	alone	meaning
on	wrong	nought	nay
own	awning	morning	pawn
home	noon	knee	amazing
noodle	mood	bean	nimble
unknown	nuisance	mean	ringing

7   Say the phrases that follow, taking care to maintain adequate oral reso nance free from excessive nasality on the italicized vowels.

Father and *I*.	Around and about.
Calm demeanor.	Only a rose.
All alone.	High noon.
Mowing the lawn.	Clean laundry.
No nonsense.	Room and board.

8   If you have not been successful in reducing excessive nasality in the preceding exercises, try this approach: Speak the phrases as if your nasal passages were completely blocked by a severe cold. When you succeed in imitating a voice lacking nasal resonance because of some obstruction to the nasal passages, you are closing the nasal port.

Stop the car.	The circus parade.
The awful author.	People will talk.
Over forty.	A pack of lies.
Soup of the day.	The paper house.
Other efforts.	Apple pie.
The twilight hour.	Fill the bucket.

If this technique proves useful, apply it to exercises 4 and 5. When you can sustain vowels fairly free of excessive nasality, attempt to do so in the phrases where nasal consonants precede or follow vowels. Thus:

palm	Say *p-ah-m*.
own	Say *ow-n*.
home	Say *ho-me*.
moan	Say *m-oa-n*.

When the vowels are satisfactory, synthesize the sounds in the words at normal rhythm. When the vowel sounds in these words are free of excessive nasality at normal speed, apply your skill to exercises 6, 7, and 8.

9   Add the following technique to any of those listed above, or use it alone: Speak the phrases in the previous exercises with great exaggeration of articulatory activity. Articulate as if your listener, hard of hearing, had to rely on lipreading. If you watch yourself in the mirror, you will discover that much of this movement feels far more conspicuous than it looks.

10   Using the most useful techniques from the preceding exercises, practice the material that follows.

a.   "I heard" is good—"I saw" is better.   [*Chinese Proverb*]

b.   If the man doesn't believe as we do, we say he is a crank, and that settles it. I mean it does nowadays, because we can't burn him.

[MARK TWAIN]

c.   When pride cometh, then cometh shame:
But with the lowly is wisdom.

Old Testament

d.   Laugh, and the world laughs with you; love, and you love alone.

[JAMES THURBER]

11   Read the following verses, applying the techniques found to reduce excessive nasality.

a.   I have a song to sing, O!
Sing me your song, O!
It is sung to the moon
By a love-lorn loon
Who fled from the mocking throng, O!
It's the song of a merry man, moping mum,
Whose soul was sad and whose glance was glum,
Who sipped no sup and who craved no crumb,
As he sighed for the love of a ladye.

WILLIAM S. GILBERT, from *The Yeoman of the Guard*

b.   Never ask of money spent
Where the spender thinks it went
Nobody was ever meant
To remember or invent
What he did with every cent.[1]

ROBERT FROST

c.   "You are old, Father William," the young man said,
"And your hair has become very white;

[1] From *Complete Poems of Robert Frost*. Copyright 1923 by Holt, Rinehart and Winston, Inc., New York. Copyright 1936 by Robert Frost. Copyright renewed 1951 by Robert Frost. Copyright renewed © 1964 by Lesley Frost Ballantine. Reprinted by permission of Holt, Rinehart and Winston, Inc., New York.

And yet you incessantly stand on your head—
Do you think, at your age, it is right?"

"In my youth," Father William replied to his son,
"I feared it might injure the brain;
But, now that I'm perfectly sure I have none,
Why, I do it again and again."

LEWIS CARROLL, from *Father William*

12   Read the prose passages that follow, practicing avoiding excessive nasality.

a.   There was once a father who had a family of sons who were always quarreling. When his exhortations failed to stop them, he determined to give them a practical lesson in the evils of disunion. One day, he instructed his sons to bring him a bundle of sticks. When they did so, he gave each one in turn the bundle and told them to break all the sticks at the same time. Each of his sons tried with all his strength, but was not able to do so. Next the father separated the sticks, one by one, and again put them in their hands. This time each son broke the sticks with ease. Then said the father to his sons, "Remember, my sons, in unity there is strength."

AESOP, from the *Fables*

b.   With malice toward none, with charity for all, with firmness in the right as God gives us to see the right, let us strive on to finish the work we are in, to bind up the nation's wounds, to care for him who shall have borne the battle and for his widow and his orphan, to do all which may achieve a just and lasting peace among ourselves and with all nations.

ABRAHAM LINCOLN, from the *Second Inaugural Address*

DENASALITY

The lack of sufficient nasal resonance, *denasality,* occurs when the speaker's nasal passages are blocked so that air cannot vibrate freely through them. Most people erroneously call this voice "nasal." Since *too much* nasal resonance characterizes the nasal voice, nasality cannot occur under these circumstances.

The person with a severe head cold is denasal. If you listen carefully to his speech, you hear that it is only the nasal consonants that are greatly affected by his inability to breathe through his nose. When the mouth-breathing speaker cannot use his blocked nasal passages to produce the nasal consonants, he substitutes the analogous oral consonant: *m* (/m/) becomes *b* (/b/), *n* (/n/) becomes *d* (/d/), and *ng* (/ŋ/) becomes *g* (/g/). Although denasality seems thus to be more a problem of articulation than of voice production, consistently denasal production of the three nasal consonants exerts a pervasive influence on the entire speech output. The denasal speaker's vowels tend to be flat and dull in quality, for that ingredient of nasal resonance that makes for superior voice is lacking.

Denasality and hypernasality sometimes occur in the same voice. This combination exists when a speaker habitually produces vocal tones with too much nasal resonance but at the same time has some obstruction in the nasal passages. If you listen closely to this kind of voice, you can hear the excessive vibration in the pharynx resulting in a nasal "twang," along with an overlay of denasality due to the lack of sufficient nasal resonance for the nasal consonants. Or the speaker may be one whose articulatory mechanism, including the soft palate, is so sluggish or tight that not enough nasal resonance exists for the *m*, *n*, and *ng* but too much exists for the other sounds. This speaker typically moves his articulators as little as possible, tending to speak with his mouth almost closed.

Since a physical obstruction may cause denasality, the problem may be a medical one. Enlarged adenoids, deviated septum, nasal polyps, or chronically swollen nasal passages due to allergy or infection may be the basis of the difficulty. Denasality can exist, however, without these conditions or can persist after their removal.

Severe denasality can be an especially irritating vocal problem. The listener finds himself wishing he could offer the speaker a handkerchief to blow his nose. The denasal speaker sounds dull or bored, and his intelligibility may suffer.

Although denasality is one of the areas where voice and articulation overlap, procedures for dealing with it are presented here.

REDUCING DENASALITY

1   Emphasize the nasal consonants, prolonging and exaggerating them until you can feel the appropriate vibration in the nasal passages. Keep mouth and throat relaxed. Prolong;

m-m-m-m-m-m-m
n-n-n-n-n-n-n
ng-ng-ng-ng-ng-ng-ng-ng (as in *sing*)

Exaggerate the nasal consonants in these phrases:

Many moons.	No, not any.
Another noun.	Not even a penny.
Normal noise.	Song of the nightingale.
Nonsense rhymes.	Singer of songs.
Mingle among them.	Under the moon.
Climbing the mountain.	Animal antics.

2   If your denasality combines with excessive nasality, learning to use a wider mouth opening for vowels and holding the tongue as low in the mouth as possible may help solve both problems. Begin with exercise 2 on page 70 and proceed to exercises 6 and 7 on page 71 to develop clear open vowels and strong nasal consonants.

3   Exaggerated articulation is also helpful for eliminating nasality-denasality combinations. Refer to exercise 9 on page 72.

4   Using the technique you have found most useful to relieve denasality, read the following sentences:

   a.   Many an author has become famous under a pen name.

   b.   Emmett Kelly is known for his role of the sad clown.

   c.   Never underestimate the power of a woman.

   d.   Ancient thinkers praised the notion of a sound mind in a sound body.

   e.   No man is justified in doing evil on the ground of expediency.

[THEODORE ROOSEVELT]

   f.   Vanity dies hard; in some obstinate cases it outlives the man.

[ROBERT LOUIS STEVENSON]

5   Read the following verses, using techniques you have found effective in earlier exercises to eliminate denasality.

   a.   The world is so full of a number of things,
       I am sure we should all be as happy as kings.

ROBERT LOUIS STEVENSON

   b.   Farewell, my own!
       Light of my life, farewell!
       For crime unknown
       I go to a dungeon cell.

       I will atone;
       In the meantime, farewell!
       And all alone
       Rejoice in your dungeon cell.

       He'll hear no tone
       Of the maiden he loves so well!
       No telephone communicates
       With his cell.

WILLIAM S. GILBERT, from *H.M.S. Pinafore*

   c.   I
       Among twenty snowy mountains,
       The only moving thing
       Was the eye of the blackbird.

        II
       I was of three minds,
       Like a tree
       In which there are three blackbirds.

        III
       The blackbird whirled in the autumn winds.
       It was a small part of the pantomime.

IV
A man and a woman
Are one
A man and a woman and a blackbird
Are one.[2]

WALLACE STEVENS, from *Thirteen Ways of
Looking at a Blackbird*

6   Read these prose selections for practice in eliminating denasality.
a.   The learned Fool writes his Nonsense in better
Language than the unlearned; but still 'tis
Nonsense.

BENJAMIN FRANKLIN

b.   Adam was but human—this explains it all. He did not want the apple for
the apple's sake, he wanted it only because it was forbidden. The mistake was in not forbidding the serpent; then he would have eaten the
serpent.

MARK TWAIN

c.   At that time there was nothing on God's earth that I could do,
except run. I had no brains, and I had no memory. When I was told to do
anything I got into such an enthusiasm about it that I couldn't remember
anything about it. I just ran as hard as I could, and then I ran back,
proud and panting. And when they asked me for the whatever-it-was
that I had run for, I started, right on the instant, and ran some more.[3]

JAMES STEPHENS, from *A Rhinoceros, Some
Ladies, and a Horse*

BREATHINESS

The excessively breathy voice commonly results from inefficient control of the
exhaled breath. In other words, not all the expelled breath is used to set the
vocal bands into vibration. The excess breath is itself audible, while the vocal
tone is relatively weak.

Actors and actresses frequently use a breathy voice to attain special effects:
Breathiness combined with a rapid rate and frequent audible gasps for renewed
air suggests hurry, fear, or astonishment. Sometimes breathiness, combined with
slow rate, suggests a certain type of feminine glamour. Perhaps the impression
of lack of energy explains this association; the languid effect of a quiet, breathy,

[2] From *The Collected Poems of Wallace Stevens*, Alfred A. Knopf, Inc., New York, 1923. Reprinted by
permission of Alfred A. Knopf, Inc.

[3] By special permission of The Macmillan Company, New York, from "A Rhinoceros, Some Ladies, and
a Horse," in *James, Scumas and Jacques*, unpublished writings of James Stephens, edited by Lloyd
Frankenburg.

slow-paced speech and voice pattern seems appropriate to a helpless, clinging female. Because it is reminiscent of whispering, breathiness also implies a feeling of intimacy in each utterance that is quite unsuitable to everyday conversations. While an actor or other speaker may occasionally use breathiness to convey these impressions, the breathy voice is ineffective for habitual use.

REDUCING BREATHINESS

The use of the outgoing breath for the production of voice was discussed in Chapter 3. If your voice is breathy, practice the basic techniques of controlled breathing and initiation of vocal tone as outlined in that chapter. When you have mastered those skills, practice applying them in connected speech as follows: In the short passages listed below, avoid running out of breath by anticipating your breath needs, taking a new breath where meaning dictates. Be sure to begin each new phrase with relaxed jaw and a well-timed release of breath.

1   Observe moderation. In all, the fitting season is best.   [HESIOD]
2   As long as war is regarded as wicked it will always have its fascination; when it is looked upon as vulgar, it will cease to be popular.   [OSCAR WILDE]
3   When I reflect upon the number of disagreeable people who have gone to a better world, I am moved to lead a different life.   [MARK TWAIN]
4   It is not the oath that makes us believe the man, but the man the oath.

[AESCHYLUS]

5   Even opinion is of force enough to make itself espoused at the expense of life.   [MICHEL DE MONTAIGNE]

Learn to articulate initial voiceless consonants without wasting breath. If your production of *p*, *t*, and *k* preceding stressed vowels is overemphasized, as when you say *pin*, *top*, and *car*, you can hear a strong *h* sound immediately after the first consonant. This habit of overaspiration both contributes to the breathy sound of your voice and causes you to be out of breath too quickly. You may also exaggerate the *s* and *h* sounds, as in *say* and *how*, so that they are noisy; this pattern, usually heard in speakers who tend to overaspirate, also contributes to a breathy voice quality.

1   Produce the initial consonants with as little breath as possible in these phrases and sentences:

Time and time again.	A party poop.
I said so.	Ten minutes past two.
My heart went pitter-patter.	Hot potatoes.
Hang up your coat and hat.	Harry and Hank.
Sing a song of sixpence.	Trailer truck.
A peck of pickled peppers.	Cut a caper.

2   Read the following verses, taking care to produce the initial consonants without wasted breath.

a.   Peas porridge hot,
     Peas porridge cold,
     Peas porridge in the pot
     Nine days old.

b.   *SONG'S ETERNITY*
     What is song's eternity?
     Come and see.
     Can it noise and bustle be?
     Come and see.
     Praises sung or praises said
     Can it be?
     Wait awhile and these are dead
     Sigh, sigh;
     Be they high or lowly bred
     They die.

                              JOHN CLARE

c.   *BUDDY*
     That kid's my buddy,
     Still and yet
     I don't see him much.
     He works downtown for Twelve a week.
     Has to give his mother Ten—
     She says he can have
     The other Two
     To pay his carfare, buy a suit, coat, shoes,
     Anything he wants out of it.[4]

                         LANGSTON HUGHES

3   The prose passages that follow contain many words beginning with the consonants *p*, *t*, *k*, *h*, and *s*. Read aloud, without wasting breath on these consonants.

    a.   Happiness consists in being perfectly satisfied with what we have got as well as with what we haven't got.

    b.   It's a great kindness to trust people with a secret. They feel so important while telling it.

                         ROBERT QUILLEN

    c.   And he gave it for his opinion, that whoever could make two ears of corn, or two blades of grass, to grow upon a spot of ground where only

---

[4]From *Montage of a Dream Deferred*. Copyright 1951. Reprinted by permission of Harold Ober Associates, Inc.

one grew before, would deserve better of mankind, and do more essential service to his country, than the whole race of politicians put together.

JONATHAN SWIFT, from *Gulliver's Travels*

d.   Apologizing is a very desperate habit—one that is rarely cured. Nine times out of ten, the first thing a man's companion knows of his short-coming is from his apology. It is mighty presumptuous on your part to suppose your small failures of so much consequence that you must talk about them.

OLIVER WENDELL HOLMES, from *The Professor at the Breakfast Table*

4   Practice controlling breathiness while reading the following passages.
   a.   Home is the place where, when you have to go there, they have to take you in.
   b.   The best horse cannot wear two saddles.
   c.   Society is a partnership in all science, a partnership in all art; a partnership in every virtue and in all perfection. As the ends of such a partnership cannot be obtained in many generations, it becomes a partnership not only between those who are living, but between those who are living, those who are dead, and those who are to be born.

EDMUND BURKE

   d.   High above the city, on a tall column, stood the statue of the Happy Prince. He was gilded all over with thin leaves of fine gold, for eyes he had two bright sapphires, and a large red ruby glowed on his sword-hilt.
      He was very much admired indeed. "He is as beautiful as a weathercock," remarked one of the Town Councillors who wished to gain a reputation for having artistic tastes; "Only not quite so useful," he added, fearing lest people should think him unpractical, which he really was not.
      "Why can't you be like the Happy Prince?" asked a sensible mother of her little boy who was crying for the moon. "The Happy Prince never dreams of crying for anything."
      "I am glad there is some one in the world who is quite happy," muttered a disappointed man as he gazed at the wonderful statue.
      "He looks just like an angel," said the Charity Children as they came out of the cathedral in their bright scarlet cloaks and their clean white faces.
      "How do you know?" said the Mathematical Master, "You have never seen one."
      "Ah! but we have, in our dreams," answered the children, and the Mathematical Master frowned and looked very severe, for he did not approve of children dreaming.

OSCAR WILDE, from *The Happy Prince*

HOARSENESS

The kind of hoarse voice with which you are most familiar occurs with a sore throat. This disorder of voice, which may range from a slight huskiness to an intermittent loss of voice, has a noisy, rough sound usually accompanied by breathiness. With a respiratory infection, the hoarseness is the result of the vocal bands being unable to vibrate smoothly and at normal speed because of swollen tissues and accumulation of excess fluid on membrane surfaces. As a cold subsides the accompanying hoarseness subsides.

In some voices, functional hoarseness is a habit associated with breathy tone production. You will remember that the vocal tone of the breathy voice is usually weak. As a speaker with this habit attempts to speak loudly, he sometimes wastes still more breath while straining to achieve sufficient power. The audible waste of breath combined with a strained, gruff tone results in a hoarseness similar to that of the speaker with laryngitis who exerts extra effort in using irritated and swollen vocal bands.

In other cases, hoarseness may stem from an organic disorder of larynx or vocal bands. Therefore, to seek the advice of a laryngologist when you have prolonged hoarseness is wise. Whether or not the medical specialist discovers a physical condition responsible for the hoarseness, he may recommend voice retraining. Since some laryngeal disorders have been found to result from habitual vocal misuse, a program of vocal reeducation is often an important step in correcting the existing condition.[5]

The hoarse voice seems to play a curious role in our culture. While hoarseness is uncomfortable to both the speaker and the listener, a hoarse voice has become the stock-in-trade of several actors, actresses, and popular singers. In some instances, this voice is associated with comedy effects; in others, with romance and drama. Perhaps the serious actress with the hoarse voice captivates her public because she always sounds as though she were about to cry. The repressed sob seems to be implicit in the voices of some of the most popular recording stars. The special effects achieved by the hoarse voices of these performers are, at all events, inappropriate to conventional speaking circumstances. That hoarseness is normally disturbing is evident when the listener empathically clears his throat.

REDUCING HOARSENESS

The recommended procedure for alleviating hoarseness combines several of the techniques already presented. A cardinal point for eliminating hoarseness is achieving an effective balance between relaxation and tension in the production of vocal tone. Most hoarse speakers have to use considerable effort to produce voice that is at all reliable and audible. They complain of a "tired" throat at the

---

[5] H. J. Rubin and I. Lehrhoff, "Pathenogenesis and Treatment of Vocal Nodules," *Journal of Speech and Hearing Disorders,* vol. XXVII, pp. 156–158, May, 1962.

end of the day. The constant use of voice under these adverse conditions produces tension and irritation, which, in turn, create the need for still greater effort in phonation.

Review the material in Chapter 3, pages 36 to 39, on posture. In addition, do the exercises on pages 37 and 38 designed to produce voice from silence with minimal effort. If your voice is hoarse, the sound that results from doing these exercises correctly may be quite weak and unsteady at first, but do not give in to the temptation to clear your throat and "belt out" a strong tone. In the long run, this mistaken procedure only aggravates hoarseness. The techniques to achieve relaxed jaw and throat during phonation are essential to the desired goal.

Yawning, as suggested in Chapter 3, also has excellent effects in relaxing the entire articulatory and phonatory musculature. Practice yawning silently at first and then with concurrent vocalization. The sound you hear on a vocalized yawn may be relatively free from hoarseness and strain. If you think you can't yawn at will, go through the motions as if faking a yawn. The pretended yawn will accomplish almost as much as a real one in achieving relaxation.

1   Yawn while producing the following vowel sounds, letting the pitch variation follow the yawn itself:

ah /ɑ/   oo /ʊ/
ee /i/   oy /ɔɪ/
ow /aʊ/   aya /aɪ/
oh /oʊ/   aw /ɔ/

2   Make sure the pitch level you use is the right one for you. Speaking habitually on a pitch level much lower or higher than the optimum pitch aggravates hoarseness. Follow the procedures in Chapter 4 for discovering optimum pitch.

With severe hoarseness, the pitch range is likely to be narrow. As you master the techniques for achieving relaxed phonation, you will probably find that your pitch range increases somewhat. *Having established a good working pitch level, use it throughout these exercises* unless otherwise specified.

3   Develop effective breathing for speech. Since hoarseness is typically associated with breathiness and air wastage, the mastery of good control over the outgoing breath for speech is basic to overcoming it. Effective breath control also contributes to relaxed use of the vocal mechanism. Review the sections on breathing for speech in Chapter 3 and the material on breathiness earlier in this chapter.

4   Learn to begin words smoothly. The way in which voice is initiated has a considerable effect on hoarseness. When the attack is too forceful, the entire utterance may sound more hoarse than it is. The special problems in attacking words arise when (a) producing voice from silence, (b) speaking syllables beginning with vowels, and (c) speaking stressed syllables beginning with consonants likely to be overaspirated.

a. *Producing voice from silence.* Review the techniques for initiating vocal tone on pages 37 and 38. Sighing and yawning into the tone are helpful. When the procedure of inserting an *h* sound before the word is used, be sure that the *h* is barely audible.

b. *Speaking syllables beginning with vowels.* Say the following words with a smooth initiation of tone on the vowel. Avoid the glottal attack.

arm	aim	unable	Alice
able	umpire	infant	over
area	elephant	open	under

The words that follow have stressed syllables beginning with vowels. These syllables are not the initial ones in the word. For these words, do not attack the stressed syllable separately, but link it with the preceding syllable to avoid the intrusion of the glottal stop.

tri umphant	idi otic
Se attle	bi annual
pi ano	be atify
pedi atrics	my opic

When a word beginning with a vowel comes at the beginning of a phrase, use your techniques of initiating tone from silence. When a word with an initial vowel is not the first word in the phrase, link it with the preceding word. This practice will solve the problem of vocal attack and will improve the speech rhythm. Observe these principles in reading the following phrases and sentences:

I am an old man.
Among the old familiar faces.
It's on my arm.
I said "up," not "cup."
Andy brought the ale, Al brought the ashtrays, and I brought the eggs.

Read the following passages, applying the techniques of initiating tone smoothly from silence where phrases begin with vowel sounds and linking initial vowels with the preceding word when they occur within phrases.

(1)   The only way to get rid of a temptation is to yield to it.

[OSCAR WILDE]

(2)   Thou canst not joke an Enemy into a Friend, but thou may'st a Friend into an Enemy.   [BENJAMIN FRANKLIN]

(3)   Every hero is a Samson. The strong man succumbs to the intrigues of the weak and the many; and if in the end he loses all patience, he crushes both them and himself. Or he is like Gulliver at Lilliput, overwhelmed by an enormous number of little men.

ARTHUR SCHOPENHAUER, from *The Fate of Samson*

(4)   I eat my peas with honey,
I've done it all my life;
It makes the peas taste funny,
But it keeps them on the knife.

ANONYMOUS

c.   *Speaking stressed syllables beginning with consonants.* You will remember that only certain consonants tend to be articulated with too
much force and, as a result, become overaspirated. Review exercises 2
and 3 on page 78. When you avoid the overly explosive production of
p, t, and *k* and the noisy production of *s* and *h*, your voice may sound
suddenly clearer. The habit of overaspirating these sounds is probably
related to the excessive effort characteristic of the hoarse speaker.

5   Work to improve your general articulatory activity. Exercise 9 on page 72 is
listed as a technique for reducing nasality because increasing activity of lips,
jaw, and tongue tends to reduce tension at the back of the mouth and
pharynx. You can treat the tension associated with hoarseness similarly.

6   Some hoarse speakers tend toward denasality. Increasing the nasal resonance, within acceptable limits, may give the voice more richness and may
mitigate the hoarse quality to some degree. If denasality is one of your difficulties, review the appropriate exercises in this chapter.

HUSKINESS, HARSHNESS, AND STRIDENCY

These terms are frequently applied to voices of defective quality, but not, unfortunately, in consistent ways. Many students who embark on a program of voice
improvement, having been told that their voices are husky, harsh, or strident,
wish to know which techniques to practice.

Some persons consider *huskiness* as synonymous with hoarseness, while
others consider any noticeably low-pitched voice husky. Sometimes the term is
used to include breathiness. Insofar as the term has any usefulness, the authors
apply it to the voice which is somewhat hoarse and breathy and at the same
time relatively low in pitch or giving the impression of low pitch. The techniques
for reducing hoarseness are fully applicable to this voice.

Harshness refers to the voice quality that appears when a speaker who is
breathy at soft volume tries to speak louder and at a relatively low pitch. The
harsh voice, with an abundance of glottal attacks and overaspiration, sounds very
tense. The speaker with a harsh voice should work for adequate pitch placement,
relaxation, and easy initiation of tone. See appropriate exercises.

The *strident* voice is similar to the harsh voice but generally has higher pitch
and even greater tension. In addition, a tendency toward excessive nasality is
usually apparent. Again, relaxation techniques, proper pitch placement, and
avoidance of hard attacks are helpful. Exercises to reduce nasality may assist in
eliminating the piercing, unpleasant quality of this voice.

THE THIN VOICE

The thin voice is quiet and has little carrying power. Some persons describe this voice as one lacking resonance or *projection*. In fact, to hear this voice at all is difficult unless you are very close to the speaker, although he does not seem to be trying to speak softly. The speaker with a thin voice typically uses little energy for speaking and has a shallow breathing pattern. He characteristically speaks with minimal articulatory activity and little change of facial expression. Although listeners associate thin voices with small, immature people, speakers with less appropriate physical makeup also use such voices.

The speaker with a thin voice needs to bring more support to his speaking by applying techniques of breathing for speech and for increasing oral and pharyngeal resonance. As the voice becomes more vigorous, it also becomes louder.

INCREASING VOCAL POWER

1   Review the material on posture on page 36. Do your vocal exercises in a standing position whenever possible.

2   Work to develop effective breathing for speech; see the exercises beginning on page 36. Avoid the type of breathing in which the shoulders and the upper chest are raised during inhalation; this shallow breathing will not give enough support to establish strong vocal tones.

3   Do the exercises involving "pushing" on page 38. The additional effort used in this exercise will probably call forth a tone unusually strong for you. Sustain that tone on *ah* so long as your breath lasts. Be sure to maintain good breath support. Avoid harshness or stridency.

4   Locate your optimum pitch level and use it in vocal exercises. Thin voices tend to sound higher in pitch than they really are. If your habitual pitch is adequate, locate it and use it in vocal exercises to ensure that you do not lower your pitch unnecessarily.

5   Develop increased resonance for vowel sounds. The techniques for improving oral activity in exercise 9, page 72, will be helpful.

6   Read the following selections, combining the foregoing techniques as they have proved effective.

    a.   I threw a penny in the air,
         It fell again—I know not where.
         But if it had been half a crown,
         I would have watched where it came down.

                      ANONYMOUS

    b.   Five miles meandering with a mazy motion
         Through wood and dale the sacred river ran,
         Then reached the caverns measureless to man,
         And sank in tumult to a lifeless ocean:
         And 'mid this tumult Kubla heard from far
         Ancestral voices prophesying war!

        SAMUEL TAYLOR COLERIDGE, from *Kubla Khan*

c.   Man is born free, and everywhere he is in chains.
Many a one believes himself the master of others, and yet he is a greater slave than they.

JEAN JACQUES ROUSSEAU, from Social Contract

d.   It is illogical to reason thus, "I am richer than you, therefore I am superior to you," "I am more eloquent than you, therefore I am superior to you." It is more logical to reason, "I am richer than you, therefore my property is superior to yours," "I am more eloquent than you, therefore my speech is superior to yours." You are something more than property or speech.

EPICTETUS

THE STRAINED VOICE

Excessive tension is generally the basis of the problem for speakers with habitually strained voices. The entire vocal mechanism, and probably other parts of the body as well, may be held in such a degree of tension that the moving parts cannot function efficiently. In extreme examples, the speaker seems to be literally choking when he tries to phonate. The continued effort of producing voice in this way is likely to lead to fatigue and tremulousness, just as the hands may begin to tremble after prolonged and tense manual activity. The entire pattern may be compared to the attempts of a beginning golfer who, as his instructor admonishes him to "relax," grows more and more tense, so that he misses his shots and tires easily.

Emotional and personality factors often underlie this tension. Recently a group of students described the circumstances under which each became tense. They listed such examples as heavy schoolwork, anticipating examinations, and being interviewed for jobs. The instructor and a visiting psychologist both noted that the students' voices became tense and strained as each contributed examples of circumstances productive of emotional tension. Some speakers, however, seem always to be overly tense. One student with a severely tense voice that sounded strained when she spoke louder, habitually held her teeth clenched and her jaw thrust forward in a pugnacious attitude. She reported one day that her lower jaw often ached when she awoke in the morning.

The material in earlier chapters designed to improve initiation of tone, posture, relaxation, and breathing for speech is appropriate to this problem. Once a good foundation for relaxed voice production has been established, the exercises on improving oral resonance should follow.

LISTENING AND OBSERVING:
THE EFFECT OF VOCAL QUALITY ON THE LISTENER

1   As you ride the bus or subway, observe some of the passengers. What kind of voice would you expect to hear from each one? Try to imagine the vocal quality which seems suitable to the individual's size, sex, appearance, and

facial expression. How do you react when the tall, portly gentleman opposite you begins to speak to his neighbor in a thin, breathy voice? When the fashionable young woman uses a denasal voice?

2   Vocal quality often changes with the situation in which the speaker finds himself. The speaker may alter his vocal quality to match what he thinks his listeners expect. A famous actress wrote on this subject:

> I am aware that I have a voice full of ersatz sunshine that makes its nauseating appearance when I am suddenly confronted by the children of my friends—young creatures on whom I've not set eyes for years. This voice with hypocritical eagerness utters banalities like "How's the new math teacher?" . . .
>
> Another locution I have recently discovered is my doctor's voice. Not the confiding mutter used in situations of illness or consultation, but the one I catch myself using when I meet one of the medical profession socially. Possibly out of a desire to give the impression that I have no need for his professional services, I talk with great animation in tones vibrant with radiant health.[6]

Listen to your own voice quality as the listeners change. What "voices" can you add to the ones described above?

3   Actors portraying unpleasant characters or unpleasant emotions may use corresponding vocal qualities. A writer describes thus the voices used by actors in a television commercial for a pill that calms the nerves:

> One of them, who has neglected to take the pill that would have prevented it, screams at her elderly mother in a voice so disagreeable that an offstage studio announcer is driven to remonstrate with her. Take the pill, he says; but the next time we see her she's bringing her children to the point of tears with just the same voice. Her husband, who doesn't know about the pill either, whines to his wife and son . . . because the boy has left his bicycle in the driveway, but it seems more likely that his trouble is not the pill or the bicycle but rather the realization of the voice he has come home to.[7]

4   Many observers of our culture have wondered why speakers are so unaware of the effect of their voices on others. A popular columnist recently emphasized this point for her women readers:

> A writer for the *Manchester Guardian* recently wondered why women worry so much about their hair and their figures. "Though their voices are as repellant as halitosis, I have yet to hear a girl wail: 'I shall never get a boy friend. My voice is so ugly.'"
>
> But a woman with a charming voice can hold a man spellbound while she tells him the horrid remark the grocer's boy made today.
>
> Women who spend huge sums on clothes, standing for many irksome hours in hot, frantic fitting rooms, may fancy that the secret of feminine allure lies in a sly satin

---

[6]Cornelia Otis Skinner, "I Keep Hearing Voices," from *Bottoms Up.* Reprinted by special permission of Dodd, Mead & Company., New York.

[7]C. W. Morton, "The Peanut Butter World," *The Atlantic Monthly,* p. 129, April, 1963.

bodice or an errant bit of lace. Such details help, of course. But its the soft inflection of a "Really, darling?" that a man remembers.

The harshness of women's voices is most apparent in the places where women gather without men. In those gaudy stores with the great chandeliers, at the hairdresser's, in the boutiques and booteries, and in the park with small children. To hear some mothers summoning their little ones from the swings is a shuddery experience.

I don't suggest that all mothers should address their young in sweet, small voices. Nor should every woman warble like a bird. But there's no denying that the voice is the truest clue to the texture of a woman's mind. Vulgar voice, vulgar mind. It never fails.[8]

[8] H. Van Horne, "New Retail Image," *New York World-Telegram & Sun,* p. 17, Jan. 27, 1966.

CHAPTER SEVEN

The Time Factor
in Effective Speaking

Speech is an event occurring in time; its occurrence is measurable in units of time, and when the speech act is finished, it cannot be recaptured for examination except by recording devices. Plutarch illustrates this ephemeral nature of speech in the following:

> Antiphanes said merrily, that in a certain city the cold was so intense that words were congealed as soon as spoken, but that after some time they thawed and became audible; so that the words spoken in winter were articulated next summer.

The time factor in speech has two major aspects: *rate* and *rhythm*. The rate of speaking is roughly the number of words spoken in a given unit of time (such as a minute), while the rhythm of speaking is the allotment of time for the words spoken. Two speakers saying the same words in about the same amount of time may use that time very differently. For example, read aloud the following paragraph according to the markings, timing each reading.

1	2
In life	there is nothing more unexpected and surprising

3	4
than the arrivals and departures of pleasure.	If we find it in one place today,

5	6
it is vain to seek it there tomorrow.	You cannot lay a trap for it.

ALEXANDER SMITH

1   Read it with a slow, steady rate, pausing briefly at the end of each sentence only.
2   Read more rapidly, but pause briefly at the end of each numbered phrase.
3   Read more rapidly still, but pause at length at the end of each numbered phrase.
4   Read the odd-numbered phrases slowly and the even-numbered phrases rapidly, pausing briefly at the end of each one.

If you follow the instructions closely, you will observe that while each reading represents a different arbitrary rhythm, all of them may consume approximately the same amount of time.

An analogy from music may further illustrate the distinction between rate and rhythm. Musical notation specifies both rate and rhythm for the instrumentalist or singer: The composer shows the rhythm or pattern of time allotment by using a time signature such as $\frac{3}{4}$ or $\frac{6}{8}$ and by writing the notes differently to show how long each lasts in relationship to the others. Any player can then translate the musical notations into the rhythm intended by the composer. To indicate the overall speed, or rate, the composer also inserts such terms as *allegro* and *adagio*.

Rate and rhythm, then, are different aspects of time as applied to sound. In speech, as in music, general configurations of rate and rhythm reflect the underlying theme; therefore, both the speaker and composer choose a slow rate and a stately rhythm to communicate sadness or gravity. In speech, as contrasted with music, rate and rhythm are not fixed in advance but rather follow the ideas and feelings of the speaker within the framework of some basic patterns of the language.

RATE

The speaker's rate varies with his immediate situation, with the content and style of his material, and with his feelings about himself and what he is saying. The speaker tends to slow down his rate when addressing a large audience, when the listening conditions are poor, such as over a bad telephone connection, or when the listener is unfamiliar with the language or is hard of hearing; his rate may become quite rapid when talking to one or two friends about everyday matters. The speaker tends to speak slowly when speaking or reading aloud weighty material using many long words, technical terms, or numbers; he speaks faster when engaged in small talk about familiar matters. He uses a slow rate when reporting someone's tragic experience; he uses a rapid rate when recounting an amusing incident. He tends to speak slowly when he is depressed, tired, or bored; he tends to speak more rapidly when he is enthusiastic or anxious.

From the listener's point of view, his evaluation of rate of speech depends also on his own expectations and needs. Tourists from small towns visiting a big city often report that folks in the city seem to talk faster than those at home. The rate of the listener's own speech may affect his judgments about the speaking rate of others. Listeners frequently believe that speakers of foreign languages talk unusually fast. Examination of the numerous factors that influence rate and perception of rate leads to the conclusion that there is no single correct rate of speech. Because of variations in speaking rate, listeners ordinarily become aware of the speaker's rate only when it is exceptionally fast or exceptionally slow.

It is possible, however, to offer guidelines for the range of acceptable rates in certain speaking situations. Fairbanks,[1] in line with previous investigators, reports that the rate of "excellent" reading lies between 160 and 170 words per minute. A study by Kelly and Steer[2] compares reading and speaking rates and shows that while the average speaking rate is approximately the same as the average reading rate, far greater variability in rate exists in speaking than in reading aloud.

Aggertt and Bowen[3] give a table which indicates the rate at which outstanding readers read poetry. Furthermore, they have compiled the average rates at which these readers read different kinds of material. They find that these readers read sonnets at the average of 125 words per minute, serious, contemplative poetry at 134 words per minute, and light, cheerful poetry at 154 words per minute. They also show that different readers vary in the rate at which they read the same material. They give the rates of four well-known readers in reading "She Walks in Beauty." Edith Evans read at the rate of 106 words per minute, Tyrone Power at 109, Eric Portman at 138, and Norman Corwin at 150.

In ordinary speaking situations, remember that factors other than the measurement of words per minute influence the listener's evaluation of rate as fast or slow. The speaker's rhythm, phrasing, and articulation affect the listener's impression of rate. If the speaker talks relatively fast with clear articulation, his rate may not be conspicuous because he is easy to understand. On the other hand, if the speaker talks relatively fast with indistinct articulation, his rate is conspicuous because he is difficult to understand.

Inappropriate habits of rate convey information about the speaker himself. Sometimes rapid speakers who talk on and on, hardly pausing for air, seem to fear silence or to be afraid of giving the other person an opportunity to reply. Perhaps the rapid rate of some of these speakers stems from a wish to avoid communication, for they never quite get to the point. The unusually slow speaker may give the impression of being reflective and earnest, but when the slow rate

---

[1] G. Fairbanks, *Voice and Articulation Drillbook*, Harper & Row, Publishers, Incorporated, New York, 1960, p. 115.

[2] J. C. Kelly and M. D. Steer, "Revised Concept of Rate," *Journal of Speech and Hearing Disorders*, pp. 222–226, June, 1949.

[3] O. J. Aggertt and E. R. Bowen, *Communicative Reading*, 2d ed., The Macmillan Company, New York, 1963, pp. 222 and 237.

is inappropriate to the content and situation, the listener may come to the conclusion that the speaker is painfully bored, ill, or unconcerned. To some listeners, an excessively slow rate implies slow thinking, as in the "Mortimer Snerd" pattern.

LISTENING AND OBSERVING: FACTORS INFLUENCING SPEAKING RATE

Compare the speaking rates of a news analyst, a theater critic, and a sports announcer heard on radio or television. Which one speaks the slowest? Which, the fastest? Why? When listening to an announcer report a sporting event, observe how his rate increases as the action grows more lively and remains relatively moderate when he interviews one of the players during an intermission.

ACHIEVING APPROPRIATE RATE

1   Listen to a recording of your spontaneous speech. Rate that is unusually fast or slow is frequently far more conspicuous to the listener than to the speaker. How well did your previous estimate of your rate match your evaluation of your rate on the recording? Do your instructor and classmates find your rate too fast or too slow?

2   Analyze your rate for oral reading: After you familiarize yourself with the following paragraph, record it. Ask your instructor or a classmate whether you are using the rate typical of your reading. Time your reading in seconds.

It is important to remember that, in strictness, there is no such thing as an uneducated man. Take an extreme case. Suppose that an adult man, in the full vigour of his faculties, could be suddenly placed in the world, as Adam is said to have been, and then left to do as he best might. How long would he be left uneducated? Not five minutes. Nature would begin to teach him, through the eye, the ear, the touch, the properties of objects. Pain and pleasure would be at his elbow telling him to do this and avoid that; and by slow degrees the man would receive an education which, if narrow, would be thorough, real, and adequate to his circumstances, though there would be no extras and very few accomplishments.[4]

THOMAS HENRY HUXLEY

The range of 157 to 170 words per minute is the most desirable rate for reading aloud material of this kind. If your time for reading the passage was between forty-six and forty-eight seconds, your rate is excellent. If your time was less than 42.5 seconds, you were reading at a rate faster than 185 words per minute. If your time was more than fifty-six seconds, you were reading at a rate slower than 140 words per minute.[5]

---

[4]From Thomas Henry Huxley, *Lay Sermons*, 1870. Reprinted by special permission from Appleton-Century-Crofts, Inc., New York.

[5]Recent studies show that syllables per minute provide a more accurate and less variable measure of rate than words per minute. For the sake of simplicity, this exercise employs the more traditional words-per-minute measurement.

Compare the results of this procedure with the evaluation of the rate of your recorded speaking in exercise 1. If your rate was consistently too fast, follow exercises 3 through 5. On the other hand, if your speaking and reading rates were both too slow, exercise 6 provides practice material.

3   To slow down rate, learn to prolong vowel sounds. At first you may try to slow down your over-all rate by pausing more frequently and at greater length, while the words you speak are as rapid as ever. This approach, producing an awkward rhythmical pattern, does little to create the impression of slower rate. Concentrate instead on lengthening vowel sounds in appropriate syllables.

Read the following phrases, prolonging the italicized vowels twice as long as is customary for you. *Do not* allow yourself to begin articulating the following sound until you have held the vowel as long as suggested.

Open the door.	Stay ahead.
The time of your life.	Look and learn.
Five and ten.	Olive branch.
The old stone face.	The fourth form.
Hands and feet.	The early bird.

4   Rapid rate, oral inactivity, and inadequate loudness often appear together. Such a speaker seems to mumble. As you learn to open your mouth wide for vowel sounds and to use more lip and tongue action for consonants, you will probably find that your rate becomes slower. Do the exercises on page 72 again, this time being conscious of their effect on your rate.

5   Rate is often implicit in the ideas to be spoken or read. Reading aloud material containing solemn or weighty ideas will encourage you to slow down. The following selections were chosen because of their affinity to a slow rate. Read them aloud, trying to match your rate to the meaning of each passage. Apply the techniques in exercises 3 and 4. Listen carefully to your reading so that you accustom yourself to hearing this slower rate.

   a.   The Lord is my Shepherd; I shall not want.   [*Old Testament*]

   b.   Sleep is the cousin of death.   [*African Proverb*]

   c.   Sweet are the thoughts that savour of content:
          The quiet mind is richer than a crown.

      ROBERT GREENE, from *Sweet Are the Thoughts*

   d.   *THE SLUGGARD*
          'Tis the voice of the sluggard; I hear him complain,
          "You have waked me too soon; I must slumber again."
             As the door in its hinges, so he on his bed,
             Turns his sides, and his shoulders, and his heavy head.

                                          ISAAC WATTS

   e.   My task is now finished. I have performed it to the best of my ability, and in word, at least, the requirements of the law are now satisfied. If deeds be in question, those who are here interred have received part of their honours already, and for the rest, their children will be brought up till manhood at the public expense: the state thus offers a valuable prize, as the garland of victory in this race of valour, for the reward both of those who have fallen and their survivors. And where the rewards for merit are greatest, there are found the best citizens.

PERICLES, from the *Funeral Oration for the Athenian Soldiers*

6   The meaning and emotional content of the material that follows are best reflected by a relatively fast rate. If you need to use a faster rate, you can probably benefit from working to match your over-all rate to these ideas.

a.   I remember your name perfectly, but I just can't think of your face.

[WILLIAM A. SPOONER]

b.   I am the very model of a modern major general.   [W. S. GILBERT]

c.   A fellow named Phineas Fly
Lived right in a muddy pig-sty;
    If you asked why this was,
    He'd reply, "Oh, because
It's none of your business, that's why!"

ANONYMOUS

d.   *ANIMAL FAIR*
I went to the animal fair,
The birds and the beasts were there.
The big baboon, by the light of the moon,
Was combing his auburn hair.

ANONYMOUS

e.   "The Duchess! The Duchess! Oh my dear paws! Oh my fur and whiskers! She'll get me executed, as sure as ferrets are ferrets! Where can I have dropped them, I wonder?"

LEWIS CARROLL, from *Alice in Wonderland*

7   In addition to the need for slowing down or speeding up over-all rate of speech, it is important to vary rate as the meaning of the material changes. Read the following, changing your rate as necessary:

a.   Don't drive so fast! Just take your time, please.

b.   When you reach the top of the mountain, you'll see five states spread out below you.

c.   He's only three years old, but he's as bright as a button!

d.   I think I'll take a walk—a long, quiet, solitary stroll down the road.
I think I'll take a walk—a brisk trot down the road.

e.   Did you see that? It was a four-car collision on the highway.
Did you see that? It was a Chinese funeral procession, with the mourners all dressed in white.

f.   I'd like to go to the party, but I'm just too weary.
     I'd like to go to the party, but I really don't have a minute to spare.

g.   *SONG OF THE OPEN ROAD*[6]
     I think that I shall never see
     A billboard lovely as a tree.
     Perhaps, unless the billboards fall,
     I'll never see a tree at all.

                              OGDEN NASH

h.   Since what is known as time immemorial it has been the custom of the
     Republican and Democratic Parties to hold conventions every four years
     and nominate candidates for the Presidency, and a month later hold
     elaborate ceremonies at which each nominee is notified that he has been
     tapped for Standard Bearer. The news comes to the nominee as a com-
     plete surprise. You could knock him over with a feather. One feather
     might even serve for both nominees. Fortunately, each happens to have
     in his pocket a typed speech of a few thousand words which, by a rare
     coincidence, just fits the occasion and saves the day.
        Nobody ever thinks of holding a notification ceremony for a defeated
     candidate, although when you look at it from a humanitarian point of
     view, he needs it a lot more than the successful candidate. His morale
     is shattered. His tongue is coated, and so is his faith in human nature.
     It would perk him up no end if a few thousand friends were to gather a
     month later and notify him officially that he did not get the nomination.[7]

                              FRANK SULLIVAN, from *Surprise!*

8   Practice using the appropriate rate in spontaneous speaking. Make im-
    promptu comments on one or more of the following topics:
    a.   The advantages of a large family.
    b.   How to relax.
    c.   "Cramming" for final examinations.
    d.   Eating foreign foods.
    e.   Speaking out of turn.
    f.   The importance of being on time.

RHYTHM
The rhythm of speech includes the duration of sounds and syllables together
with the arrangement and duration of pauses. These variables depend both on

[6] By special permission of Little, Brown and Company, Boston. Copyright 1932 by Ogden Nash; originally
appeared in the *New Yorker*.
[7] By special permission from Frank Sullivan.

the ideas and feelings of the speaker and on the conventions of his language. Duration of sounds and syllables is one of the factors contributing to *stress;* arrangement and duration of pauses comprise *phrasing.*

The discussion of duration will begin with the smallest unit of speech, the individual speech sound. Speech sounds differ from one another in average duration. Vowels are usually held longer than consonants. Among the consonants, sounds like *m, l, r* are longer in duration than sounds like *p, t, k.* The duration of vowels varies depending on the sounds that precede or follow. A given vowel sound is longer when it appears at the end of a phrase than when it precedes a consonant; a vowel preceding a voiced consonant is longer than the same vowel preceding a voiceless consonant. For example, the vowel in *see* is longer in the phrase *I see* than in the phrase *see that* or in the word *seek,* and the vowels in *pig* and *mean* are longer than the same vowels in *pick* and *meat.*[8]

Investigations show that listeners rely largely on durational aspects of speech production to identify the sounds they hear. In an experiment with artificial speech, listeners identified as different sounds vowels that were alike in every respect but length.[9] It follows that the expected length of speech sounds is one factor contributing to the intelligibility of speech.

The duration of individual speech sounds, particularly vowels, varies further within the expected limits according to the amount of *stress* they receive. Chapter 18 treats the combined factors of pitch, loudness, and duration as they contribute to *stress.*

The duration factor includes not only the time allotted to the sounds of speech but also the time allotted to silence. The speaker's arrangement of pauses and the duration of his pauses make up his distinctive pattern of *phrasing.* That pauses allow the speaker to replenish his breath supply is obvious. However, most pauses in speaking or reading aloud are not accompanied by inhalation but rather serve the purpose of dividing the total utterance into shorter units of thought that permit increased intelligibility. Within the limitations imposed by the need for renewed breath, the speaker determines where and how long to pause as he chooses his combinations of words. Phrasing, like stress, must follow the intellectual and emotional content of speech; inappropriate phrasing reduces intelligibility and disguises feeling.[10] Speak these words:

Did the patient come to the doctor asked the nurse.

When spoken with no indication of phrasing, this sentence makes no sense. You may read the sentence as:

"Did the patient come to the doctor?" asked the nurse.

---

[8] A. J. Bronstein, *The Pronunciation of American English,* Appleton-Century-Crofts, Inc., New York, 1960, p. 143.

[9] P. B. Denes and E. N. Pinson, *The Speech Chain,* Bell Telephone Laboratories, New York, 1963, p. 138.

[10] The concept of phrasing also implies intonation contours, which are discussed in Chapter 18 in the section on *juncture.*

or as:

"Did the patient come to?" the doctor asked the nurse.

These two arrangements suggest a possible pause either after *doctor* or after *to;* as a result, the different meanings of the sentence are clear. If you pause at any other point, however, neither of these meanings emerges.

Various types of distortion of rhythm exist. Some speakers use a staccato, "machine-gun" kind of rhythm with abruptly cut-off vowels, where all words seem to receive equal stress and where pauses occur briefly and infrequently. Other speakers use an uneven, irregular rhythm; a typical example includes rapid phrases broken unexpectedly by long pauses. Still other speakers use a monotonous, repetitive rhythm in which the rate and length of phrases vary little.

All these distortions of rhythm detract from meaning and from the impression the speaker desires to create. Although the staccato speaker sounds more energetic than the monotonous speaker or the one with an irregular rhythm, all three are difficult to understand. Awkward, irregular rhythm makes meaning especially hard to follow. Staccato speakers may appear to have a great deal of nervous tension; the speaker with awkward rhythm may appear uncomfortable, distracted, or unsure of himself; the monotonous speaker may appear tired, disinterested, or not too bright.

LISTENING AND OBSERVING:
CONTRIBUTIONS OF RHYTHM TO MEANING AND FEELING

1   Listen to a courtroom scene in a movie or play or television drama. How do the actors' rhythms help you to distinguish between the attorney for the prosecution and the attorney for the defense?
2   Listen to the voices of people arguing angrily. What patterns of rhythm do you hear in these angry voices?
3   Speak, instead of sing, the words of a familiar song. How does the speaking rhythm compare with the singing rhythm for the same words? Note differences in duration of sounds and in phrasing.
4   When attending a church service, listen to the rhythm of the minister's reading and speaking. In your judgment, is his style meaningful and interesting? Describe the pattern of rhythm that you hear in relation to the effectiveness of his style. Analyze the aspects of rhythm that differentiate his speaking from his reading aloud.

ACHIEVING MEANINGFUL PHRASING

1   To evaluate your phrasing, tape-record a lecture by an effective speaker on television or radio or secure a commercial recording of such a lecture. After typing or writing out a portion of the lecture, tape your reading of it. Compare the differences between your own phrasing and that of the speaker.

2   Because your awareness of language tends to be tied to the written word, you may assume that punctuation determines phrasing. Remember that no punctuation marks exist for speaking. While in the written language punctuation marks such as periods, commas, and semicolons do often indicate ends of phrases, the many exceptions make these marks unreliable for phrasing. For example, the sentences that follow are punctuated with commas that do *not* imply pauses:

Oh, no.
Why, John?
Oh, Mary, don't you weep.
One, two, three, four, five.
I said, "Shut up."

If you pause at every comma in the above sentences, the rhythm becomes awkward and the content difficult to follow. On the other hand, you will often find you need to pause where no punctuation mark appears. Examine these sentences to discover where pauses help to clarify the meaning:

a.   Every man takes the limits of his own field of vision for the limits of the world.   [ARTHUR SCHOPENHAUER]

b.   Meat eaten without either mirth or music is ill of digestion.

SIR WALTER SCOTT

c.   The scholar digs his ivory cellar in the ruins of the past and lets the present sicken as it will.   [ARCHIBALD MACLEISH]

d.   I got a religion that wants to take heaven out of the clouds and plant it right where most of us can get a slice of it.   [IRWIN SHAW]

3   You may be able to analyze a sentence into its component phrases and yet need practice in speaking the sentences accordingly. In the following sentences, the single stroke (/) marks the ends of phrases and the double stroke (//) marks the longer pauses, such as at the ends of sentences. Read these sentences aloud, taking care to pause as marked and only as marked.

a.   It is better to be able neither to read nor write/than to be able to do nothing else.//

WILLIAM HAZLITT

b.   We may affirm absolutely/that nothing great in the world has been accomplished without passion.//

GEORG HEGEL

c.   You can't appreciate home till you've left it,/money till it's spent,/your wife till she's joined a woman's club,/nor Old Glory till you see it hanging on a broomstick/in the shanty of a consul in a foreign town.//

O. HENRY

d.   I disapprove of what you say,/but I will defend to the death/your right to say it.//

VOLTAIRE

GALVESTON COMMUNITY COLLEGE LIBRARY

4   Analyze the following passages for appropriate phrasing and read them aloud accordingly. Try more than one possibility.

  a.   It is singular how impatient men are with over-praise of others, how patient with over-praise of themselves; and yet the one does them no injury, while the other may be their ruin.

JAMES RUSSELL LOWELL

  b.   Why may not a goose say thus: "All the parts of the universe I have an interest in: the earth serves me to walk upon, the sun to light me; the stars have their influence upon me; I have such an advantage by the winds and such by the waters; there is nothing that yon heavenly roof looks upon as favourably as me. I am the darling of Nature! Is it not man that keeps, lodges, and serves me? . . ."

MICHEL DE MONTAIGNE

  c.   If a man has a talent and cannot use it, he has failed. If he has a talent and uses only half of it, he has partly failed. If he has a talent and learns somehow to use the whole of it, he has gloriously succeeded, and won a satisfaction and a triumph few men know.

THOMAS WOLFE

  d.   As felicitous an instance of futile classicism as can well be found is the conventional spelling of the English language. English orthography satis-fies all the requirements of reputability under the law of conspicuous waste. It is archaic, cumbrous, and ineffective; its acquisition consumes much time and effort; failure to acquire it is easy of detection.

THORSTEIN VEBLEN

ACHIEVING VARIETY IN RHYTHM

1   Some ideas are best expressed when spoken in short phrases and staccato rhythm; other ideas lend themselves to longer phrases and smooth rhythm. Rhythm is smooth, or *legato,* when the vowels of each syllable are prolonged and the words within each phrase seem to flow from one to the next with no break between. Staccato rhythm is achieved by cutting the syllables short and detaching the words from one another. Staccato rhythm is usually associated with rapid rate, while smooth rhythm is associated with slower rate.

  a.   Read the following sentences with staccato rhythm:

  (1)   The car skidded, swerved across the road, and smashed into a truck parked at the curb.

  (2)   We'll be late if you don't hurry!

  (3)   Don't give me any more of your lip.

  (4)   I need five hundred dollars immediately, or I'll miss a real bargain.

b.   These sentences should be read with a smooth, or legato, rhythm:
    (1)   I stared into the horizon as far as I could see.
    (2)   There's nothing so cozy as sitting by the fire on a winter's day.
    (3)   Close your eyes and go to sleep.
    (4)   The silent shadows stretched across the ground.
c.   Sometimes the rhythm of speech carries as much information as the words themselves. For example, if you say

I received fourteen ties for Christmas.

with staccato rhythm, the listener would probably understand that you were dissatisfied or annoyed with the gifts; if you spoke the same sentence with a smooth rhythm, the listener would probably understand that you were resigned to your fate. While other factors such as pitch contours and vocal quality play a role here, rhythm certainly contributes to the speaker's message.
    Read each of the following sentences twice, first with staccato rhythm and then with smooth, legato rhythm. Observe the shift in meaning that occurs along with the shift in rhythm.
    (1)   Use the back door, please.
    (2)   George said he'd be back by midnight.
    (3)   Have you ever seen such weather?
    (4)   I think I'll go outside for a while.

2 Students frequently need practice in using smooth rhythm. Read the following passages, avoiding any break between words within each phrase. Choose long phrases where possible.
    a.   The finest music in the room is that which streams out to the ear of the spirit in many an exquisite strain from the little shelf of books on the opposite wall. Every volume there is an instrument which some melodist of the mind created and set vibrating with music.

JAMES LEE ALLEN

    b.   The far peaks sleep, the great ravines,
        The foot-hills, and the streams,
        Asleep are trees, and hived bees,
        The mountain beasts, and all that the dark earth teems,
        The glooming seas, the monsters in their deeps;
        And every bird, its wide wings folded, sleeps.

ALCMAN

3 Another source of variety in rhythm is the combined use of long and short phrases. A lengthy utterance is dull when pauses occur at almost equal intervals. The speaker achieves variety of phrasing by careful choice of language and of the phrasing appropriate to that language. The reader does not choose his words, but he uses alternative possibilities for phrasing to achieve variety

in length of phrases. When you read well-written prose, however, you notice that variation in length of phrases is often inherent in the material.

Study the following passage carefully for meaningful phrasing. Then read the paragraph aloud. You will find that short phrases are soon followed by a longer one; that long sentences, broken into two or three phrases, may soon be followed by a shorter sentence of only one phrase; that some phrases are made up of two or three words, while other phrases are eight or ten words long.

Books are the best of things, well-used; abused, among the worst. What is the right use? What is the one end which all means go to effect? They are for nothing but to inspire. I had better never see a book than to be warped by its attraction clear out of my own orbit, and made a satellite instead of a system. The one thing in the world, of value, is the active soul. This every man is entitled to; this every man contains within him, although in almost all men obstructed and as yet unborn. The soul active sees absolute truth and utters truth, or creates. In this action it is genius; not the privilege of here and there a favorite, but the sound estate of every man.

RALPH W. EMERSON, from *The American Scholar*

4   Study and read aloud the following passages to achieve variety in phrasing.

a.   The first proof a man gives of his interest in a woman is by talking to her about his own smart self. If the woman listens without yawning, he begins to like her. If she flatters the animal's vanity, he ends by adoring her.

RUDYARD KIPLING

b.   It is better to be able neither to read nor write than to be able to do nothing else. A lounger who is ordinarily seen with a book in his hand is (we may be almost sure) equally without the power or inclination to attend either to what passes around him or in his own mind. Such a one may be said to carry his understanding about with him in his pocket, or to leave it at home on his library shelves. He is afraid of venturing on any train of reasoning, or of striking out on any observation that is not mechanically suggested to him by passing his eye over certain legible characters; shrinks from the fatigue of thought which, for want of practice, becomes insupportable to him; and sits down contented with an endless and wearisome succession of words and half-formed images, which fill the void of the mind, and continually efface one another. Learning is, in too many cases, but a foil to common sense; a substitute for true knowledge.

WILLIAM HAZLITT, from *On the Ignorance of the Learned*

c.   All the great evils which men cause to each other because of certain intentions, desires, opinions, or religious principles, are likewise due to nonexistence, because they originate in ignorance, which is absence of wisdom. A blind man, for example, who has no guide, stumbles constantly, because he cannot see, and causes injury and harm to himself and others. In the same manner various classes of men, each man in proportion to his ignorance, bring evils upon themselves and upon other individual members of the species. If men possessed wisdom, which stands in the same relation to the form of man as the sight to the eye, they would not cause any injury to themselves or to others; for the knowledge of truth removes hatred and quarrels, and prevents mutual injuries.

MOSES MAIMONIDES

5 The foregoing principles of variety and meaningfulness in phrasing apply not only to reading aloud but also to speaking your own ideas. Spontaneous speech does not have the faultless, planned phrasing of oral reading because the speaker develops his ideas and chooses his words as he goes along. However, the patterns of rhythm still illuminate the speaker's meaning.

Use one or more of the following statements to develop some impromptu comments. As you choose the words and phrases to express your ideas, apply what you have learned about phrasing. Where possible, use a tape recorder so that you can study and improve your product.

a. Education is an end in itself.
b. Working mothers are a major cause of juvenile delinquency.
c. Organized competitive sports do not belong on a college campus.
d. Prospective teachers should have a five-year undergraduate program.
e. Men make better drivers than women.
f. Deafness is a more serious handicap than blindness.
g. If a person is honest with you, he can always explain his motivations.
h. If a person speaks English fluently, he has no need to learn a second language.

PART THREE

Acquiring Effective
Pronunciation

CHAPTER EIGHT

Standards of Speech

Interest of the public in language usage is evident from the furor raised after the publication of Webster's *Third New International Dictionary, Unabridged* [Philip B. Gove, (ed.), G. & C. Merriam Company, Springfield, Mass., 1961]. An editorial writer of *the New York Times* says the dictionary will "accelerate the deterioration" of the language. Other writers have been just as critical. One of the more conservative calls the dictionary a "disappointment"; another, less conservative critic calls it a "scandal and disaster." Many critics are sceptical of some of the pronunciations listed in this dictionary. For example, *Life Magazine* complains of the inclusion of the pronunciation (hīth) for (hīt) *height,* even though (hīth) is listed as a dialectal variant. On the other hand, professors of linguistics, defending the policy of the dictionary's editors, have used the columns of the *New York Times, Life,* and *The Atlantic Monthly* to say that the critics do not know whereof they speak and that the "pontifications" prove that they do not. They base their defense of the dictionary on the principle that it is a comprehensive and accurate record of current usage.

Not only is the interest in usage in spoken English evident in the columns of newspapers and magazines, but it is also evident in conversation. When the president of a large corporation says *athalete* for *athlete,* people note it, talk about it, and often feel a little superior because they "know better." When a radio announcer uses a British pronunciation, people remark about it. Matters of usage are frequent conversational topics.

Why this interest? Probably because speech is an important clue to the speaker's background. Who generally possess superior educational and cultural backgrounds in a community? The lawyers, business leaders, writers, artists, and public servants—those who hold positions of worth, of responsibility, and of importance. Most of these people are college graduates; furthermore, their speech represents the educated speech of a specific community. In other words, the prestige of patterns of speech depends upon those who use them.

DEFINITION OF STANDARD SPEECH

This concept reveals itself in definitions of standard English. For example, Webster's *Third New International Dictionary* defines *standard English* as "the English that with respect to speaking, grammar, pronunciation and vocabulary is substantially uniform though not devoid of regional differences, that is well-established by usage in the formal and informal speech and writing of the educated, and that is widely recognized or acceptable wherever English is spoken or understood." Similarly, *standard speech* is that which is in actual use among the persons who are the conservers of the approved social traditions of the community.

On the other hand, *substandard usage* is defined by Webster's *Third* as "conforming to a pattern of linguistic usage existing within a speech community but not that of the prestige group in that community in choice of word (as *set* for *sit*), form of word (as *brung* for *brought*), pronunciation (as *twicet* for *twice*), construction (as the boys is growing fast) or idiom (as *all to once* for *all at once*)." The speaker who says "Awri' I dint" is using *nonstandard speech* and is calling attention to his lack of education and culture.

Eliminating nonstandard pronunciation patterns and adopting those of the cultured, educated man of the community may, however, pose problems for you. Your democratic ideals may suggest the acceptability of almost all speech patterns. Or, while you may wish to sound like an educated, cultured individual, you may fear that you are spurning the values of those with whom you grew up. If, however, you view your patterns as part of a useful tool of communication for most situations and if you recognize that when necessary you can revert to former patterns, you can accept change. Walter Loban tells of a young lady on Kaui who said, "Using the Island dialect, for me, is like taking off my high-heeled shoes and getting into comfortable slippers. It's the real me; it's my deepest feeling."[1]

ALTERNATE PRONUNCIATIONS

Although educated speakers sound, on the whole, somewhat alike, pronunciations in their speech do differ. Bergen Evans writes:

[1] Walter Loban, "Teaching Children Who Speak Social Class Dialects," *Elementary English*, vol. XLV, p. 594, May, 1968.

A citizen listening to his radio might notice that James D. Conant, Bernard Baruch, and Dwight D. Eisenhower pronounce *economics* as *eckuhnomiks* while A. Whitney Griswold, Adlai Stevenson, and Herbert Hoover pronounce it *eekuhnomics*. A citizen turns to his dictionary to see which of the two pronunciations is "right" and finds that they both are acceptable.[2]

Educated people use alternate, equally acceptable pronunciations of the same word. For *either,* some say *eether* /'iðɚ/ and others say *eyether* /'aɪðɚ/. For *research,* some say *reesearch* /'risɚtʃ/ and others say *ruhsearch* or *rihsearch* /rə'sɚtʃ/ or /rɪ'sɚtʃ/, using the schwa /ə/ or the short *i* /ɪ/ for the first vowel. Some educated speakers use the short *a* /æ/ not the long *a* /e/ for the first *a* in *data* /'dætə/, put the emphasis in *abdomen* on the second not the first syllable, do not pronounce the *n* in *government,* and say *childern* /'tʃɪldɚn/ not *children* /'tʃɪldrɪn or -rən/. These variant pronunciations are all acceptable according to Kenyon and Knott's *A Pronouncing Dictionary of American English.*

Some words have many more pronunciations than those listed in any dictionary. In the word *almond,* you may pronounce the first *a* as the *a* in *hat* /æ/ or in *father* /ɑ/; you may omit the *l* or put it in; you may pronounce the *o* as the *i* in *hit* /ɪ/ or a schwa /ə/, the sound of the first *a* in *about.* A mathematician with a knowledge of the theory of permutations and combinations can compute how many different pronunciations, all equally acceptable, result.

THE CHANGING NATURE OF LANGUAGE

Language changes constantly. A pronunciation which is prestigious today may not be so tomorrow. In the eighteenth century, Dr. Samuel Johnson confessed that as he began his dictionary he had hoped to standardize the English language but soon discovered that no dictionary could "embalm his language and secure it from corruption." Changes are still taking place. Some of them have just been noted in the different acceptable pronunciations of *data, research, government,* and *children.* Some are less recent, as the loss of the sound *k* in the pronunciations of *know, knight,* and *knee;* this loss began in the seventeenth century and was completed in the eighteenth century. Whereas in Tennyson's time *blooming* connoted glowing, lovely, it later connoted just the opposite. In Chaucer's time the double negative was accepted. In the fifteenth century *women* was spelled *wymmen; gentle, jentyle.* Most changes in spelling ended in the sixteenth century.

The discrepancy between the spoken and the written word has caused some of you to try to make the sound conform to the spelling. Some few of you may pronounce both the *p* and *b* in *cupboard* or all the letters in *indict.* Many more of you pronounce the *t* in *often* and the *l* in *almond* or *palm,* thus reversing the historical process of the elimination of these *t*'s and *l*'s. Thomas says, "It is hard to avoid the suspicion that spelling pronunciations originate with those

---

[2]B. Evans, "But What's a Dictionary For," *The Atlantic Monthly,* vol. CCIX, p. 59, May, 1962.

people who are not quite at ease in their literacy. Neither the illiterate nor the highly literate are likely to place so high a value on the authority of spelling."[3]

SOUNDS IN CONNECTED DISCOURSE

Words are almost always spoken in a phrase or sentence, seldom singly. Occasionally one may answer a question with a single word. For example, one speaker asks, "Is that a red or yellow rose?" Another responds, "Red." Normally, however, even in answering questions one speaks in phrases or sentences. Speech moves or flows onward from word to word within a phrase. In onflowing speech, an assimilative process is at work and the sounds of syllables of different words may be linked, as in *takegoodaim* /tekəgʊdem/ for *take a good aim*. Or *What is* may become *whats* /ʍɑts/. Other examples of linking occur in the sentence "The children arrived with thin black coats." *With thin* may become *within* /wɪθɪn/; *black coats* may become *blackoats* /blæk:ots/.

PHONETIC SYMBOLS

These words and phrases are made up of individual speech sounds, each represented by a symbol of the International Phonetic Alphabet. The phrases have been written as they might be heard, that is, according to sounds that might be uttered by a speaker. The study of sounds and their combinations is a necessary tool in your examination of spoken language. A discussion of speech sounds and their representation appears in Chapters 9 through 16. In the next chapter, the term *phoneme* is used and explained. Briefly, the families of sounds belonging to individual vowels and consonants are called *segmental phonemes*. In addition, there are *suprasegmental phonemes*, represented by symbols of stress, of variation of pitch, and of clausal terminals. These phonemes are discussed in Chapter 18.

ASSIMILATION

The onward flow of speech results in *assimilation,* the modification of pronunciation because of adjacent sounds. While in Chaucer's day the past tenses of verbs were pronounced with an *ed* sound, now they are pronounced with either a /d/ or a /t/. For example, whereas the past tense of *grabbed* is pronounced with a d /græbd/, the past tense of *tapped* is pronounced with a t /tæpt/. The final sound in *grab,* /b/ is voiced, and the *ed* occurs as a voiced /d/. But /p/, the final sound in *tap,* is unvoiced, and as a result, the *ed* occurs as an unvoiced /t/.[4] The /p/ influences the unvoicing of the sound /d/ that follows. A similar

---

[3] C. K. Thomas, *Phonetics of American English,* 2d ed., The Ronald Press Company, New York, 1958, p. 10.

[4] A voiced sound is one where the vocal bands vibrate. An unvoiced sound is one where they do not vibrate.

influence exists in plurals of nouns: *Caps* is pronounced with a final unvoiced /s/, whereas *cabs* is pronounced with a final voiced /z/. The use of /z/ rather than /s/ is due to the voicing influence of /b/. Assimilation, an integral part of the onward flow of speech, makes for ease and economy of utterance.

This economy is evident in many of the common assimilations. For *nature,* no one says *naytyer* /'netjɚ/; rather, we say *naytcher* /'netʃɚ/. For *education,* no one says *edyukayshun* /ˌɛdjuˈkeʃən/; we say *ejikayshun* /ˌɛdʒəˈkeʃn̩/. This type of economy is exemplified in Ogden Nash's lines:

> What would you do if you were up a dark alley with Caesar Borgia
> And he was coming torgia.

It also occurs when someone carelessly asks *jeet* /dʒit/ for *did you eat* and is answered with *jew* /dʒu/ for *did you.*

This last phrase shows the influence of neighboring sounds not only within a word but also within a phrase. Assimilation within phrases occurs frequently in ongoing speech. C. K. Thomas gives this example:

> The usual pronunciation of *income* is /'ɪnˌkʌm/, with primary stress on the first syllable, secondary stress on the second syllable and a distinct syllabic division between /n/ and /k/. When we use the word as an adjective, however, in the phrase *income tax,* the pronunciation may be /'ɪnˌkʌm 'tæks/ but often it changes to /'ɪŋkəm tæks/. The reduced vowel represents reduced stress. The change from /n/ to /ŋ/ illustrates what is known as assimilation.[5]

Thomas goes on to explain that when *income* becomes part of the phrase *income tax,* the speaker scans the details more rapidly. He telescopes the phrase within itself, and the amount of time available for the shift from one syllable to the next is shortened. Since the shift from /n/ to /k/ takes more time than the shift from *ng* /ŋ/ to /k/ (both /ŋ/ and /k/ being made in the same position), the tongue, anticipating the /k/ position, makes only one contact, *ngk* /ŋk/, instead of two.

Assimilation, or the change of sounds under the influence of a third sound, is illustrated by what has occurred in derivatives of words with the Latin prefix *cum.* The /m/ remains in *complicate* and *comfort,* has become /n/ in such words as *conspire* and *consign,* and is *ng* /ŋ/ in such words as *congregate* and *conquer.* In *complicate* and *comfort,* /m/, /p/, and /f/ all involve the lips. In *conspire, consign,* and *contain,* /n/, /s/, and /t/ all involve the tip of the tongue and the gum or alveolar ridge. In *congregate* /'kɑŋgrɪˌget/ and *conquer* /'kɑŋkɚ/, the *ng* /ŋ/, /k/, and /g/ all involve the back of the tongue and the soft palate.

TYPES OF ASSIMILATION

In general, assimilation includes regressive assimilation, progressive assimilation, and reciprocal assimilation. *Regressive assimilation* is assimilation where a sound

---

[5] Thomas, *op. cit.,* p. 170.

influences the one preceding it. The change of the *n* in the prefix *con* to *ng* /ŋ/ in the words *congregate* and *conquer* exemplifies this type of assimilation, where the influence is backward in the word or phrase. This is the most frequent form of assimilation.

In *progressive assimilation,* a sound retains its identity but influences the following sound. The examples of /tæpt/ (*tapped*) as the past tense of *tap* and of /kæbz/ (*cabs*) as the plural of *cab,* noted earlier, represent progressive assimilation. *Open the door* may become /'opm̩ ðə 'dɔr/. /p/ being made with both lips has influenced /n/ to become /m/, also a bilabial sound. The nasal characteristic of the sound[6] has been maintained. This same type of assimilation, where the /n/ takes over the /t/, is evident in Ogden Nash's lines:

> I sit in an office at 244 Madison Avenue
> And say to you, Have a responsible job, havenue?

In these instances, the influence is forward.

In *reciprocal assimilation,* both forward and backward influences are at work; two sounds influence each other so that a third sound, a compromise between the two, is introduced. The examples given earlier of pronunciations of *nature, education,* and /dʒit/ for *did you eat* represent reciprocal assimilation. The /t/ or /d/ and the *y* sound /j/ interact in such a way that the *ch* /tʃ/ or *j* /dʒ/ sound results. In the word *tissue,* the *sh* was originally *sy,* but the *sy* /sj/ required more careful articulation than most speakers are willing to make. Consequently, speakers today say *tishoe* /tɪʃu/.

DISSIMILATION

Dissimilation is a change where a sound is dropped or made different from the original to make it less like its neighbor. The modern English word *turtle* is the result of the change of the final *r* in the original *turtur* to *l.* A present-day example is the loss of the first *r* in *library* or in *February.*

Some assimilations and dissimilations are acceptable; others are not. Your best guide to acceptability lies in the usage of cultured people. Listen carefully to discover which assimilations they use and which they avoid.

INFLUENCE OF PURPOSES OF SPEAKING ON SPEECH PATTERNS

The kind of onflowing language you use depends on the purpose of your speaking and on the occasion. If you are working in a road gang during summer vacation, you will probably use and hear many nonstandard pronunciations such as *Jawannago?* for *Do you want to go?* You will speak quickly and with little care.

---

[6] /m/, /n/, and /ŋ/ all possess nasal resonance.

Your vocabulary may be striking and colorful, appropriate to the ears of your fellow workers but inappropriate to the ears of most others. Such speech might well be likened to "overalls" speech. On the other hand, if you have been asked as student council president to deliver the main address to members of the student council and the faculty advisors of all campus organizations at a formal banquet in a large dining hall, you will speak formally. You will have prepared what you are going to say with the audience and the occasion in mind. On this occasion you will probably speak more precisely, slowly, carefully, and deliberately than you usually do. You will use more stresses. You probably will not say *won't* for *will not*. You will choose your language to fit the formality of the occasion.

The speech patterns used with the road gang and those used at the formal banquet represent both ends of a continuum of speech from nonstandard to formal. Most speech, however, is of the informal variety. This middle section of the continuum shows variation. In a bull session you will speak more rapidly, use more assimilations, be less careful of your choice of words than you would if you were being interviewed for a job. Your classroom speech patterns probably fall on the continuum between those of the interview and those of the bull session, although the size of the class, the type of room, and the degree of formality of your instructor influence the position of the patterns on the nonstandard-to-formal continuum. Martin Joos[7] notes that people use a wide variety of speech styles—varying from the most intimate to the most formal and that they automatically shift to whatever is most appropriate to the social situation. He points out that informal language fits small-group activity.

REGIONAL DIFFERENCES

A "standard" or "acceptable" speech does exist, and speech patterns do vary with the purpose and the occasion of the speaking. Another important influence on speech patterns, however, is that of region. Conspicuous differences exist among the speech patterns of the uneducated of varying regions. John Steinbeck points up the differences when he has Ivy from "Oklahomy" in *Grapes of Wrath* comment:

> "Ever'body says words different," says Ivy. "Arkansas folks says 'em different, and Oklahomy folks says 'em different. And we seen a lady from Massachusetts, an' she said 'em differentest of all. Couldn't hardly make out what she was saying."

Few (but clearly discernible) differences exist among the speech patterns of the educated of varying regions. The educated in a particular city may have characteristic pronunciations that are all their own. For example, in Philadelphia the middle vowel in words like *beautiful, citified,* and *attitude* is usually pro-

[7] Martin Joos, "The Five Clocks," *International Journal of American Linguistics*, vol. XXVIII, no. 2, part V, 1962.

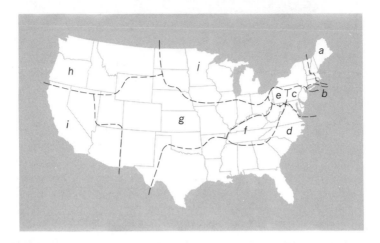

Map 1.   The ten major regional speech areas: (*a*) eastern New England, (*b*) New York City, (*c*) Middle Atlantic, (*d*) Southern, (*e*) western Pennsylvania, (*f*) Southern Mountain, (*g*) Central Midland, (*h*) Northwest, (*i*) Southwest, (*j*) North Central. (With permission from C. K. Thomas, *An Introduction to the Phonetics of American English,* 2d ed., p. 232. Copyright 1958, The Ronald Press Company, New York.)

nounced as a long *e* /i/. To delineate areas thus finely does not make sense for a text such as this. Thomas' classification of speech areas, however, is helpful to the student of pronunciation. Thomas reports that the geographical divisions in American speech are most clearly defined along the Atlantic Coast, which he divides into eastern New England, the Middle Atlantic area, and the South. He adds to these the New York City area, which he says is anomalous because its speech resembles both the Middle Atlantic and the Southern types and because its type was never reflected further west. In addition, he notes the North Central area; western Pennsylvania, with Pittsburgh as its cultural and economic center; and the Southern Mountain area, containing most of the mountain settlements of some Southern states. Finally, he names the Central Midland, a large area in the heart of the country the boundaries of which are not clearly defined and in which the speech characteristics are similar to those of western Pennsylvania and the Southern Mountain area; the Northwest, which includes everything from the central Dakotas westward to the Pacific Coast and down the Coast to include part of northern California; and the Southwest Coastal area, which includes most of Nevada and Arizona and all of California except the northern tier of counties.[8] (See Map 1.)

The following are a few of the regional differences: A New Englander and a Southerner may say *bahn* /bɑn/ for *barn*, whereas the Ohioan is likely to pronounce the *r* in the same word. A Bostonian approaches *pahth* /pɑθ/ for *path*,

[8]Thomas, *op. cit.*, pp. 216–242.

whereas the Ohioan is likely to use the same vowel in *path* /pæθ/ that he uses in *cat*. In the South, the *o* in *glory* /glorɪ/ is usually the same *o* as in *tote*, whereas in some other regions, it may be the *aw* sound in *law* /glɔrɪ/. In western Pennsylvania, the *o* in *doll* is usually the *aw* sound /dɔl/, whereas in New York City, in the Middle Atlantic area, and in the South, it is usually the *ah* sound /dɑl/. In *greasy* and the verb *grease*, the New Englander uses the *s* sound, whereas the Southerner uses the *z* sound.

These differences are representative of many others. Do you say *dawg* /dɔg/ or *dahg* /dɑg/? Do you use identical vowel sounds in *merry, marry,* and *Mary*? Do you say *ahn* /ɑn/ or *awn* /ɔn/ for *on*? Do you say *wawter* /wɔtɚ/ or *wahter* /wɑtɚ/ for *water*? Do you use /ɪ/ as in *hit* or /ɛ/ as in *let* in *any, many,* and *penny*? When you say *food, moon,* and *spoon,* do you make them sound more like *fyood* /fɪud/, *myoon* /mɪun/, and *spyoon* /spɪun/? Some of you follow one pattern, and some a different pattern, depending upon the region from which you come.

If you, a Southerner, move to Boston, you may almost unconsciously adapt your speech to that which surrounds you. On the other hand, you may stand out as "the Southerner" in the firm for which you work. Some individuals readily adopt the pronunciation patterns of the region in which they live; others do not. The pronunciation patterns of many persons as they live in various areas of our country take on a national flavor; differences are ironed out. Listen carefully to the pronunciation patterns of those of your region whom you respect, who show good taste, and who have social assurance. Such persons will be using patterns of speech which meet the demands of any situation and which do not call undue attention to themselves.

Walter Loban points out that what causes problems in communication and in social and personal relationships is not American regional accents but social-class dialect which differs from standard structure and usage. He indicates that in every region of this nation, Americans speak with rhythms and intonations that vary from New England to the South to the Far West. He notes that in Hawaii, educated and cultured people have—as in all other regions—a delightful and special way of speaking standard English. That in Georgia, teachers and community leaders speak *their* standard English—like Georgian Southerners. He goes on to support the concept of the acceptance of various educated regional patterns with:

> A man can speak with one of the New England accents and become President of the United States. President Kennedy never voiced the *r* in "Hahvahd" but he had no difficulty putting it in in "idear." Similarly one can speak with the regional accents of Texas and be elected to the highest office in the land. In any sizable nation, regional variation is inevitable, with syntax or grammar remarkably standard but with pronunciations, rhythms, and subtle idiosyncracies of usage providing a desirable range of variety.[9]

[9] Walter Loban, "Teaching Children Who Speak Social Class Dialects," *Elementary English,* vol. XLV, p. 592, May, 1968.

In summary, many influences are at work on your pronunciation patterns. Those with whom you work and play and the region from which you have come make a difference. Furthermore, the purpose and occasion of your speaking help determine your choice of usage. In all your speech you, as others have in the past, economize effort. As a result, changes in pronunciation are occurring and have occurred, for assimilative forces are always at work on onflowing speech. The best guide for acceptable speech patterns is the pronunciation used by the educated, cultured members of your own community. After you have heard and noted the acceptable pronunciations, you should learn to utter them with accuracy but without ostentation.

EXERCISES
LISTENING FOR STANDARD AND SUBSTANDARD SPEECH: OBSERVING ITS CHARACTERISTICS
1   Watch a television show such as *Gomer Pyle*. On the basis of speech, judge the cultural level of the characters. How did you arrive at your decisions?
2   Watch a news broadcast. Indicate the social, cultural level of the broadcaster and of the persons whom he interviews. How did you arrive at your decisions?

ANALYZING ATTITUDES TOWARD CHANGE
Allen Hubbell, a noted authority on dialectal speech in New York City, has said, "An individual's linguistic usage is among other things the outward sign of his most deepseated group loyalties." Support or attack this statement.

OBSERVING CHANGES IN LANGUAGE
1   What do you mean by "fulsome" praise? Look the meaning up in the diction-ary. Do you agree with the meaning in the dictionary?
2   Read some of Alexander Pope. From an examination of the rhyming words, what are some of the changes in pronunciation that have occurred since Pope's day?
3   Read some of Chaucer. Note differences in the language usage then and now.

LISTENING FOR ASSIMILATIVE CHANGES
Listen carefully to one of your professors. Write down some of his phrases just as spoken. Note how some of his words were linked to other words. Note how some of his sounds gave evidence of assimilation, as "Didja get the assignment?"

LISTENING FOR REGIONAL VARIATIONS
Listen to a professor who comes from a section of the country different from yours. List five words he pronounces differently from you. Contrast your pronun-ciations with his.

LISTENING FOR VARIANT PRONUNCIATIONS

Listen for pronunciations which you believe are unacceptable. Look up the pronunciations of these words in a dictionary with a copyright date no earlier than 1960. Report on your findings.

OBSERVING ENVIRONMENTAL INFLUENCES ON SPEECH

1   You normally greet people with "Hello," "Hi," or "Good morning." Do you consistently use one of these greetings for all whom you meet on campus? Or do you use different greetings? Explain.

2   First assume you are going into the remote areas of your state to find ghost stories. You meet with a laborer of little education. Then assume that you are to introduce the Secretary of State of the United States to a large assemblage of students. Compare your speech patterns in the two assignments.

CHAPTER NINE

Analysis of Sounds
of American English

That English spelling does not represent exactly and consistently the sounds in spoken American English is evident from these two ditties:

A teacher whose spelling's unique
Thus wrote down the days of the wique.
   The first he spelt "Sunday."
   The second day "Munday"—
And now a new teacher they sique.

Whenever she looks down the aisle,
She gives me a beautiful smaisle:
   And of all her beaux
   I am certain she sheaux
She likes me the best of the paisle.[1]

Other examples of inconsistency are prevalent: Letters are ignored in pronouncing *castle, know, debt, lamb,* and *palm.* For the spelling *ough,* the sound is pro-

---

[1] Spelling Reform Association, *Rimes without Reason*, Lake Placid Club, New York, pp. 1 and 6.

nounced /u/ in *through,* /ɔf/ in *cough,* /ʌp/ in *hiccough,* and /ʌf/ in *tough.*
Conversely, for the sound /ɪ/ as in *hit,* different spellings are represented in the
words *build, myth, women, been,* and *business.*

Quite obviously, since English spelling does not suffice for an accurate representation of pronunciation, its study involves the use of either diacritical symbols
or the International Phonetic Alphabet (IPA). Elementary and high school students generally use diacritical symbols—sometimes successfully but often unsuc-
cessfully. One of the reasons for the lack of success is that in this system
several symbols represent a single sound. For instance, a single sound, the
schwa /ə/ of the IPA, is represented by several diacritical markings including ŭ
in *circus* (sûr' kŭs), à in *ago* (à gō'), ă in *nasal* (nā-zăl), and ė in *mathematics*
(măth'-ė-măt' ĭks). This text, concerned with sounds and not orthography, uses
the IPA, a set of symbols with only one symbol for each sound. The IPA is more
helpful to the student interested in a sound-by-sound analysis of spoken utterances because it provides for more accurate representation than do diacritical
markings. Furthermore, the IPA serves as a tool for the representation of sounds
in the one pronouncing dictionary of American English now in print.[2]

Sounds are frequently divided into three groups: consonants, vowels, and
diphthongs. A *consonant* is a sound which is the result of the action of articulating agents interrupting in some way the expiring breath stream, with the vocal
bands sometimes vibrating, sometimes not. *Vowels* are sounds uttered with little
or no stoppage of the breath stream; their quality comes from the vibration of
the vocal bands and from the shape and size of the resonating chambers in the
throat and mouth. *Diphthongs* are combinations or rapid blends of two vowels
in which the combination usually begins with one vowel and glides or gradually
changes into another, with the first of the two vowels being stressed. For example,
in "Go, call Roy" the diphthong in *Roy* usually begins with /ɔ/, the vowel in *law,*
but glides into an /ɪ/, the vowel in *hit;* the diphthong is /ɔɪ/.

CONSONANTS

When you say *tab, dab,* and *nab,* you hear three distinct words because the first
consonant of each of the three combinations of sounds is different. When, however, you examine what articulatory agents you use in /t/, /d/, and /n/, most of
you find that they are the tip of the tongue and the gum (alveolar) ridge. What,
then, makes the difference in your hearing of these three sounds? As you say
tab and *dab,* you find that the /t/ and /d/ are alike not only in the agents of
articulation involved but also in the manner of articulation; both are held and
then quickly released. That /t/ is made without voice whereas /d/ is made with
voice accounts for the difference. As you say /t/ and /d/, notice this difference.

[2] J. S. Kenyon and T. A. Knott, *A Pronouncing Dictionary of American English,* 2d ed., G & C. Merriam
Company, Springfield, Mass., 1949.

What, then, makes /n/ unlike /t/ and /d/? When you say *dab* and *nab*, you again use the same articulatory agents, and furthermore, both /d/ and /n/ are voiced. Here, however, the difference lies in the manner of production. If you hold your nose while you say *dab* and *nab*, you find that saying *nab* becomes difficult. The /n/ has nasal resonance, whereas /d/ does not; in addition, /n/ is not held and released as /d/ is but is continued. Thus, the manner of production of /n/ results in acoustic features enabling the listener to distinguish it from /d/.

From this discussion, you may conclude that three factors are important in the production and perception of consonants: (1) the involvement of particular articulatory agents, (2) the presence or absence of voice, and (3) the manner of production.

An individual, however, makes a sound such as /t/ differently as he combines it with other sounds. As noted in the preceding chapter, the position of a sound in a syllable and its proximity to other sounds inevitably bring about a difference in it. When you place /s/ before *tab*, making the word *stab*, the /t/ in *stab* is somewhat different from the /t/ in *tab*, for the /t/ in *tab* is fully aspirated. Again, when you say *taut*, the initial and final /t/'s do not sound identical, for the initial /t/ is fully aspirated whereas the final /t/ is not. When you say *bat the ball*, you do not even use the articulatory agents you normally use in /t/, for the /t/ in this phrase is made not with the tip of the tongue on the alveolar ridge but with the tip of the tongue against the teeth. This change occurs because the *th* sound /ð/ which follows is usually made with the tip of the tongue against the cutting edges of the teeth.

The differences which distinguish the initial consonantal sounds of *tab*, *dab*, and *nab* are significant, for as a result of the three initial sounds, each word has a distinct meaning. Differences such as these are called *phonemic*. Since, however, the /t/'s in *tab* and *stab* and the final /t/ in *cat* do not vary significantly from one another, they are included in the phoneme /t/. A *phoneme* is a linguistic unit significantly different from all other sounds.

The term *allophone* is applied to the variety of /t/'s in the words *tab*, *stab*, and *taut*. These allophones are all sounds which help make up the phoneme /t/. Obviously, there are many other /t/ allophones than those listed here.

INVOLVEMENT OF ARTICULATORY AGENTS   (See Figure 9.)

In the initial sounds of the words *tab*, *dab*, and *nab*, the articulatory agents involved are the tip of the tongue and the gum (alveolar) ridge. In *pop*, *bop*, and *mop*, the articulatory agents involved in both the initial and the final consonants are the lips. In *back*, *bag*, and *bang*, the articulatory agents involved in the final consonants are the middle or back of the tongue and the soft palate. In *fan* and *van*, the articulatory agents involved in the initial sounds are the lower lip and the upper teeth. In *thin* and *then*, the articulatory agents in the initial sounds of

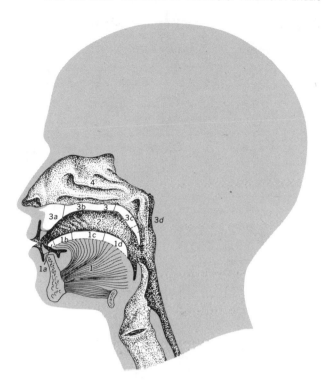

FIGURE 9.   The articulatory mechanism.

1. Tongue	1c. Front of tongue
2. Mouth (oral) cavity	1d. Back of tongue
3. Palate	3a. Gum or alveolar ridge
4. Nasal cavity	3b. Hard palate
1a. Tongue tip	3c. Soft palate
1b. Blade of tongue	3d. Uvula

(Adapted from Jon Eisenson and Mardel Ogilvie, *Speech Correction in the Schools,* The Macmillan Company, New York, 1963, p. 90; by permission of the publishers.)

these words involve the tip of the tongue and the teeth. In *hay,* the articulatory agent involved is the glottis, the space between the vocal bands which are located in the larynx. In consonantal sounds, the tip or the center or back of the tongue, the lips, the teeth, the soft palate, and the glottis may be involved. When you know that *lingua* represents *tongue; dental, teeth; alveolar, alveolar* or *gum ridge; palatal, palate; velar, velum* or *soft palate; glottal, glottis* or space between the vocal bands, you can understand the terminology applied to sounds. For instance, /t/, /d/, and /n/ are tip-of-tongue–gum-ridge, or lingua-alveolar, sounds, whereas /p/, /b/, and /m/ are lip, or bilabial, sounds. (See the "Involvement of Articulatory Agents" column in Chart 1.)

CHART 1   PRODUCTION OF AMERICAN ENGLISH CONSONANTS

MANNER OF PRODUCTION	INVOLVEMENT OF ARTICULATORY AGENTS						
	Lips (Bilabial)	Lip-Teeth (Labio-dental)	Tongue-Teeth (Lingua-dental)	Tongue Tip Alveolar Ridge (Lingua-alveolar)	Tongue and Hard Palate (Lingua-palatal)	Tongue and Soft Palate (Velar)	Glottis (Glottal)
Voiceless stops	p			t		k	
Voiced stops	b			d		g	
Voiceless fricatives	ʍ	f	θ	s*	ʃ†	ʍ¶	h
Voiced fricatives		v	ð	z*	ʒ†		
Nasals	m			n		ŋ	
Lateral semivowel				l			
Glides	w				r‡ j	w¶	
Voiceless affricate					tʃ		
Voiced affricate					dʒ		

* In /s/ and /z/, the channel is narrow.
† In /ʃ/ and /ʒ/, the channel is broad.
‡ The tongue tip in many instances is curled away from the gum ridge to the center of the palate.
¶ In /ʍ/ and /w/, both the lips and the back of the tongue are involved.

THE MANNER OF PRODUCTION

STOPS

When you say *tab, dab,* and *nab,* you note that in /t/, /d/, and /n/, the same articulatory agents are used but the words are produced differently. In /t/ and /d/, you compress the breath and then suddenly release it. /t/ and /d/ are called *stops.* Other stops are /p/, /b/, /k/, and /g/. Included in this category is the glottal stop /ʔ/. Normally, the listener does not hear the glottal stop as a separate sound, and therefore, in American English it is not a consonantal phoneme. It may be substituted for the medial /t/ in *bottle,* or it may appear initially before a vowel or diphthong, as in the word *ask* /ʔæsk/.

CONTINUANTS

All other consonant sounds are *continuants*. Continuants are classified as (1) frictionless consonants or semivowels and (2) fricatives. The /n/ which you hear in *nab* not only continues but also possesses nasal resonance since you lower your velum or soft palate and direct the voiced breath stream through the nose. /n/, /m/, and /ŋ/ as in *sing* comprise the nasal consonants, which are semivowels. The glides and the lateral /l/ are also classified as semivowels. The glides /r/ as in *rate*, /j/ as in *yellow*, and /w/ as in *warm* are not made by the action of one articulatory agent upon another but by the movement of the articulatory agents from one position to another. /l/, the lateral semivowel, is made with the voiced breath stream forced over the sides of the tongue. All these sounds are frictionless. But other sounds have a frictionlike quality: In /f/, /v/, /s/, /z/, /h/, the two *th* sounds /θ/ as in *thin* and /ð/ as in *then*, /ʃ/ as in *shall*, and /ʒ/ as in *azure*, the breath is impeded on its way out, with a resulting noise that suggests friction. Such sounds are called *fricatives*.

AFFRICATES

Lastly, American English sounds include *affricates*, or the consonantal blends /tʃ/ as in *child* and /dʒ/ as in *Jack*.

Consequently, each sound achieves some of its characteristic quality because of the way it is produced. The listener utilizes these acoustic cues in distinguishing and identifying the segmental phonemes in ongoing speech.

PRESENCE OR ABSENCE OF VOICE

As already noted, although the articulatory agents used and the manner of production in the /t/ and /d/ of *tab* and *dab* are the same, the difference lies in the presence or absence of voice. When you put the tips of your fingers on your Adam's apple and utter /t/ without adding a vowel, you feel no laryngeal vibrations. When, however, you do the same thing with /d/, you do feel laryngeal vibrations. You note this difference clearly when you continue a fricative sound /θ/ as in *cloth*, which is unvoiced, and /ð/ as in *clothe*, which is voiced. You feel no vibration on the /θ/ in *cloth*, but you do feel vibration on the /ð/ in *clothe*. Both in /d/ and in /ð/, the vocal bands have been producing vibrations which you can feel. Almost all the stops and fricatives have voiced and voiceless counterparts. All semivowels are voiced. (See Chart 1 for sounds which are voiced and voiceless.)

As each category of consonants is discussed, you will find that you produce most of them accurately, for college students do pronounce most sounds acceptably. Some students, however, have trouble with /t/, /d/, /s/, /z/, /ʃ/ as in *shore*, /ʒ/ as in *azure*, /θ/ as in *thin*, /ð/ as in *then*, /l/, and /r/. Considerably more drill material for these sounds than for the others will, therefore, be included in the chapters that follow.

CHART 2   CONSONANTS OF AMERICAN ENGLISH

/p/	pit	/v/	van	/ʒ/	azure	/l/	lemon
/b/	bit	/θ/	thin	/h/	hill	/r/	ran
/t/	lea	/ð/	then	/ʍ/	where	/j/	yard
/d/	day	/s/	sea	/tʃ/	church	/m/	may
/k/	can	/z/	zero	/dʒ/	judge	/n/	no
/g/	go	/ʃ/	shall	/w/	won	/ŋ/	rang
/f/	fan						

VOWELS

Whereas consonants are important in determining intelligibility for listeners, vowels through their variables of quality, pitch, time, and loudness are important in determining emotional intent for the listener. Dictionary meanings of *so* as an interjection include expressions both of approval (*let it be so*) and of surprised dissent. The vowel sound in *so* through its variables makes both the intended meaning and the feeling clear to the listener. The concept of conveying emotional intent to the listener through the variables in voice is discussed in the section on voice and in Chapter 18.

Vowels are normally voiced sounds; the vocal bands vibrate as they are uttered. Furthermore, in all vowels the nasal port is closed. The differentiating characteristics of vowels are (1) the place of articulation or the section of the tongue raised to narrow the oral passage at a particular point, (2) the height of the tongue, (3) the degree of lip-rounding, (4) the degree of muscular tension, and (5) the degree of stress.

Vowels are more variable than consonants. The influence of neighboring sounds is greater for vowels. And the effect of the continuing movement of the vocal articulators during the utterance of a vowel in context makes for differences both in acoustic results and in articulatory position. Consequently, although the authors describe vowels according to the above characteristics, you must remember that these characteristics are based on norms and that many individual variations exist.

PLACE OF ARTICULATION

Say /i/ as in *meet* and then /u/ as in *boot*. In /i/, the blade of the tongue is bunched and raised toward the hard palate. In /u/ as in *boot,* the back part of the tongue is bunched and raised toward the velum or soft palate. In /ɝ/ as in *burn,* the central portion of the tongue is bunched. Now look at Chart 3. You will find the terms *front, central,* and *back.* In the front vowels listed at the left, the blade, or front part, of the tongue is raised toward the hard palate. In the central vowels listed in the middle section, the center part of the tongue is raised to a spot toward the back of the hard palate and forward from the soft palate. In the back vowels listed on the right side, the back of the tongue is raised toward

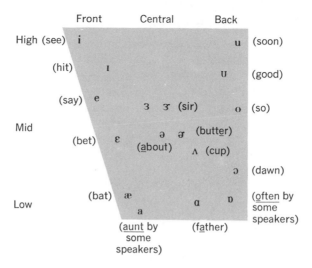

CHART 3   DIAGRAM OF VOWELS

the soft palate. Remember that the articulatory positions of vowels show variability. Whereas in most consonants the articulatory positions remain somewhat
definite, in vowels the positions are adjusted with no articulatory constriction
existing.

THE HEIGHT OF THE TONGUE

Say /i/ as in *beat,* /e/ as in *mate,* and /æ/ as in *hat.* Then say /u/ as in *boot,*
/o/ as in *obey,* and /ɑ/ as in *father.* In both the first and the second series, the
tongue goes from a comparatively high position to a mid-position and then to a low
position. Furthermore, in both series, the jaw drops as the second and third
sounds in the series are uttered. The terms *high, mid,* and *low* refer to the differences in the height of the tongue as represented by the sounds in these
words. As you examine the chart depicting the vowels of American English, you
find that /i/, /ɪ/, /u/, and /ʊ/ are high vowels, that /e/, /ɛ/, /ɝ/, /ə/, /ɚ/, /ʌ/,
and /o/ are mid-vowels, and that /æ/, /a/, /ɔ/, /ɑ/, and /ɒ/ are low vowels.
Again, to attribute an exact level to a vowel is impossible, for the height varies
with phonetic context.

LIP-ROUNDING

Lip-rounding alone does not distinguish one American vowel from another. A
degree of lip-rounding usually accompanies most back vowels. This lip-rounding
occurs in /u/ as in *loot,* /ʊ/ as in *look,* /o/ as in *obey,* /ɔ/ as in *law,* and /ɒ/ as
sometimes heard in *often.*

MUSCLE TENSION OR LAXNESS

Say /i/ as in *heat* and /ɪ/ as in *bit*, then /u/ as in *boom* and /ʊ/ as in *look*. Repeat the sounds, placing your hand under your chin. In /i/ and /u/ you feel the muscles tense; you do not feel the tenseness in /ɪ/ and /ʊ/. /i/ and /u/ are tense vowels; /ɪ/ and /ʊ/ are lax vowels.

DEGREE OF STRESSING

Vowels with greater stress tend to be longer than those with less stress; in fact, the stressed vowel sometimes becomes diphthongized. For example, where /e/ is stressed, as in *trade* or *maid*, it is diphthongized /eɪ/. Where /e/ is not stressed, as the first *a* in *vacate* and the second *a* in *mandate*, it is monophthongal /e/. Context again plays a role. For example, as a speaker utters a syllable with less stress than usual in a phrase, /eɪ/ tends to become /e/, as in *play* in "a definitely superior play performance." On the other hand, the diphthongal variant /eɪ/ is present in the *play* in "Are you going to the play?" In the South, the monophthongal /e/ is characteristic of the pronunciation of many persons. A second example involves /o/. When a speaker utters /o/ in a stressed syllable, it is diphthongized /oʊ/, as in "The wind doth blow." In an unstressed syllable, as in *okay* or *fellow*, it is monophthongal /o/. Here, too, context plays a role. In "The lawn must be mowed" the /o/ in *mowed* is diphthongal /oʊ/. But in the *mow* in "Your lawn is lovely. Did Bobby mow it yesterday?", /o/ tends to become monophthongal. In this text, /e/ and /o/ will be considered phonemes which have variants.

DIPHTHONGS

A diphthong is a vocalic glide uttered in a single breath impulse in which two vocal resonances can be identified. The first phonetic symbol represents the first vocal resonance, and the second symbol, the second resonance. The organs of articulation modify themselves to give a continuous change of sound until the diphthong is completed. A diphthong, then, is a blend of two vowels wherein the first vowel slowly changes and glides into the position and acoustic value of a second vowel. In the discussion of /i/ and /u/, the authors indicate that these vowels in positions of stress often become diphthongized /ɪi/ and /ʊu/. Where the unstressed element begins the glide, it is called an *on-glide*. In the discussion of /o/ and /e/, the authors indicate that, similarly, these vowels in positions of stress become /oʊ/ and /eɪ/. Since the unstressed part of the diphthong ends the glide, it is called an *off-glide*.

A diphthong is a phonemic diphthong when the sound unit is distinctive. For example, in the phonemic diphthongs in *cow* /kaʊ/, *kite* /kaɪt/, or *boy* /bɔɪ/, the sound units are distinctive. In the nonphonemic diphthongs in /roʊ/ and /deɪ/, the sound units are not distinctive. Whether you say *row* as /roʊ/ or /ro/ and *day* as /deɪ/ or /de/, the meaning remains the same. Since /ou/ and /eɪ/ are allophones of /o/ and /e/, in this text the authors have transcribed them as monophthongs /o/ and /e/. On the other hand, the phonemic diphthongs must always be transcribed as diphthongs.

CHART 4   VOWELS AND DIPHTHONGS OF AMERICAN ENGLISH

/i/	see, beat, machine, people, mien, dece*i*t	/ʌ/	cup, love, touch, blood
/ɪ/	hit, busy, women, built, bicycle	/u/	soon, through, shoe, blew, blue
/e/	say, same, rain, reign, great, they	/ʊ/	good, should, full
/ɛ/	bet, friend, many, stationary, stealth	/o/	so, sew, soap, row, though
/æ/	bat, bade	/ɔ/	dawn, ought, daughter
/a/	aunt, dance, path (regional)	/ɒ/	often (regional)
/ɝ/	sir, colonel, world, fern, learn, turn	/ɑ/	father, psalm, hearth, sergeant
/ɜ/	by some regional speakers	/aɪ/	ride, sky, high, height, eye, aisle
/ɚ/	butter, doctor, measure	/au/	how, about
/ə/	about, sofa, attention, circus, collect, relative	/ɔɪ/	boy, spoil

EXERCISES
DISTINGUISHING SPELLING FROM SOUND REPRESENTATION

1   List three different pronunciations for the letters *u, a,* and *i*. (*Example:* Three different pronunciations for the letter *o* occur in *hot, obey,* and *women*.)

2   List four spellings for the sound of /e/ as in *day*.

NOTING ALLOPHONES OF PARTICULAR PHONEMES

Listen to the following consonantal sounds in these pairs of words:

/k/	key, coke	/t/	late, eighth	/k/	Kay, sky
/l/	lemon, William	/p/	paid, ape		

Do you hear differences in the sounds in each pair? In which pairs do you feel differences in where the sounds are made?

DETERMINING INVOLVEMENT OF ARTICULATORY AGENTS, PRESENCE OR ABSENCE OF VOICE, AND MANNER OF PRODUCTION

1   Note where you make these sounds. What articulatory agents are involved?

/m/	as in *may*	/f/	as in *fan*	/θ/	as in *think*
/g/	as in *go*	/ʃ/	as in *shall*		

2   Indicate whether the italicized consonantal sounds are voiced or unvoiced: *K*ay, *d*ay, *th*in, *th*en, *th*istle, ba*th*e, *r*oar, clip*s*, fad*s*, co*ll*ege, *f*un, *v*an.

3   *a.*   Underline *stops* in: Pick a peck of pickled peppers.

    b.   Underline *continuant sounds* in: Mary had a little lamb,
                                  Its fleece was white as snow.
    c.   Underline *fricatives* in: This is the day I take my Middle-English exam. I
        hope I don't fail. Two failures, and back I go to working in a garage.
    d.   Underline *nasals* in: Millicent is a popular singer at the Club. Millicent—
        a funny name for a singer.
    e.   Underline *laterals* in: Calm yourself, Lolita. Your call is late, but you'll
        get it eventually. Go on building castles in the air.
    f.   Underline *glides* in: Row, row, row your boat gently down the stream.
                       You'll be surprised what fun rowing gently can be.

DISTINGUISHING AMONG FRONT, CENTRAL, AND BACK VOWELS

In the following selection, note whether each vowel is front, central, or back. Then note whether each is high, low, or central:

> Johnny sat in the car waiting for his girl friend Mary. She was shopping for a new dress to wear to the Fall Prom. She couldn't decide between a beautiful long blue dress and a short white one. Johnny said to himself. "Learn to stay home—away from a shopping girl."

LOCATING PHONEMIC DIPHTHONGS

In the following selection, pick out the phonemic diphthongs:

> While paperbacks of cheap price are found in an enormous number of outlets, they nonetheless suffer, as magazines do, a rapid turnover. Each competes desperately for display space at the newsstand or drugstore, and each is held in stock only briefly, with a life cycle scarcely greater than a fruit fly's. . . . A decade ago . . . it was found necessary to destroy 60,000,000 paperbacks within a single year.
>
> WILLIAM JOVANOVICH, from *Now Barabbas*

PRINCIPLES OF CONTROL OF PRONUNCIATION

You are now ready to examine patterns of speech sounds, compare your patterns with those of others, and make the changes you desire. In the chapters on voice, the term *feedback* and its application to voice improvement were stressed. The concept is equally important in changing pronunciations. Authorities who discuss therapy for articulatory defects often emphasize the need for three functions in correcting errors: scanning, comparing, and correcting.

    In *scanning*, the speaker receives information through sensory channels about how his speech mechanism is performing and about the result of the performance, the utterance. For speech improvement, the speaker listens to and hears his utterance. In addition, he feels what articulatory agent works with what other articulatory agent and is aware of such a factor as the fricative manner of production of /f/ and /v/. The speaker who does not scan effectively is not examining the product of his speech motors.

In *comparing*, you match your speech patterns against the standard you desire to achieve. You examine the dominant features of an utterance and match what you say against what you wish to say. Since there is obviously not time to match every sound before uttering the next, key features of entire patterns of sounds rather than individual sounds are compared. As you watch the expert typist, you can understand the comparison of the backflow of message against a standard pattern. The typist places her fingers on the eight designated keys, turns on "feedback," and proceeds to hit the necessary keys to type the words that correspond to the pattern she is following. In her almost automatically controlled typing, a discrepancy between her pattern and her copy can take place. She discovers the error through her "feel" that she has hit the wrong key or through her visual inspection of her typed copy. The feel is all-important for speed in typing. The expert typist often knows through feel that she is about to make an error; she may then correct it before it actually occurs, thereby maintaining her rhythm and speed. But when the error has occurred, she confirms her impression of error through visual inspection and proceeds to correct the error. In this instance, the rhythm has been broken. Thus the corrector function becomes involved. In speech improvement, the discrepancies between the desired speech patterns and the actual speech patterns (error signal) are what determine the amount and kind of improvement. Here, too, the correcting is involved.

The third function, then, is *correcting*. It is based on information obtained through scanning and comparing. You are aware of this function in correcting slips of the tongue, for you are often immediately conscious that you have mispronounced a word or uttered a sound inaccurately. You then correct the mispronunciation by stressing a different syllable or the misarticulation by changing the position of the tongue to what feels right and sounds right to you. In other words, you vary the way you utter the syllable or sound until no difference exists between the pattern you are producing and the one you desire to produce (zero error signal). The same kind of correction occurs in eliminating speech patterns you judge to be undesirable. Having become aware of what speech patterns need to be changed and having found for yourself patterns which you believe should be standard for you, you adjust your mechanism through hearing, feeling, and seeing so that it produces the desired patterns. Then you proceed to practice until the control becomes automatic.

When the expert typist started to learn to type, her control was far from automatic. She probably began with a-s-d-f space, semi-l-k-j space; she practiced until she no longer had to look at the keys. The almost automatic "feel" took over. As in typing, the control for speech is learned. In childhood you compared the self-hearing of your own utterances with the sounds that the adults around you produced. When you matched them fairly well, you were rewarded. The kinesthetic and tactual messages from your placement and from the operation of parts of the articulatory mechanism became satisfying and vivid. Soon the kinesthetic and tactual feedback was so well established that the auditory feedback played a secondary role. You came to rely almost completely on the feel of the movements of your speech mechanism rather than on your hearing.

In the correcting phase, you are substituting conscious control for automatic control in order to change your speech patterns. You must match the auditory feedback from your mouth with the auditory patterns coming from the mouths of the educated. You adjust your mechanism by hearing, seeing, feeling. In hearing, a tape recorder is helpful. Working with another student adept at mimicking your pattern is also helpful. In seeing, a mirror aids you in discovering what articulatory agents are at work. For example, if your /s/ does have some of the /θ/ qualities, the tongue is visible. In feeling, you need to become aware of the tactile and kinesthetic sensations. If you wish not to dentalize /t/ and /d/—that is, if you wish to make the sounds on the alveolar ridge instead of against the teeth—you can feel whether the tongue tip is on the alveolar ridge or on the teeth.

Your choice of the auditory pattern against which to match yours is important. Having found out how the speech patterns of the educated differ from yours, you must then make value judgments on the desirability of certain changes. The material that is presented in the following chapters should make you aware of the differences. Undoubtedly, if you say *dis* and *dat* for *this* and *that,* you will change your patterns to *this* and *that* because you will not find many educated people saying *dis* and *dat.* But in many instances, you will make decisions different from those of some of your classmates. You may want to eliminate intrusive r's, as in *idear* and *lawr,* but a classmate, aware that many of the educated in his community say *idear* and *lawr,* may decide not to make the change. You make your value judgments on the basis of current linguistic information, on what you hear the educated in your community utter, and on personal preference.

Having made the decision and being able to make the change, you then work toward an automatic control. Just as in learning to type, the first efforts will be slow, sometimes clumsy. And just as in typing, practice is essential. Use readily available time for practice. As you drive or walk to class, say some of the phrases, recite some of the poetry, make up limericks or ditties with the sound you are changing. If you cannot say the words out loud, imagine you are uttering them. "Feel" yourself going through the imaginary movements. Involve your classmates in practice. Several pairs of students before and after speech class can walk from one campus building to another practicing. With practice, the automatic control does take over.

CHAPTER TEN

Stops: /p/, /b/, /k/, /g/, /t/, /d/, /ʔ/

Certain characteristics apply to all the voiceless stops. The speaker in pronouncing /p/, /k/, and /t/ does not vibrate his vocal bands but obstructs his breath with certain articulatory agents, and then releases the sound as he utters the next sound. He keeps the nasal port closed so that there is little or no emission of air. The presence or absence of aspiration in the unvoiced plosives varies with the position of the particular sound in relation to other sounds. At the beginning of a word or of a stressed syllable, /p/, /k/, and /t/ are fully aspirated, as in *pen, repeal, couch, recover, tar,* and *return.* But when /p/, /k/, or /t/ occurs as a final sound at the end of a syllable (*lap, lick, mat*), as an initial sound of a lightly stressed or unstressed syllable (*sleeper, slacker, rater*), or preceded by /s/ (*spar, scale, stale*) or followed by a consonant (*mopped, licked, actress*), it is not fully aspirated.[1]

A tendency to insert a /p/ or a /t/ between /m/ and some consonantal sounds occurs often. An *excrescent* /p/ occurs in such words as *something* /sʌmpθɪŋ/, *warmth* /wɔrmpθ/, and *comfortable* /ˈkʌmpfɚtəbl/. This assimilation is evident in

---

[1] In this text, the allophonic symbols of voiceless plosives are not indicated in environments where they are not fully aspirated. For a discussion of the distinctions among weakly aspirated, unaspirated, and imploded voiceless stops, consult a text on phonetics.

the spelling of such words as *empty, exempt,* and *glimpse.* Similarly, an excrescent /t/ occurs between /n/ and /s/ or /θ/ in such words as *tense* /tɛnts/, *prance* /prænts/, *dance* /dænts/, *mince* /mɪnts/, and *tenth* /tɛntθ/. The excrescent /p/ and /t/ occur so frequently in educated speech that they are acceptable.

Certain characteristics also apply to all the voiced stops. The speaker vibrates his vocal bands, obstructs his vocal stream with certain articulatory agents, and then releases the sound as he utters the next sound. These sounds are always unaspirated. Like /p/, /k/, and /t/, the voiced stops /b/, /g/, and /d/ are more strongly exploded when they occur at the beginning of a stressed syllable and are less so as a final sound or as an initial sound of an unstressed syllable. The voiced stops, because of their voicing, are less strongly exploded than their voiceless counterparts.

/p/ AS IN *PIT* AND /b/ AS IN *BIT*

The /p/ and /b/, which are *bilabial* (made with the two lips), are usually uttered acceptably. Occasionally, /p/ is too weakly articulated, so that it is perceived as somewhat like a /b/. If *pie* sounds like *buy,* then /p/ may not be aspirated strongly enough. This weak aspiration takes place sometimes in the speech of those whose native language is other than English. On the other hand, a too carefully articulated /p/ can result in an aspirate quality in words like *cap* or *captain.* A partially devoiced /b/ occurs in a phrase like *throw away the tab.* This /b/ should not, however, become /p/.

Consequently, in practicing the following material, keep in mind these suggestions:

1 Make sure that you pronounce /p/ and /b/ relatively distinctly and precisely. Close your lips firmly so that you cannot be accused of being "lip-lazy,"— especially where /p/ and /b/ occur finally. Be careful that your /p/ and /b/ are not confused with /f/ and /v/. Do not allow your /p/ to become a /b/.
2 On the other hand, do not pronounce /p/ and /b/ with too much vigor. Be sure that you do not pronounce them with so much vigor that /p/ is aspirated where it should not be or that /p/ or /b/ has a schwa /ə/ after it.
3 After you have pronounced the phrase, use it in a sentence.
4 After practicing the /p/ and /b/ in the phrases listed, carry the correction over into reading and finally into conversation.

PHRASES WITH /p/ AND /b/ FOR DRILL

/p/ INITIATING A STRESSED SYLLABLE	/p/ TERMINATING A SYLLABLE; /p/ INITIATING AN UNSTRESSED SYLLABLE; INITIAL /sp/; AND FINAL /pt/
Panic buying.	Step aside.
A severe penalty.	A complete flop.

/p/ INITIATING A STRESSED SYLLABLE	/p/ TERMINATING A SYLLABLE; /p/ INITIATING AN UNSTRESSED SYLLABLE; INITIAL /sp/; AND FINAL /pt/
Grave peril.	You hope.
Call the porter.	Upward movement.
Great pain.	Spot the garment.
Enemy occupation.	Spoke well.
Perpetual motion.	Slapped hard.
Impart the news.	Kept quiet.
A soft pillow.	Ripped badly.
A large pail.	The tipsy stroller.

/b/ INITIATING A STRESSED SYLLABLE	/b/ TERMINATING A STRESSED SYLLABLE; FINAL /bd/; AND /b/ INITIATING AN UNSTRESSED SYLLABLE
Bet a dollar.	Club meeting.
Bargain basement.	Pick up the tab.
A new bulletin.	The cub scouts.
Off base.	Tubbed and cleaned.
Abuse the privilege.	Dubbed a moron.
The ambassador to France.	A mob of men.
A ballot wasted.	Rubbed hard.
Boston, Massachusetts.	Tubby the Tuba.
A bicycle race.	Believe your teacher.
Bacon and eggs.	Subway stairs.

/k/ AS IN *CAN* AND /g/ AS IN *GO*

The voiceless /k/ and the voiced /g/ are cognates which are *lingua-alveolar* stops, made by bringing the middle or back of the tongue firmly into contact with the velum. /k/ and /g/, like all other sounds, are influenced by the sounds around them. When /k/ is followed by a front vowel, as in *keel,* the tongue touches further forward on the palate than when it is followed by a back vowel, as in *cool.* When /k/ or /g/ is followed by /l/, as in *tackle* or *gargle,* the /k/ or /g/ may be exploded laterally because of the influence of /l/, which is a lateral sound. When /k/ or /g/ is followed by /n/, as in *chicken coop* or *dragon fly,* the /k/ or /g/ may be exploded nasally because of the influence of /n/, which is a nasal sound.

   /k/ can be carelessly articulated just as /p/ can. It should not be weakened to a constricted velar fricative, somewhat like an exaggerated /h/, in a word such as *technical* or to a /g/, as in /sɪg'nɪfəgənt/ for /sɪg'nɪfəkənt/. The speaker must articulate /k/ well enough for it to be clear. But he must not aspirate /k/ strongly where unnecessary, such as in *lick* or *faction.* Furthermore, he must not allow his final /g/ to become /k/ even though some unvoicing does occur. Consequently, in the following phrases:

1   Say /k/ and /g/ relatively distinctly and precisely. (Be sure that enough contact between the back or middle of the tongue and velum exists so that air pressure as released produces adequate explosion.)

2   Do not pronounce /k/ and /g/ with too much vigor. (Do not press the tongue so tightly against the palate that the release is overly explosive.)

3   After practicing the /k/ and /g/ phrases listed below and after using the phrases in sentences, carry the correction over into reading and finally into conversation. If you have worked on /p/ and /b/, be sure to maintain your acceptable articulation of these sounds.

PHRASES WITH /k/ AND /g/ FOR DRILL

/k/ INITIATING A STRESSED SYLLABLE	/k/ TERMINATING A SYLLABLE; INITIAL AND FINAL /sk/, /kt/, AND /ks/; AND /k/ INITIATING AN UNSTRESSED SYLLABLE
Kansas City.	An important link.
Corning glass.	A picnic table.
Accustom yourself.	Skim the surface.
A good mechanic.	Squeeze the tube.
Overcome your fear.	Ask the conductor.
A speedy recovery.	A brick house.
Unconsciously greedy.	Attract attention.
Carve the meat.	Poor brakes.
Conquer your fear.	Defect of hearing.
Carrots and peas.	Tax collector.

/g/ INITIATING A SYLLABLE	/g/ TERMINATING A SYLLABLE; FINAL /gz/ AND /gd/; AND /g/ INITIATING AN UNSTRESSED SYLLABLE
Disguised as an angel.	Snug as a bug in a rug.
Beginning of time.	Catalogue of fishing materials.
Gambling tables.	Ignorant proceedings.
Ghastly mistakes.	The ugly picture.
Premium gasoline.	The dog show.
A goal of a million dollars.	Lags behind.
Forget the date.	Rigged election.
Regard it as a favor.	Bagged a deer.
Again and again.	Shaggy dog.
Undergoing surgery.	Meager dinner.

/t/ AS IN *TEA* AND /d/ AS IN *DAY*

The cognates /t/ and /d/, the unvoiced and voiced stops made with the tip of the tongue and the alveolar ridge, are called *lingua-alveolar* sounds. /t/ and /d/ are influenced by the sounds around them: In some contexts, the /t/, with its lack of aspiration, seems to the uninitiated ear to be a /d/. These cases usually occur when (1) /t/ precedes /n/ or /l/ which are syllables by themselves, as in *kitten* or *little* (in the first instance, the /t/ is exploded nasally because of the nasal /n/; in the second, the /t/ is exploded laterally because of the lateral /l/); (2) the final /t/ precedes the stressed vowel of the next word, as in a phrase like *let out the dog;* (3) /t/ precedes an unstressed vowel, as in *sitting, city,* or *cutting.* In some instances, speakers do change the /t/ to a weakly articulated /d/ or to a glottal stop /ʔ/ (formed by closing the vocal bands, then releasing the compressed air at the glottis). These speakers utter *latter* and *ladder* with the same medial consonant. You can, however, usually strengthen the /t/ in these words without being accused of being affected. In formal cultivated speech, the glottal stop is not used. The authors suggest that you listen to yourself saying an unaspirated medial /t/, as in *battle* and *kettle,* to find out whether you do use a glottal stop in these words.

In many languages, /t/ and /d/ are made with the tip of the tongue against the upper front teeth. In American English, most speakers make the /t/ and /d/ in this manner only when /t/ and /d/ are followed by /θ/ as in *thin* or by /ð/ as in *then.* The phrases *at the door* and *add the number* and the words *eighth* and *width* exemplify /t/ and /d/ as linguadental sounds. Speakers with direct or indirect foreign influences, such as those living in major urban areas, often make /t/ and /d/ with their tongue on their teeth in other combination of sounds. You can check yourself by looking in a mirror with your mouth open while you say *tea.* If the tip of the tongue is touching the teeth, you can change your mode of articulation by moving the tip of your tongue to the alveolar (gum) ridge.

The omission of the /d/ is common in words like *grandmother, bandstand,* and *handsome,* for the /n/ and /d/ are made in the same place. Many educated speakers use these assimilated forms. But in other words or phrases, the same speakers do not use somewhat similar assimilated forms. Only those using over-assimilated speech say /aɪ ʃʊnt go/ for *I shouldn't go* and /wʊnt jə dʊ ɪt/ for *wouldn't you do it.*

A poorly articulated /t/ often occurs in phrases like *sit down* and *let go.* You are likely to drop the /t/ in these phrases and move to the next sound. In other phrases, such as *last night* and *past the gate,* many educated people do omit the /t/. In formal situations, however, the /t/ is likely to be used in both instances.

Consequently, practice the words and phrases listed below, paying attention to these directions:

1   Look, as suggested earlier, to see where you make /t/ and /d/.
2   Listen to hear whether your /t/ sounds like /ts/ and your /d/ like /dz/. If they do, place your tongue tip on the alveolar position and release it quickly.

3   Make /t/ and /d/ relatively distinct and clear, but do not overaspirate /t/ or overexplode /d/ so as to call attention to the sounds.
   a.   Where /t/ and /d/ occur in the middle of a word, as in *bottle*, note whether you substitute a glottal stop for the /t/ or /d/. Furthermore, listen to discover whether your medial /t/ in words such as *better* sounds too much like a /d/.
   b.   Where /t/ and /d/ occur finally in a word used alone, finally in a phrase, or in words such as *rats* or *cads*, retain the /t/ and /d/.
   c.   Observe whether the final /d/ becomes a /t/ in a phrase such as *a smooth forehead*.
4   While reading the prose and poetry, be careful to use the patterns of plosive sounds that you believe are acceptable in your community. Try, however, to make your reading sound conversational. Finally, carry over your improved patterns into conversation. Topics have been provided for this purpose.

/t/ AND /d/ WORDS AND PHRASES FOR DRILL[2]

/t/ AND /d/ INITIATING A STRESSED SYLLABLE		/t/ AND /d/ TERMINATING A SYLLABLE; /t/ AND /d/ IN CLUSTERS, MEDIAL POSITION, AND PRECEDING UNSTRESSED SYLLABLES			
tale	dainty	await	fed	faculty	ladder
temper	deaf	stable	aboard	hospitality	medal
meantime	dark	staff	aloud	kettle	fiddle
tore	dam	combat	code	matter	hoarding
tar	ordeal	fright	slid	meeting	cloudy
routine	condemn	omit	upward	notice	hinder
retire	adopt	rat	lads	butter	madam
until	damp	bats	lids	beauty	riddle
attend	darken	kept	tobacco	delight	saddle
attention	daylight	wrapped	tomorrow	desire	spender
attempt	endeavor	laughed	city	hidden	trader
contend	undo	parts	mountain	laden	fodder
entire	redeem	confide	settle	ladle	ridden
sometime	adopt	forbid	flatter	lady	Daddy

PHRASES

With /t/
Wait your turn.
Take attendance.

With /d/
An advanced academy.
Read aloud.

[2]Since /t/ and /d/ are frequently troublesome, the authors have included lists of words with these sounds. They suggest, however, that you use each word in a phrase or sentence after you have said it acceptably.

With /t/
Attract attention.
Sit down.
Eighteen faculty members.
A dramatic editorial.
A kettle of victuals.
A tan kitten.
Eighteen dollars.
Literary critic.
A neutral country.
The mantle of greatness.
Seventy-two tapes.
A rotten tomato.
A subtle difference.
The eighth person.

With /d/
Good candy.
The hidden garden.
Identical twins.
The middle child.
A medical problem.
Solve the riddle.
Put on the saddle.
Slide down.
A tendency to fade.
A trader of repute.
A timid boy.
A dull undertaking.
A reward of fifty dollars.
The width of the door.

VERSE

1   *THE LITTLE KITTENS*[3]
"Where are you going, my little kittens?"
"We are going to town to get us some mittens."
    "What! Mittens for kittens!
    Do kittens wear mittens?
Who ever saw little kittens with mittens?"

"Where are you going, my little cat?"
"I am going to town to get me a hat."
    "What! A hat for a cat!
    A cat get a hat!
Whoever saw a cat with a hat?"

ELIZA LEE FOLLEN

2   A tutor who tooted the flute
    Tried to tutor two tooters to toot.
    Said the two to the tutor:
    "Is it harder to toot, or
    To tutor two tooters to toot?"

ANONYMOUS

3   A woman to her son did utter,
    "Go, my son, and shut the shutter."
    "The shutter's shut," the son did utter,
    "I cannot shut it any shutter."

ANONYMOUS

---

[3]Students who plan to teach in elementary school will find this type of material useful.

4   *SPRING RAIN*[4]

The storm came up so very quick
   It couldn't have been quicker,
I should have brought my hat along.
   I should have brought my slicker.

My hair is wet, my feet are wet,
   I couldn't be much wetter.
I fell into a river once
   But this is even better.

MARCHETTE CHUTE

5   Use it up and wear it out,
Make it do, or do without.

ANONYMOUS

6   The mountain sheep are sweeter,
But the valley sheep are fatter;
We therefore deemed it meeter
To carry off the latter.

THOMAS LOVE PEACOCK, from *The War Song of Dinas Vawr*

PROSE

1   The following article by Sylvia Wright describes a heroic effort to help a bank
   understand that running a house is much more complicated than managing
   investments—especially when a couple of women and a cookie jar and a
   country carpenter get mixed up with it:

You sound cross. How, you coldly ask, can anyone have spent so much more money
than she told the Fiduciary Trust Company she was going to? Don't think, you intimate
to me, that you can play fast and loose with funds, even if they are your own funds.

   The tone of your letter indicates that for you this is standard procedure. You assume
you are something quite usual, even something I should accept. I can't. I find you
peculiar. Look at it from my point of view. Here is our family, owning a delightful, if
dilapidated, house by the seashore. I own a sixth, and my brother owns a twelfth, and
one of my aunts owns a third, and the other of my aunts owns five-twelfths. Things
are simple.

   My aunt who owns the third dies, and things are still simple, because I am expect-
ing to inherit it. Suddenly you leap into the picture, and it's your third of a house. I
have inherited it, but you have it, in trust for me.

   You don't know anything about the house. You've never seen it. You don't intend to
see it. You don't know its beautiful view of the sound ("We must cut down that dead

---

[4]Copyright 1946 by Marchette Chute. From *Around and About*, by Marchette Chute. Published 1957
by E. P. Dutton and Co., Inc., New York, and reprinted with their permission.

tree"). You've never been swimming here ("It's the getting in that's difficult"), or felt the breeze on the piazza in summer ("This must be a scorcher on the mainland"). You don't know the house's individual smell—wood, salt air, soap, and something unidentifiable. . . . And you have no notion of my Aunt Maria, who knows where everything is and the minute it isn't. . . . ink bottles are put in the potties that have covers, in case they freeze and bust. If they do, you can always wash the potties. And if they don't, there is your ink for next summer.[5]

2   The following is the first paragraph of an article by B. J. Chute:

Language, like gunpowder, is an invention; and, like gunpowder, it is a very lively one. It marches with the times out of necessity, and any new biological, medical or electronic discovery demands new words to describe it.[6]

3   In an article in the *New York Times,* Dr. Philip Gove, editor-in-chief of Webster's *Third New International Dictionary,* explains that his editorial principles are sound:

The criticisms involve less than one percent of the words in the dictionary, he said in an interview. He goes on to say that the purpose of the dictionary is to describe objectively the meanings and values of words as educated people use them today. He makes an interesting comment about *finalize.* He says that he is impatient with the furor over the third edition's acceptance of *finalize.* He sees no reason why *finalize* should be graded below "anglicize" or "macadamize."[7]

4   The artist must yield himself to his own inspiration, and if he has a true talent, no one knows and feels better than he what suits him. I should compose with utter confidence a subject that sets my blood going, even though it were condemned by all other artists as anti-musical.

GIUSEPPE VERDI, from *On Composing*

QUOTATIONS TO STIMULATE IMPROMPTU TALKS OR CONVERSATION
The following quotations are intended to inspire talks—singly or in groups:
1   History makes one shudder and laugh by turns.   [WALPOLE]
2   A good name is better than riches.   [*Bible*]
3   Speech is the gift of all, but thought of few.   [CATO]
4   A noble mind disdains not to repent.   [HOMER]

[5] By permission of S. Wright, "Dear Fiduciary Trust Company," *Harpers Magazine,* vol. 215, p. 27, July, 1957.
[6] B. J. Chute, "How Dictionaries Grow," *Inside the ACD,* vol. 9, p. 1, March, 1957.
[7] *New York Times,* March 1, 1962, p. 28.

5   Modesty is the only sure bait when you angle for praise.
                                                    [EARL OF CHESTERFIELD]
6   Travelling teaches toleration.   [BENJAMIN DISRAELI]
7   Wit is the salt of conversation, not the food.   [WILLIAM HAZLITT]
8   A prating barber asked Archelaus how he would be trimmed. He answered,
    "In silence."   [PLUTARCH]
9   Time is the image of eternity.   [DIOGENES LAERTIUS]
10 I never met a man I didn't like.   [WILL ROGERS]
11 Politics has got so expensive that it takes lots of money to even get beat
    with.   [WILL ROGERS]
12 The man that hath a tongue, I say, is no man, if with his tongue he cannot
    win a woman.   [WILLIAM SHAKESPEARE]
13 My method is to take the utmost trouble to find the right thing to say, and
    then to say it with utmost levity.   [G. B. SHAW]
14 He that is slow to anger is better than the mighty; and he that ruleth his
    spirit than he that taketh a city.   [Bible]
15 Train up a child in the way he should go; and when he is old he will not
    depart from it.   [Bible]
16 Grow up as soon as you can. It pays—the only time you really live fully is
    from thirty to sixty.   [HERVEY ALLEN]
17 Poverty is the parent of revolution and crime.   [ARISTOTLE]
18 Where's the man could ease a heart like a satin gown?   [DOROTHY PARKER]
19 If liberty and equality are chiefly to be found in a democracy, they will be
    best attained when all persons alike share in the government to the utmost.
                                                    [ARISTOTLE]
20 The best, the most exquisite automobile is a walking-stick; and one of the
    finest things in life is going a journey with it.   [ROBERT CORTEST HOLLIDAY]

DISCUSSION
Hold brief discussions on the following topics:

  Should typewriting be required of all high school students?
  Does an honor system in college eliminate cheating?
  Should a year abroad be substituted for a year of college study?
  Should a student delay on the choice of his career until he has completed his
  first two years of college?

/ɔ/ GLOTTAL STOP
The glottal stop results from the compression and sudden release of air at the
glottis, the opening between the vocal bands. It is unvoiced and unaspirated. When

speakers utter sounds with a high degree of laryngeal tension, it occurs frequently before words beginning with vowels or diphthongs. For example, when you tense your throat and say "Eat your oatmeal" emphatically, you may hear a clicking sound before *eat* and before *oatmeal*. As already noted, some speakers also substitute /ʔ/ for /t/ in words like *cotton, batten,* and *bottle.*

CHAPTER ELEVEN

Fricatives and Affricates

FRICATIVES: /f/ **AS IN** *FAN*, /v/ **AS IN** *VAN*, /θ/ **AS IN** *THIN*, /ð/ **AS IN** *THEN*, /h/ **AS IN** *HILL*, /s/ **AS IN** *SEA*, /z/ **AS IN** *ZERO*, /ʃ/ **AS IN** *SHALL*, /ʒ/ **AS IN** *AZURE*, **AND** /ʍ/ **AS IN** *WHERE*

As noted in Chapter 9, a fricative is a continuant sound in which the breath is impeded on its way out, with a resulting noise that suggests friction. With the exception of /h/, this noise is caused by the direction of the breath against the hard palate, alveolar ridge, teeth, and/or lips.

/f/ AS IN *FAN* AND /v/ AS IN *VAN*

The voiceless /f/ and the voiced /v/ are cognates that are labiodental fricatives (made with the cutting edges of the upper teeth and the lower lip). In both sounds, the noise of friction results from forcing the breath stream out through the spaces between the teeth or between the upper teeth and the lip; in /v/, as in other voiced fricative cognates, the voiced sound has less friction than the unvoiced sound. For both /f/ and /v/, the nasal port is closed.

In connected speech, /f/ and /v/ are influenced by the sounds around them. For example, when a bilabial sound precedes /f/ or /v/, it tends to become a labial fricative. This assimilation occurs in words like *campfire*, *comfort*, and *obviate* and in such phrases as *tame fox*, *lame fighter*, *cab fare*, and *mob vengeance.* Although many careful speakers avoid this assimilation, it is not particularly noticeable in informal speech. As in all fricatives, when a voiceless consonant follows the /v/ or when the /v/ occurs at the beginning or end of a phrase, /v/ is partly devoiced. This devoicing occurs in such phrases as *value of the land, more to give,* or *live fish.* Similarly, "I have to do it" or "I have to see about that" may sound like "I haf to do it" or "I haf to see about that" in the speech of many educated people.

/f/ and /v/, although generally made acceptably, may cause some difficulty; nonnative speakers sometimes confuse /v/ with /b/ or /w/. Since both /f/ and /v/ are readily visible, the correction is fairly simple.

DRILL MATERIAL FOR /f/ AND /v/

DIRECTIONS FOR DRILL

1   Make sure that you do not substitute /b/ or /w/ for /v/.
2   Articulate /f/ and /v/ distinctly enough so that /f/ or /v/ where preceded by a bilabial does not become a bilabial fricative sound. This change should not occur in formal speech in the first five phrases in both the /f/ and the /v/ lists. Remember, however, that in informal speech, this assimilation is common.
3   Be careful that the initial or final /v/ does not become completely unvoiced.
4   Be sure that for formal speaking purposes, the /f/ and /v/ in the last group of phrases and sentences are not omitted.
5   After you have said each phrase, incorporate it in a sentence.
6   Include in your drill any changes that you have made so far.

PHRASES

INITIATING A WORD OR SYLLABLE

/f/	/v/
Cupful of sugar.	The same voice.
Room fan.	Top van.
Tame fox.	To obviate the act.
Delicious comfit.	Blame Vi.
Comforting thought.	Glum villager.
Face the facts.	Value for your money.
A good farm.	Voice of the people.
Defeat the candidate.	November the first
A good performer.	A good provider.
Can't afford it.	Avenge the wrong.

TERMINATING A WORD OR SYLLABLE

/f/	/v/
A good wife.	Give her a gift.
Enough pain.	Have to go.
Laugh out loud.	Move at once.
Life of the party.	Prove it.
Roof over her head.	Save your stamps.
The difference between the two.	Seven of them.
A great effort.	Evening news.
A different scheme.	A new discovery.

/v/ TERMINATING AN AUXILIARY VERB

I would have bought it.	I should have remembered.
I would have to think about it.	I should have tried.

/θ/ AS IN *THIN* AND /ð/ AS IN *THEN*

The voiceless /θ/ and the voiced /ð/ are cognates that are linguadental fricatives (made with the tip of the tongue against the cutting edge of the teeth). Differences, however, do exist in the exact positions of the articulators of these sounds. Sometimes the tongue tip is placed between the teeth; at other times it is in contact with the lower portion of the back surface of the upper teeth. But the sound of friction in both instances results from air being directed by the tongue against the hard surface of the teeth, and consequently, the sound you hear is the same. As in other fricatives, the voiced /ð/ has less friction than the unvoiced /θ/. In /θ/ and /ð/, the nasal port is closed.

In the other fricative sounds, the differences between the voiced and unvoiced cognates are obvious, but you may have difficulty in discerning the difference between /θ/ and /ð/. Say *thin*, prolonging the /θ/; then say *then*, prolonging the /ð/. Place your fingers on your larynx as you say the words, and feel the difference in the two sounds. No hard-and-fast rules exist which will help you to distinguish between these two sounds. In general, however, the *th* at the beginning of nouns, verbs, adjectives, and adverbs is /θ/. For example, the *th* in *thank you, you bit your thumb, cut me a thick slice,* and *a pretty Scotch thistle* are all unvoiced. In pronouns such as *them, they, this,* and *these,* in the adverb *then* and the article *the,* and in words with a silent e following /ð/, as in *breathe,* the *th* is voiced.

Like other fricatives, the /θ/ and /ð/ are affected by the sounds around them. The /ð/ is somewhat devoiced when it begins or ends a word in a phrase or when it is followed by a voiceless consonant. For example, /ð/ in the sentences *They will do it, A verb ending with a silent e is breathe,* and *I loathe pickles* is partly devoiced.

Most American speakers have little trouble with these sounds, although some who have grown up in an area where dental /t/ and /d/ are substituted for /θ/

and /ð/ may retain traces of this substitution. For example, they may say /θ/ and /ð/ acceptably in all words except *with,* which may be consistently /wɪt/ or /wɪd/. Many of you, however, do tend in rapid conversation to substitute sounds somewhat like dental /t/ or /d/ for /θ/ and /ð/. You may also omit /θ/ in words such as *fifths, sixths, sevenths, eighths,* and *ninths* in very informal or very rapid speech. Speakers learning English frequently find the /θ/ and /ð/ unfamiliar sounds. Consequently, they substitute either dental /t/ and /d/ or /s/ and /z/ for them.

DRILL MATERIAL FOR /θ/ AND /ð/

DIRECTIONS FOR DRILL

1   Make sure that you do not substitute /t/ and /d/ or /s/ and /z/ for /θ/ and /ð/. If you do make such substitutions, say the words first with the substitution and then with the desired sound. Finally, incorporate the acceptably pronounced words in the phrases.
2   Listen to hear whether you articulate /θ/ and /ð/ distinctly enough so that they are heard in the last group of phrases, which contain words where these sounds are frequently omitted.
3   Discover whether you completely unvoice /ð/ in initial or final positions or when it is followed by an unvoiced sound.
4   Read the verse and prose incorporating your changes. Be sure to include the changes you have already made on other sounds.
5   Using the quotations, incorporate your changes in conversation or an impromptu talk.

PHRASES WITH /θ/

INITIATING A WORD OR SYLLABLE	TERMINATING A WORD OR SYLLABLE
Good theater.	A plain truth.
Thank you.	Worth a great deal.
Thin slice.	Faith in your country.
Think of it.	Month of July.
A thousand ships.	Going north.
Through a door.	Easy path.
Theme of the play.	A birthday party.
Something exciting.	A breathless moment.
A Scotch thistle.	A faithful dog.
One-third of a pie.	A monthly allowance.
Didactic authority.	Going southwest.
Cathedral on Third Avenue.	A terrifying earthquake.
An infectious enthusiasm.	A ruthless dictator.
An apathetic listener.	A pithy statement.

PHRASES WITH /ð/

INITIATING A WORD OR SYLLABLE	TERMINATING A WORD OR SYLLABLE
The big day.	Bathe your dog.
Better late than never.	The baby will teethe soon.
That ship.	Cut with a scythe.
Finding them.	Breathe deeply.
These texts.	Soothe the invalid.
Those students.	Pay your tithe.
They are late.	Gather moss.
Thus I prove my point.	Your mother.
Thereafter do better.	Your brother.
Thereupon I rest my case.	Altogether now.
Be true to thyself.	Don't bother.
Neither of you.	Feather your nest.

WORDS IN WHICH /θ/ OR /ð/ IS LIKELY TO BE OMITTED OR AFFECTS THE OMISSION OF ANOTHER SOUND

The *breadth* of the land.	*Paths* to find.
A *hundredth* anniversary.	An *eighth* of the estate.
Twelfth night.	A *sixth* of a pie.
Six *months* away.	A *seventh* sense.
Many *mouths* to feed.	Five *sixths*.
Three *fifths*.	Christmas *wreaths*.

VERSE

1   . . . *THE WINTER IS PAST*
    For lo, the winter is past,
    The rain is over and gone,
    The flowers appear on the earth;
    The time of the singing of birds is come,
    And the voice of the turtle is heard in our land.

                    From *The Song of Solomon*

2   The earth is the Lord's and the fullness thereof:
    The world, and they that dwell therein.
    For he hath founded it upon the seas,
    And established it upon the floods.
    Who shall ascend into the hill of the Lord?
    Or who shall stand in his holy place?
    He that hath clean hands, and a pure heart;
    Who hath not lifted up his soul unto vanity,
    Nor sworn deceitfully.

He shall receive the blessing from the Lord,
And righteousness from the God of his salvation.

From *Psalm 24*

3   *HIS OWN EPITAPH*
Life is a jest, and all things show it;
I thought so once, and now I know it.

JOHN GAY

PROSE
Herbert Asbury tells of the growth of the old Bowery, originally an Indian trail, as a recreation center. He explains that the Bowery Theater, the largest playhouse in New York City in the early 1800s, was burned three times and again caught fire some fifteen years before the Civil War. The police, who had recently been uniformed, appeared on the scene resplendent with suits trimmed with brass buttons. He writes:

> They ordered the spectators to make way for the firemen, but the Bowery gangsters jeered and laughed at them as liveried lackeys, and refused to do their bidding. The thugs attacked with great ferocity when someone howled that the policemen were trying to imitate the English bobbies, and many were injured before they were subdued. So much ill feeling arose because of this and similar incidents that the uniforms were called in and for several years the police appeared on the streets with no other insignia than a star-shaped copper shield, whence came the names coppers and cops. After weathering many storms the theater was finally renamed the *Thalia* and [in 1927] still stands in the shadow of the Third Avenue elevated railroad, devoted to moving pictures and Italian stock with occasional performances by traveling Chinese troupes.[1]

QUOTATIONS TO STIMULATE IMPROMPTU TALKS OR CONVERSATION
1   Nothing is so much worth as a mind well instructed.   [*Bible*]
2   Speech is the gift of all, but thought of few.   [CATO]
3   True courage is to do without witnesses everything that one is capable of doing before all the world.   [LA ROCHEFOUCAULD]
4   Do not threaten a child. Either punish or forgive him.   [GEMARA]
5   A little thing in hand is worth more than a great thing in prospect.   [AESOP]
6   Truth is the secret of eloquence and of virtue, the basis of moral authority; it is the highest summit of art and of life.   [HENRI-FRÉDÉRIC AMIEL]

---

[1] By permission from Herbert Asbury, *The Gangs of New York, An Informal History of the Underworld*, Alfred A. Knopf, Inc., New York. Copyright 1927, 1928.

7   That judges of important causes should hold office for life is not a good thing, for the mind grows old as well as the body.   [ARISTOTLE]

8   Said old Gentleman Gay, "On a Thanksgiving Day,
If you want a good time, then give something away."
                    ANNIE DOUGLAS GREEN ROBINSON

9   I assert that nothing ever comes to pass without a cause.
                    [JONATHAN EDWARDS]

10   I do then with my friends as I do with my books, I would have them where I can find them, but I seldom use them.   [RALPH WALDO EMERSON]

11   For where there are Irish there's loving and fighting,
And when we stop either, it's Ireland no more.
                    RUDYARD KIPLING

12   A pun is a pistol let off at the ear; not a feather to tickle the intellect.
                    [CHARLES LAMB]

13   But O the truth, the truth!
        The many eyes.
    That look on it! The diverse things
        They see.
                    GEORGE MEREDITH

14   There is no cure for birth and death save to enjoy the interval.
                    [GEORGE SANTAYANA]

15   She wears her clothes as if they were thrown with a pitchfork.
                    [JONATHAN SWIFT]

/h/ AS IN HALL

/h/, a glottal fricative made by exhaling breath through vocal bands partially closed for audible friction, takes on the quality of the vowel sound that follows. For example, when you say *heat, hat,* and *hoot,* you will note that the articulators anticipate the positions of /i/, /æ/, and /u/ even before you utter /h/. A few phoneticians prefer to classify /h/ as a voiceless vowel. Since this text is concerned with the function of /h/ as a consonant, it is included here.

Normally, when a syllable possesses some stress, the /h/ is retained, as in the word *comprehend.* But in an unstressed syllable, it is dropped, as in *prohibition, annihilation,* and *shepherd.* This same loss occurs in onflowing speech in auxiliary verbs such as *have, has,* and *had* and in the pronouns *he, his, him,* and *her.* The loss is not the result of carelessness but rather the result of highlighting the stressed words and placing in shadow the unstressed words. For instance, consider /h/ in these three sentences:

Harry has learned to hit his nails hard by holding the hammer at the end of its handle. At first, his nails had to be removed, straightened, and rehammered. But now he is holding his hammer correctly.

In these sentences, the /h/ in *has* would normally be omitted but the /h/ in *had* might well be retained if *had* is to be given some stress because the nail's *having* to be removed is considered significant. If the significance is on the nail's being removed, the /h/ would be omitted. In all three *his's* and in *he*, the /h/ is probably omitted, for none of these pronouns is stressed. The /h/'s in *Harry, hit, hard, holding, hammer, handle*, and *rehammered* are all present, for these words are lexical items which are stressed and which have low predictability. If the /h/ in the first *has*, in the three *his's*, and in the *he* are included, the speech sounds pedantic and overly careful.

In some words, the /h/ is normally omitted, as in *heir, honor, hour, honest*, and *homage*. In other words, less uniformity exists. Most careful speakers include /h/ in words like *hue, Huguenot, humiliate*, and *Huron*. Many educated speakers omit the /h/ in rapid, connected speech in *huge, human, humane, humble*, and *humor*.

DRILL MATERIAL FOR /h/

Go through the following paragraphs deciding which /h/'s may be omitted and which are likely to be retained. Be sure that not too much breath escapes before the following vowel. Then read the paragraphs aloud.

HELEN'S FAME

While Helen's husband, a famous historian, was in the hospital, she had to help him with his research. The possibility of telling some historical facts in story form presented itself to her. Therefore, with her few free hours, she outlined an historical story based on her research and then hurried to write it. She had a way with words, a delightful sense of humor, and a kindly sympathetic feeling for all humanity. Helen was a humble soul who was loath to show her short novel to anyone, even her husband. But when he finally read it, he enjoyed its humor, its humane quality, its charm. He approached his publisher, who, after reading the story, believed he had a hit on his hands. And he did. After publication, a great hue and cry was raised about the story. It became a best seller and finally a vehicle for a moving picture. The moving picture almost annihilated the original story. But Helen and her husband, with their quiet senses of humor, enjoyed her newfound fame and all the homage paid her. Her husband would say, "Let me tell you about my operation and Helen's historical novel."

HUGO AND HIS UNCLE

Hugo, the heir to his uncle's huge fortune, was a gourmet. He liked to cook, and he liked to eat. On holidays he took over the household cooking chores, prohibiting his wife from even entering the kitchen. His uncle, a great humanitarian, hoped that Hugo would become interested in humane charitable projects and would forget his interest in food. He, therefore, had Hugo invited to the local children's hospital board meetings to stir his interest in this activity. And Hugo, while retaining his interest in cooking with herbs, did begin to give financial and administrative help to a small handful of agencies. Even with this concession, his uncle threatened to disinherit Hugo as his heir unless Hugo gave up his herbs. But one holiday, Hugo brought his uncle's hidden talent in cooking to light. And now both engage in this harmless pastime. Hugo remains the heir to his uncle's fortune.

/s/ AS IN SO AND /z/ AS IN ZERO

The voiceless /s/ and the voiced /z/ are cognates that are lingua-alveolar fricatives. Along with /ʃ/, /ʒ/, /tʃ/, and /dʒ/, these sounds are called *sibilants*. As in other fricatives, the voiced counterpart /z/ has less friction than the unvoiced /s/. In both instances, as the sounds are emitted, there is little or no escape of air through the nose; the nasal port is closed.

The /s/ is one of the most difficult sounds to articulate; it is among the last sounds to be stabilized in adult form in children's speech. The following positions and movements are a composite of those used by acceptable native speakers of the language:

1   The sides of the tongue are in contact with the upper teeth and gums from the back of the tongue to the canine teeth. The tongue is grooved to provide a narrow channel along its midline through which breath is forced.
2   The tip of the tongue may be placed slightly in front of the alveolar ridge and somewhat behind the upper teeth. The tip may also be placed against the lower gum below the lower teeth or behind the lower teeth at various levels. Several positions can produce an acoustically satisfactory /s/.
3   The teeth are brought almost together, with the upper teeth slightly ahead of the lower teeth.
4   The breath stream is directed along the groove to strike the alveolar ridge. It then passes downward over the back surface of the upper teeth and outward to the cutting edges of the lower teeth.

The sounds around /s/ and /z/ affect them. For example, as noted in Chapter 8, when, in the plurals of words, the last sound before the letter s is voiced, the plural is spoken with /z/; when unvoiced, with /s/. For instance, the final sound in *cabs* is /z/, whereas in *caps* it is /s/. Likewise, the third person singular in a verb is spoken with /z/ when the last sound before the letter s is voiced but is spoken with /s/ when the last sound before the letter s is unvoiced. The final sound in *packs* is /s/, whereas in *lags* it is /z/. Other assimilative changes occur. *I will miss you* frequently becomes /aɪl ˈmɪʃu/; *associate* becomes /əˈsoʃɪˌet/. The /s/ and /j/ interact, and the sound /ʃ/ results.

Many conspicuous variants occur in the production of the /s/ and /z/ sounds. They include:

1   The resulting sound is a strident one, with /s/ having a whistling quality. This /s/ may be due to excessive breath pressure or to too deep a grooving of the tongue in the middle as the /s/ position is reached.
2   The resulting sound has a quality of lateral emission. The sides of the tongue have not maintained a light contact with the upper teeth and gum ridge, so that air escapes laterally over the tongue.
3   The resulting sound has some of the characteristics of the voiceless *th* /θ/. The tip of the tongue approaches the cutting edges of the teeth, assuming an interdental position.
4   The resulting sound has a kind of mushy quality. The teeth are not or cannot be, because of teeth formation, brought together. Consequently, the /s/ is not the result of friction against the cutting edges of the teeth but of air escaping broadly.
5   The resulting /s/ has a dull and heavy quality. This /s/ can be due to an excessively low position of the tongue in the mouth or to too wide a groove of the tongue.

If your /s/ draws attention to itself, find out whether it belongs in any of the five categories listed above. If it does belong in one of them, see that the conditions listed earlier are met. Listen to the sharp, distinct quality of /s/ in other speakers. Then try to improve your /s/ by adjusting your articulators and by listening to the end result. Use a mirror so that you are sure that your tongue is not protruding in the front or at the sides and that your teeth are brought almost together. Do not assume that you cannot change the sound if you have an underbite, overbite, or other malocclusion. Experiment with the /s/ using a tape recorder that will reproduce accurately the high-frequency /s/ components.

Make sure that your /s/ is not too prolonged. Shorten it if it is. That your breath pressure be not excessive is equally important. Since your ability to hear the sound is essential, practice /s/ in some nonsense syllables. Some of these nonsense syllables involve the /n/ sound, for the tongue in one type of /s/ is close to the position that it normally is in for /n/. You must, however, move the tip of your tongue away and slightly forward from the /n/ position. Or you may use /t/ as a guide, provided you make /t/ with the tip of the tongue on the alveolar ridge.

DRILL MATERIAL FOR /s/

DIRECTIONS FOR DRILL
1   Listen to your /s/ as you read the phrases in the drill material aloud; then record the same material. Listen again to decide whether your /s/ has any of the undesirable characteristics listed earlier.
2   If you are not satisfied with your /s/, follow the directions given earlier for making an acceptable /s/. Then try saying /s/ in nonsense syllables. Listen to see how the sound changes.

3   After you have said /s/ in isolation satisfactorily, include it in words where the /s/ is in the initial position. Then include it in words where /s/ is in the final position. Finally, try the words with the /s/ clusters.

4   After saying /s/ in words satisfactorily, use the words in phrases. Then practice phrases with words which include /s/. Then carry over your change into conversation based on the quotations and discussion questions. Be sure that you incorporate the changes already made in other sounds in your reading and conversation.

NONSENSE DRILL

/sn i/,/s i/	(ee as in *meat*)
/snæ/,/s æ/	(a as in *cat*)
/snɛ/,/s ɛ/	(e as in *met*)
/snu/,/s u/	(u as in *true*)
/sno/,/so/	(o as in *no*)
/snɔ/,/s ɔ/	(aw as in *law*)
/snɑ/,/s ɑ/	(a as in *father*)

WORD DRILL

/s/ WHICH INITIATES A WORD OR SYLLABLE

sail	second
salt	sell
same	senate
center	century
circle	certain
single	sit
scene	sold
facility	decide
insane	absolute
considerably	assemble
ascent	consume
assail	deceive
assault	descent

/s/ WHICH TERMINATES A WORD OR SYLLABLE

divorce	kiss
fierce	loss
fireplace	nurse
immense	pass
impress	else
malice	actress
face	coarse
housekeeper	possible
ambassador	announcement
classwork	escort
facelifting	Alaska
distrust	aspect
sassafras	isthmus

WORDS OR SYLLABLES BEGINNING AND ENDING WITH /s/

necessary	analysis
sense	ancestor
assess	nonsense
access	suspect
absence	Swiss

WORDS WITH /s/ CLUSTERS

/sk/ Clusters

school	screen
scare	screw
skin	risk
ask	skunk
brisk	task

/sl/ Clusters

sleep	slavery
asleep	slay
slap	sleeve
slow	slice
slip	sly

/sm/ Clusters

small	smooth
smile	smock
smoke	smirk
smash	smudge
smite	smart

/sn/ Clusters

snow	snowy
snake	snarl
snap	sneak
snare	sneer
snort	sniff

/sp/ Clusters

space	inspire
speak	spark
special	sparrow
spend	spun
spring	spray

/st/ Clusters

stay	install	cost
abstain	stale	amongst
stall	first	next
starve	interest	August
steamer	last	past

/sw/ Clusters

swam	sweetness
sweat	swore
Sweden	swung
sweep	sway
swear	swallow

Final /fs/

life's	roofs
Biff's	laughs
wife's	beliefs
proofs	graphs
coughs	cliffs

Final /ks/

box	lacks
coax	exclude
complex	expand
flax	laxative
tax	backs

Final /ps/

caps	types
ropes	snipes
tapes	drapes
reaps	maps
leaps	cups

Final /ts/

coats	bouts
boats	kites
mats	flights
floats	lots
rates	meets

Final /ns/

rinse	tense
France	fence
romance	mince
enhance	since
glance	dance

Final /sts/

tests	masts
arrests	casts
lasts	costs
vests	rests
pests	ghosts

Final /sks/

asks	masks
risks	tasks
casks	basks
frisks	flasks
disks	desks

PHRASES

The publicity given to the Post Office.
A parcel sent to the Pacific.
A manuscript with malice.
Sauce for the salmon.
Secondary restraints.
Respectable scientists.
A sly kind of slavery.
Soup and a sandwich.

A traffic snarl caused by the snow.
Signature of the minister.
A stanza of verse.
Solitary Simon.
Risks of the voice.
Sixth son.
An inspiring historian.
A song of sixpence.

VERSE

1   *CHRISTMAS*

Christmas is coming, the geese are getting fat,
Please to put a penny in an old man's hat;
If you haven't got a penny, a ha'penny will do,
If you haven't got a ha'penny, God bless you.

MOTHER GOOSE

2   *JENNY KISSED ME*

Jenny kissed me when we met,
    Jumping from the chair she sat in;
Time, you thief, who love to get
    Sweets into your list, put that in!
Say I'm weary, say I'm sad,
    Say that health and wealth have missed me.
Say I'm growing old, but add,
    Jenny kissed me.

LEIGH HUNT

3   *FISHERMAN'S LOVE*
When the wind is in the East
'Tis neither good for man nor beast.

When the wind is in the North
The skillful fisherman goes not forth.

When the wind is in the South
It blows the bait in the fish's mouth.

When the wind is in the West,
Then it is at its very best.

ANONYMOUS

4   *I DO NOT ASK—FOR YOU ARE FAIR—*
I do not ask—for you are fair—
   That you should never have a lover,
But only that I be not there
   You to discover.

I am no censor to demand
   That you should always virtuous be,
I only ask that you should stand
   Upon some decency.

OVID, from *Amores*, 111, 14
(translated by F. A. Wright)

5   Sigh no more, ladies, sigh no more,
   Men were deceivers ever,
One foot in sea and one on shore,
   To one thing constant never:
Then sigh not so, but let them go,
   And be you blithe and bonny,
Converting all your sounds of woe
   Into Hey nonny, nonny.

WILLIAM SHAKESPEARE, from *Much Ado About Nothing*

6   *A CLEAR MIDNIGHT*
This is thy hour, O soul, thy free flight into the wordless,
Away from books, away from art, the day erased, the lesson done,
Thee fully forth emerging, silent, gazing, pondering the
   themes thou lovest best,
Night, sleep, death, and the stars.

WALT WHITMAN

7 *OLD MAN OF ST. BEES*
There was an old man of St. Bees,
Who was stung in the arm by a wasp;
   When they asked, "Does it hurt?"
   He replied, "No, it doesn't,
But I thought all the while 'twas a hornet!"

W. S. GILBERT

8 *NIGHT*[2]
Stars over snow,
   and in the west a planet
Swinging below a star—
   Look for a lovely thing and you will
      find it,
It is not far—
   It never will be far.

SARA TEASDALE

PROSE

1 Friends, fellow cockneys and sardines, this department is homesick for New York.
   I want to walk on Fifth Avenue at five o'clock of a cool blue September afternoon. I want to go to a first night and see the actors act again. I want to relive the magic moment when the house lights go down and the footlights go up and the play starts, and you know that in half an hour the socialites will begin to arrive.[3] [FRANK SULLIVAN]

2 In one of the skyscrapers the wires of the Associated Press were closing down. . . . The whistles rolled out in greeting, a chorus cheerful as the April dawn; the song of labor in a city built—it seemed—for giants.

SINCLAIR LEWIS from *Babbitt*

3 Your reason and your passion are the rudder and the sails of your seafaring soul. . . .
   If either your sails or your rudder be broken, you can but toss and drift, or else be held at a standstill in mid-seas.

KAHLIL GIBRAN from *The Prophet*

---

[2]Reprinted with permission of the MacMillan Company, New York, from Sara Teasdale, *Stars Tonight*. Copyright 1930 by Sara Teasdale Filsinger. Renewed 1958 by the Guaranty Trust Company of New York.

[3]"In a Rock in Every Snowball," from *Nostalgia*, The Universal Library, Grosset & Dunlap, Inc., New York, 1946, p. 111.

4 *FREEDOM OF EXPRESSION*

To crush a contrary opinion forcibly and allow it no expression because we dislike it is essentially of the same genus as cracking the skull of an opponent because we disapprove of him. It does not even possess the virtue of success. The man with the cracked skull might collapse and die, but the suppressed opinion or idea has no such sudden end and it survives and prospers the more it is sought to be crushed with force.

JAWAHARLAL NEHRU, from *The Unity of India*

QUOTATIONS TO STIMULATE IMPROMPTU TALKS OR CONVERSATION

1   The secret of success is constancy to purpose.   [BENJAMIN DISRAELI]
2   No one can give you better advice than yourself.   [CICERO]
3   Eat to please thyself, but dress to please others.   [BENJAMIN FRANKLIN]
4   The art of silence is as great as that of speech.   [German Proverb]
5   Discretion in speech is more than eloquence.
6   Success is a result, not a goal.   [GUSTAVE FLAUBERT]
7   That government is the strongest of which every man feels himself a part.

[THOMAS JEFFERSON]

8   Get for your studies both a teacher and a fellow student.

[JOSHUA OF PERAHYAH]

9   Who has lost his freedom has nothing else to lose.   [German Proverb]
10   Cats make exquisite photographs. . . . They don't keep bouncing at you to be kissed just as you get the lens adjusted.   [GLADYS TABER]
11   Courage is the price that life exacts for granting peace.

[AMELIA EARHART PUTMAN]

12   It is better to have less thunder in the mouth and more lightning in the hand.   [GEN. BEN CHIDLAW]
13   I haven't been abroad in so long that I almost speak English without an accent.   [ROBERT BENCHLEY]
14   The test of our progress is not whether we add more to the abundance of those who have much; it is whether we provide enough for those who have too little.   [FRANKLIN DELANO ROOSEVELT]
15   He is the greatest artist who has embodied in the sum of his works, the greatest number of the greatest ideas.   [JOHN RUSKIN]
16   Money is the seed of money, and the first guinea is sometimes more difficult to acquire than the second million.   [JEAN-JACQUES ROUSSEAU]
17   Liberty exists in proportion to wholesome restraint.   [DANIEL WEBSTER]
18   Women have served all these centuries as looking-glasses possessing the magic and delicious power of reflecting the figure of man at twice its natural size.   [VIRGINIA WOOLF]
19   If a house be divided against itself, that house cannot stand.   [Bible]
20   It is indeed a desirable thing to be well descended, but this glory belongs to our ancestors.   [PLUTARCH]

DRILL MATERIAL FOR /z/

DIRECTIONS FOR DRILL

1   When you have difficulty with /s/, your /z/ may also prove troublesome. Because /z/ is voiced, the /z/ difficulties usually are not as apparent to the listener as the /s/ difficulties. Try, however, to make the same changes for /z/ that you made for /s/.

2   Make sure that your final /z/ is not fully unvoiced.

WORDS

/z/ BEGINNING A WORD OR SYLLABLE		/z/ ENDING A WORD OR SYLLABLE	
zeal	Brazil	abuse	misery
zero	resort	amaze	miserable
zinc	deserve	arouse	pleasing
zone	dissolve	bronze	riser
zealous	horizon	cheese	Roosevelt
zebra	resign	Chinese	salesman
zest	museum	confuse	despise
Arizona	Zion	trousers	realize
position	zither	indoors	refuse (as a verb)
zigzag	zoo	poise	suppose
zodiac	resembles	tease	Tuesday
reserve	reside	visible	wisely

Final /vz/
gives	saves
lives	serves
loves	wives
moves	knives
proves	waves

Final /gz/
bags	gags
begs	Meg's
dogs	sags
eggs	vogues
tags	fags

Final /bz/
cabs	disturbs
robs	mobs
tabs	sobs
sobs	rubs
labs	verbs

Final /dz/
foods	maids
ponds	needs
heads	reads
sounds	rides
hides	adds

Final /nz/
bans	guns
cans	returns
loans	trains
tons	frowns
runs	learns

PHRASES WITH /z/

Suppose we go to the zoo.

Zoom ahead.

Resent the adviser.

Reside abroad.

A plush resort.

The result of our endeavors.

A wise enterprise.

The visitor from Mars.

Hazel broke the vase.

Analyzing the reaction of our allies.

Because of the rain.

VERSE

1   There was an Old Man in a tree,
     Who was horribly booted by a bee.
         When they said, "Does it buzz?"
         He replied, "Yes, it does.
     It's a regular brute of a bee."

                                        EDWARD LEAR

2   *WHEN I HEARD THE LEARNED ASTRONOMER*
     When I heard the learned astronomer,
     When the proofs, the figures, were ranged in columns before me.
     When I was shown the charts and diagrams, to add, divide, and measure
         them,
     When I sitting heard the astronomer where he lectured with much applause
         in the lecture room,
     How soon unaccountably I became tired and sick,
     Till rising and gliding out I wandered off by myself,
     In the mystical noise night-air, and from time to time,
     Looked up in perfect silence at the stars.

                                        WALT WHITMAN

3   Of all the causes which conspire to blind
     Man's erring judgment, and misguide the mind,
     What the weak head with strongest bias rules,
     Is pride, the never failing vice of fools.

         ALEXANDER POPE, from *Essay on Criticism*

QUOTATIONS TO STIMULATE IMPROMPTU TALKS OR CONVERSATION

   1   Knowledge comes, but wisdom lingers.   [ALFRED, LORD TENNYSON]
   2   Big words seldom go with good deeds.   [*Danish Proverb*]
   3   He too serves a certain purpose who only stands and cheers.
                                        [HENRY BROOKS ADAMS]

4   Of all the diversions of life, there is none so proper to fill up its empty spaces as the reading of useful and entertaining authors.

[JOSEPH ADDISON]

5   Let us not be pygmies in a case that calls for men.   [DANIEL WEBSTER]
6   Every man desires to live long but no man would be old.   [JONATHAN SWIFT]
7   True humour springs not more from the head than from the heart; it is not contempt; its essence is love; it issues not in laughter, but in still smiles, which lie far deeper.   [THOMAS CARLYLE]
8   'Tis the part of a wise man to keep himself today for tomorrow and not venture all his eggs in one basket.   [MIGUEL DE CERVANTES]
9   We have not journeyed all this way across the centuries, across the oceans, across the mountains, across the prairies, because we are made of sugar candy.   [WINSTON CHURCHILL]
10   A man's diary is a record in youth of his sentiments, in middle age of his actions, in old age of his reflections.   [JOHN QUINCY ADAMS]

/ʃ/ AS IN *SHALL* AND /ʒ/ AS IN *AZURE*

The voiceless /ʃ/ as in *shall* and the voiced /ʒ/ as in *azure* are cognates that are often considered lingua-alveolar fricatives like /s/ and /z/. But some phoneticians label /ʃ/ and /ʒ/ *linguapalatal* or *alveopalatal* because the palate is involved. In these sounds, the tip and the blade of the tongue are raised toward but not touching the alveolar ridge or the front part of the soft palate. The tongue is slightly further back than for /s/ and /z/, and the channel over which the breath stream (made between the tongue and the palate) is directed is wider for /ʃ/ and /ʒ/ than for /s/ and /z/. Most speakers round the lips in varying degrees on these two sounds. As in /s/ and /z/, the air must not escape laterally over the tongue and the nasal port is closed off.

The speaker may make errors in pronouncing /ʃ/ and /ʒ/ similar to those made in pronouncing /s/ and /z/, although he is less likely to make an unacceptable /ʃ/ and /ʒ/ than an unacceptable /s/ and /z/. One of the commonest difficulties is the escape of the breath over the sides of the tongue. Another common problem occurs when teeth are not brought together or when the tongue protrudes between the teeth as the sound is made.

DRILL MATERIAL FOR /ʃ/ AND /ʒ/

DIRECTIONS FOR DRILL

1   If you make /s/ and /z/ with lateral emission, be sure to check your /ʃ/ and /ʒ/. If necessary, adapt the directions for making an acceptable /s/ and /z/ to /ʃ/ and /ʒ/.
2   Listen to discover whether the final sound in words ending with /ʒ/ does not become /ʃ/. These words occur in phrases at the end of the column entitled "/ʒ/ *Ending a Word or Syllable.*"

PHRASES

/ʃ/ INITIATING A WORD OR SYLLABLE
A well-worn shoe.
True chivalry.
Visibly shaken.
William Shakespeare.
A famous shrine.
Shrug your shoulders.
The motion of the car.
A dictatorial administration.

/ʒ/ INITIATING A SYLLABLE[4]
A northerly exposure.
The invasion of the enemy.
Nuclear fission.
Going to Persia.
Her version of the story.
Persian melon.
Azure blue.
True confusion.

/ʃ/ ENDING A WORD OR SYLLABLE
Finish your work.
Accomplish the task.
The clash of personality.
A foolish notion.
Perish the thought.
Wash the car.
A true accomplishment.
The usher at the wedding.

/ʒ/ ENDING A WORD OR SYLLABLE
Measure for measure.
Giving pleasure.
Treasure your knowledge.
The treasurer of the organization.
Using rouge.
A corsage of orchids.
Fantastic mirage.
Lost prestige.

AFFRICATES: /tʃ/ AS IN *CHURCH* AND /dʒ/ AS IN *JUDGE*

/tʃ/ and /dʒ/, combining a stop and a fricative, are called *affricates*. According to Bronstein, the affricate results from the "slow and nonimpulsive release of the stop sound into a fricative sound made in the same part of the mouth.[5] In other words, each sound is held as in a plosive sound, but it is then exploded into a fricative sound. For both sounds, the nasal port is closed.

The lateral emission that occurs in /ʃ/ and /ʒ/ may occur in the affricates. In addition, /dʒ/ may become the unvoiced /tʃ/. This unvoicing, occurring in such words as *language* and *college,* is unacceptable in formal speech.

DRILL MATERIAL FOR /tʃ/ AND /dʒ/

DIRECTIONS FOR DRILL
1   Make sure that you are carrying over into /tʃ/ and /dʒ/ any changes you made in /ʃ/ and /ʒ/.
2   In formal speech be careful that you do not change /dʒ/ into /tʃ/ where /dʒ/ occurs finally.

---

[4] No English words exist which begin with /ʒ/. The distinction between /ʒ/ initiating or ending a syllable is sometimes arbitrary.

[5] A. J. Bronstein, *The Pronunciation of American English,* Appleton-Century-Crofts, Inc., New York, 1958, p. 91.

PHRASES

/tʃ/ INITIATING A WORD OR SYLLABLE

Chocolate cake.
Chairman of the committee.
The champion of them all.
Chancellor of the university
The state of Massachusetts.
Inferior merchandise.
A costly miniature.
An apple orchard.
The exchange student.
A righteous individual.

/tʃ/ ENDING A WORD OR SYLLABLE

Beseech your advisor.
A birch tree.
Coach of the team.
Digging a ditch.
Eating your lunch.
Doing research.
Riches or rags.
Richmond, Virginia.
Pinching pennies.
Scratching the surface.
The watchful dog.

/dʒ/ INITIATING A WORD OR SYLLABLE

The lost generation.
George the Fifth.
A genuine stone.
The Jeffersonian tradition.
A bad joke.
Adjourn the meeting.
An ingenious invention.
Cordial relations.
Reader's Digest.
A well-known engineer.

/dʒ/ ENDING A WORD OR SYLLABLE

Finding a bandage.
Besiege your President.
Losing her baggage.
Portraying an image.
Corned beef and cabbage.
An English carriage.
Being at a disadvantage.
Encourage your talent.
Being an agitator.
The broken hinge.
Lodging for the night.

VERSE FOR DRILL ON /ʃ/, /ʒ/, /tʃ/, /dʒ/

1   Deedle, deedle, dumpling, my son John
    Went to bed with his breeches on;
    One shoe off, and one shoe on,
    Deedle, deedle, dumpling, my son John.
                MOTHER GOOSE

2   There was a Young Lady whose chin
    Resembled the point of a pin;
    So she had it made sharp, and purchased a harp,
    And played several tunes with her chin.
                EDWARD LEAR

3   So new-fashioned jacks,
    With broad flaps in the necks,
    And so gay new partlets,
      Saw I never,
    So many sluttish cooks

So new-fashioned tucking-hooks,
And so few buyers of books,
   Saw I never.

JOHN SKELTON, from *The Manner of the World Nowadays*

4   *A DESCRIPTION OF A CITY SHOWER*
Careful observers may foretell the hour
(By sure prognostics) when to dread a shower.
While rain depends, the pensive cat gives o'er
Her frolics, and pursues her tail no more.
Returning home at night you find the sink
Strikes your offended sense with double stink.
If you be wise, then go not far to dine,
You spend in coach-hire more than you save in wine.
A coming shower your shooting corns presage;
Old aches throb, your hollow tooth will rage:
Sauntering in coffee-house in Dulman seen;
He damns the climate, and complains of spleen.

JONATHAN SWIFT

5   *THE LITTLE VAGABOND*
Dear Mother, dear Mother, the church is cold,
But the ale-house is healthy and pleasant and warm;
Besides I can tell where I am used well,
Such usage in Heaven will never do well.

But if at the church they would give us some ale,
And a pleasant fire our souls to regale,
We'd sing and we'd pray all the live-long day,
Nor ever once wish from the church to stray.

WILLIAM BLAKE

FOR DISCUSSION
1   Which type of test do you prefer—those involving short answers with many questions of multiple choice or those involving essays?
2   How satisfying were your high school experiences with Caesar and Cicero?
3   How would a teacher, an engineer, and a minister profit from having had sales experience?
4   How selfish are most highly successful women?
5   Does Cezanne's spirit find its purest expression in watercolor?

/ʍ/ AS IN *WHIP*
In words like *when* and *where,* the pronunciation may be /hw/. Here the speaker blends the two sounds, but the aspirate quality of /h/ is audible. Or he may use

/ʍ/, a voiceless fricative labiovelar sound, which is the result of the blending of /h/ and /w/ so that each sound loses its individual identity. The back of the tongue is raised almost to the soft palate, and the lips are rounded. Again the nasal port is closed off.

Many speakers distinguish clearly between *wh* and *w* in pairs like *which, witch; where, wear;* and *why, y.* Many other speakers, however, do not distinguish between the two sounds in these pairs. This lack of distinction is so widespread among educated speakers that either pronunciation is acceptable. In some geographic areas, the distinction is made much more frequently than in other areas. Although the distinction between /w/ and /ʍ/ seems to be on the wane, some speakers maintain the difference in formal situations but use only /w/ in informal ones.

DRILL MATERIAL FOR /ʍ/

If you wish to distinguish between /w/ and /ʍ/, practice the following pairs of words. Then carry the distinction over into phrases; then into conversation. Be sure to include the changes you have already made on other sounds.

/ʍ/ INITIATING WORDS; COMPARISON OF /w/ WITH /ʍ/

whale	wail	What are you doing?
when	wen	A whatnot in the living room.
where	wear	Why there?
whet	wet	Wherefore art thou?
which	witch	When did you see her?
whig	wig	Whistle at the girls.
while	wile	The cat's whiskers.
whine	wine	Whirl her around the room.

CHAPTER TWELVE

Nasals, Lateral, and Glides

NASALS: /m/ **AS IN** *MAY,* /n/ **AS IN** *NO,* **AND** /ŋ/ **AS IN** *RANG*
The three nasal sounds, /m/, /n/, and /ŋ/ as in *rang*, are labeled *nasal contin-uants* because they can continue so long as the voiced breath lasts and because all three possess nasal resonance. The nasal resonance results from lowering the velum and directing voiced breath through the nose. All three sounds are con-sidered semivowels. Thomas indicates that the free escape of air through nasal passages in /m/, /n/, and /ŋ/ is similar to the free escape of air through the mouth in vowels.[1]

/m/ AS IN *MAY*
/m/ is a voiced bilabial nasal continuant (made with closed lips). The context in which /m/ occurs affects its utterance. When /m/ is immediately preceded by a voiceless consonant sound, as in *smoke*, it is partially devoiced. /m/ exists as an unstressed syllabic sound in such words as chasm /kæzm̩/, and it can exist as a syllabic in such a phrase as /kipm̩ əwe/ for *keep him away*. In such instances, the articulatory position for /m/ is anticipated and no vowel sound

[1]C. K. Thomas, *An Introduction to the Phonetics of American English*, 2d ed., The Ronald Press Com-pany, New York, 1958, p. 45.

occurs before it. In rapid connected speech, /m̩/ is often heard, but in some pronunciations, for example, /kæpm̩/ for /kæptɪn/ (*captain*), it sounds non-standard. As noted earlier, in words like comfort, the /m/ may influence the /f/ to become bilabial. Similarly, the /f/ may influence the /m/ to become labiodental. Note the examples on page 140.

/m/ is usually uttered acceptably. In some instances, however, /m/ lacks nasal resonance. This condition, affecting not only /m/ but also /n/ and /ŋ/, the other two nasal sounds, is discussed in detail in Chapter 6.

DRILL MATERIAL FOR /m/

DIRECTIONS FOR DRILL

1   As you practice the following material, be sure that you incorporate any changes you have made in the plosives or fricatives.
2   If you worked on increasing nasal resonance earlier, pay particular attention to the articulation of /m/ in these phrases.
3   Be aware of the bilabial position of /m/ before /f/ or /v/ in the two phrases at the top of each column.
4   After saying the phrase, incorporate it into a sentence.
5   After you have practiced the phrases with /m/ and /n/, carry over all your changes into the reading of the prose and poetry.

PHRASES

Some fire.	Plum van.
Bum fare.	Tom veered.
An ambitious man.	Diminishing returns.
Genuine amusement.	A mannerly employer.
Contemporary movements.	In my lifetime.
A comedy of manners.	An imaginary tale.
Building a dam.	A traffic jam.
The village blacksmith.	An immense mansion.
The Monroe Doctrine.	A gleam of interest.
Monthly payments.	A municipal court.
A mellow millionaire.	A catch of salmon.
The Pilgrim Laundry.	Remain here.

/n/ AS IN NO

/n/, a voiced lingua-alveolar nasal continuant, is made with the tip of the tongue on the alveolar ridge. As in all other sounds, the phonetic context influences /n/. When /n/ is immediately preceded by a voiceless consonant, as in *snake*, the

/n/ is partially devoiced. When it precedes /θ/ or /ð/, it is made with the tongue on or between the teeth. This dental /n/ occurs in words like *eleventh* and in a phrase like *in the house.* When /n/ is followed by a high front vowel, for example, by /i/ or /ɪ/ in the words /nid/ (*need*) or /nɪt/ (*knit*), it sounds somewhat different from the /n/ which is followed by a low back vowel, as in /nɔt/ (*nought*). When /n/ is followed by /k/, it may become /ŋ/ because of the influence of the placement of /k/. For instance, *handkerchief* is acceptably pronounced /'hæŋkɚˌtʃɪf/. In formal speech, the /n/ in a phrase such as *in case* remains /n/ and does not become /ŋ/.

/n/, like /m/, can exist as an unstressed syllabic sound, as in the word *kitten,* and is then written /n̩/. /n̩/ regularly occurs in words like *cotton* and *written* and possibly in *fasten* and *listen.* The syllabic /n/ also occurs in phrases such as /'bɛd n̩ 'bɔrd/ (*bed and board*) or /'ti n̩ 'kɔfɪ/ (*tea and coffee*). To insert either an /ɪ/ or the schwa /ə/ before the /n/ in such words as *cotton* and *written* gives the speech an affected, overly careful sound. For example, note the pedantic effect when the schwa is inserted between the /t/ and the /n/ in the following: /ðə 'kɪtənz wɔr ðɛɚ 'lɪtəl 'katən 'mɪtənz/ (*The kittens wore their little cotton mittens*).

Also like /m/, /n/ is usually uttered acceptably but is not always given enough nasal resonance. Or some of you who have lived in neighborhoods with certain foreign influences may consistently use a dental /n/, one made with the tip of the tongue against the teeth. This is probably symptomatic of general dentalization.

DRILL MATERIAL FOR /n/

DIRECTIONS FOR DRILL
1   Find out how you habitually say /n/. As you say *knee,* watch to see where you place your tongue. If you place your tongue tip against your upper or lower teeth and wish to avoid dentalization, change its position, placing the tip on the alveolar ridge. Practice /n/ before vowels in syllables, then in words, then in the phrases listed, and finally in reading and conversation. But remember that when /n/ precedes /θ/ or /ð/, it is dental.
2   Be careful if you have worked earlier on acquiring more nasal resonance to give sufficient nasal resonance to /n/ and /m/.
3   Make sure that you do not insert /ɪ/ or /ə/ before /n/ where /n/ is syllabic, as in *kitten.*
4   In the phrases listed where /n/ is followed by /k/ or /g/, assuming that your speech is occurring in a somewhat formal situation, be sure that you do not change the italicized /n/ to /ŋ/.
5   Maintain all the improvements you have already made.
6   Carry over all the changes into the reading of the prose and poetry.

PHRASES

The main attraction.	The dignity of man.
Anticipate the ban.	A failing economy.
The ascending stairway.	Essential services.
A countless number.	Infinite pains.
Channels of interest.	A small kitten.
Consumer's concern.	A hidden tax.
Blending the butter.	A hound dog.
A bright candle.	An important inquiry.
The ninth hole.	A lonely man.
Nicely done.	A ton of dynamite.

/n/ FOLLOWED BY /k/ OR /g/

In case of fire.	On guard.
Come and go.	On glide.
Plane gear.	In court.
Sing on key.	Tan coat.
Lone girl.	Rain gear.

DRILL MATERIAL FOR /m/ AND /n/

VERSE

1   When I was a lad I served a term
    As office boy to an Attorney's firm.
    I cleaned the windows and I swept the floor,
    And I polished up the handle of the big front door.
        I polished up that handle so carefullee
        That now I am the Ruler of the Queen's Navee.

                    W. S. GILBERT, from *H.M.S. Pinafore*

2   So many pinkers,
    So many thinkers,
    And so many good ale-drinkers,
        Saw I never:
    So many wrongs,
    So few merry songs,
    And so many ill tongues,
        Saw I never.

                    JOHN SKELTON, from *The Manner of the World Nowadays*

3   *BURNS*

Had we two met, blythe-hearted Burns,
 Though water is my daily drink,
 May God forgive me but I think
We should have roared out toasts by turns.
Inquisitive low-whispering cares
 Had found no room in either pate,
 Until I asked thee rather late,
Is there a hand-rail to the stairs?

        WALTER SAVAGE LANDOR

PROSE

1   The influence of advertising is often too great—even if that influence is one-tenth as potent as many assume it to be. The editorial function should be as entirely free of non-editorial influences as possible.[2]

        LEO ROSTEN

2   Today television viewing is dropping off, especially among older people, educated people and smaller families. The medium, therefore, may have lost certain important minorities. Obviously we can expect the industry to make vigorous efforts to regain the attention of those groups. In short, there are countertrends which may help to redistribute programming balance. The point to keep in mind, however, is that no one, broadcaster, sponsor or publisher, can survive if he gets too far in front of public taste.[3]

        THOMAS M. GARRET

3   I lunched with Lovat Dickson, author of *The House of Words*, at the Garrick and had the pleasure of telling him how much I had enjoyed this book. In return he told me this story of a London publisher and famous angler known to us both. Our friend was fishing for salmon on the Scottish river he loved best. As he was about to cast, he stumbled and fell. "Take it easy, Sir!" said his gillie. But he had gone. In the haste of finding a doctor and of carrying the angler back to the lodge, the long fourteen-foot rod was forgotten. But when in sorrow they went back to the riverbank to recover it in the late afternoon, there it was, and fast to the fly, a salmon.[4]

        EDWARD WEEKS

/ŋ/ AS IN *RANG*

/ŋ/, a voiced linguavelar nasal continuant, is made with the middle or back of the tongue raised toward the soft palate. /ŋ/ is represented orthographically by

---

[2] From "The Intellectual and the Mass Media," *Daedalus*, p. 350, Spring, 1960.

[3] From "TV: Who's to Blame?" *America, The National Catholic Weekly Review*, p. 557, Jan. 27, 1962.

[4] From "The Peripatetic Reviewer," *Atlantic Monthly*, vol. 212, p. 126, June, 1963. By special permission.

the two letters *n* and *g*. Historically, the older pronunciation is /ŋg/, but /g/ has been dropped in words ending with *ng*. The /ŋg/ is still heard in words such as *finger* or *anger*. Guidelines for the conventional use of /ŋ/ and /ŋg/ follow:

1   When the *ng* sound occurs at the end of a word, as in *thing, ring*, and *tongue*, the *ng* is pronounced /ŋ/.
2   When inflectional forms or compound words are made from a root word ending in *ng*, the *ng* is pronounced /ŋ/. Examples include *banging, singing, wrongs, wronged, singer, hanger, Springfield, Washington, Binghamton*, and *Allingham*.[5]

> *Exception:*   The exceptions to this rule are the comparative and superlative of such adjectives as *longer, longest, younger, youngest, stronger, strongest*, and words ending with *al, ate, ation*, and *ize* as *diphthongal, elongate, prolongation*, and *diphthongize*.

3   When *ng* occurs in the middle of the root form, as in *angle, mangle*, and *linger*, the *ng* is pronounced /ŋg/.
4   Final *nge*, as in *fringe, range*, and *cringe*, is pronounced /ndʒ/.

The substitution of /n/ for /ŋ/ in words like *running, flying*, and *having* is fairly common. Historically, the /n/ was undoubtedly frequently used, as evidenced by the spelling *landyn* for *landing*.

DRILL MATERIAL FOR /ŋ/, /ŋk/, /ŋg/ AND /ndʒ/

DIRECTIONS FOR DRILL

1   In the phrases that follow, determine from the guidelines given earlier where /ŋ/, /ŋk/, and /ŋg/ occur. Having determined the pronunciation, listen to make sure that you have not included in your pronunciation of /ŋ/ a trace of the /k/ or /g/ sound, particularly in words like *singer* and *singing* or in a phrase like *going away*. A recording will help you to listen objectively. If you do hear a click, you are building pressure between the back of the tongue and the soft palate and releasing it.
   a.   Hear the contrast in /ŋ/ and /ŋk/ or /ŋg/ between:

singer	sinker	thing	think
ting-a-ling	link	hang	Hank
among	monk	hanger	anger
banger	banker	singer	linger
sung	sunk	bringer	finger

---

[5] The endings *ham* and *ton* are the unstressed forms of the older pronunciations *home* and *town*.

b. In words like *singer* and *singing*, separate the root form from the suffix /sɪŋ/, /ɚ/; then join the root and the suffix without a click /sɪŋɚ/. Proceed to say the word alone, then use it in a phrase, then in a sentence.

c. Where the /ŋ/ is a final sound of a word preceding a word beginning with a vowel, separate the two words, as in *going away* /'goɪŋ ə'we/. Then blend the two together, as /'goɪŋə'we/. These phrases will serve for practice:

Wrong attitude.   Owning a dog.
Young eagle.   Pacing away.
Sing a song.   Amazing oil.
Being alone.   Swing at him.

2 If you use /n/ for /ŋ/ in words like *fading*, be aware of what part of the tongue you use to make /n/ and what part to make /ŋ/.

3 Read the phrases. Use the phrases in sentences.

4 If you have worked on nasal resonance, be sure to give sufficient nasal resonance to /ŋ/. If you have changed your articulation of any of the plosives or fricatives, include the change or changes.

5 After you have practiced the sound in the phrases, incorporate your corrections in the reading of the prose and poetry. Finally, using the quotations as a basis, incorporate your changes in short impromptu speeches or in conversation.

PHRASES

Alongside the house.   Learning all about it.
Amongst the singers.   A streak of lightning.
A new angle.   Longing to go abroad.
A true angel of mercy.   Mingling with the crowd.
Bang away.   The length of the string.
Chase Manhattan Bank.   A pang of pain.
Being away.   A plunge into the sea.
The clinging-vine type.   The ringer of the bell.
During the war.   A mountain range.
The little finger.   Running around.
Flattering the prof.   A single girl.
The last fling.   Saying the right thing.
A gang of boys.   Seeing all.
Going to Allingham.   Singing carols.
A gingham dress.   A folk singer.
Hanging the effigy.   A singular action.
Hearing it anew.   Standing alone.
Knowing all.   Stopping at Birmingham.
The longest way around.   Strongly advise.
The youngest of them all.   The stronger of the two.

VERSE

1   *INTRODUCTION*
    Piping down the valleys wild.
    Piping songs of pleasant glee,
    On a cloud I saw a child
    And he laughing said to me:
    "Pipe a song about a Lamb!"
    So I piped with merry cheer.
    "Piper, pipe that song again";
    So I piped: he wept to hear.

    WILLIAM BLAKE, from *Songs of Innocence*

2   *NIGHTMARE*
    When you're lying awake with a dismal headache, and repose is taboo'd by
        anxiety,
    I conceive you may use any language you choose to indulge in, without
        impropriety;
    For your brain is on fire—the bedclothes conspire of slumber to plunder you:
    First your counterpane goes, and uncovers your toes, and your sheet slips
        demurely from under you;
    Then the blanketing tickles—you feel like mixed pickles—so terribly sharp is
        the pricking.
    And you're hot, and you're cross, and you tumble and toss till there's
        nothing 'twixt you and the ticking.
    Then the bedclothes all creep to the ground in a heap, and you pick 'em all
        up in a tangle;
    Next your pillow resigns and politely declines to remain at its usual angle!
    Well, you get some repose in the form of a doze, with hot eyeballs and head
        ever aching,
    But your slumbering teems with such horrible dreams that you'd very much
        better be waking.

    W. S. GILBERT

3   Ring out, wild bells, to the wild sky,
        The flying cloud, the frosty light;
        The year is dying in the night;
    Ring out, wild bells, and let him die.

    Ring out the old, ring in the new,
        Ring, happy bells, across the snow;
        The year is going, let him go;
    Ring out the false, ring in the true.

Ring out the grief that saps the mind,
    For those that here we see no more;
    Ring out the feud of rich and poor
Ring in redress to all mankind.

ALFRED, LORD TENNYSON, from *Ring out, Wild Bells*

4   *SONG*
    The year's at the spring
    And day's at the morn;
    Morning's at seven;
    The hill-side's dew-pearled;
    The lark's on the wing;
    The snail's on the thorn:
    God's in his heaven—
    All's right with the world!

    ROBERT BROWNING, from *Pippa Passes*

5   *I HEAR AMERICA SINGING*
    I hear America singing, the varied carols I hear,
    Those of the mechanics, each singing his as it should be, blithe and strong,
    The carpenter singing his as he measures his plank or beam,
    The mason singing his as he makes ready for work or leaves off work,
    The boatman singing what belongs to him in his boat, the deckhand singing
        on the steamboat deck.
    The shoemaker singing as he sits on his bench, the hatter singing as he
        stands,
    The woodcutter's song, the ploughboy on his way in the morning, or at noon
        intermission or at sundown.
    The delicious singing of the mother, or the young wife at work, or the girl
        sewing or washing,
    Each sings what belongs to him or her and to none else,
    The day what belongs to the day—at night the party of young fellows, robust,
        friendly,
    Singing with open mouths their strong melodious songs.

    WALT WHITMAN

6   *SING-SONG*
    Wrens and robins in the hedge,
        Wrens and robins here and there;
    Building, perching, pecking, fluttering,
        Everywhere!

    CHRISTINA ROSSETTI

7   Tell me the tales that to me were so dear,
     Long, long ago, long, long ago.
     THOMAS HAYNES BAYLY, from *Long, Long Ago*

PROSE

1   *HARK! HARK! THE TURNCOATS*
     (An Open Letter to the Association of National Advertisers)

     Gentlemen:

     . . . Who started the idea of American fear, anyway, if it wasn't you? . . . Who
     scared me into supposing I was intestinally sick, almost dead? . . . Who
     roused in me the fear that I was perspiring at a dance? Who kept telling me
     my flat silver wasn't of the correct design, . . . and that my throat was being
     burned by smoking the wrong brand of cigarettes. . . ? Gentlemen, I am
     asking!

     E. B. WHITE, from *Quo Vadimus or the Case for the Bicycle*

2   *LEARNING IN SCHOOLS*
     Schools have therefore never been places for the stimulation of young minds;
     they are the central conserving force of the culture, and if we observe them
     closely, they will tell us much about the cultural pattern that binds us.
     Much of what I am now going to say pivots on the inordinate capacity of a
     human being to learn more than one thing at a time. A child writing the word
     "August" on the board, for example, is not only learning the word "August,"
     but also how to hold the chalk without making it squeak, how to write clearly,
     how to keep going even though the class is tittering at his slowness, how to
     appraise the glances of the children in order to know whether he is doing it
     right or wrong. If a classroom can be compared to a communications system
     —a flow of messages between teacher (transmitter) and pupils (receivers)—
     it is instructive to recall another characteristic of the communications system
     applicable to classrooms; their inherent tendency to generate noise. *Noise,*
     in communications theory, applies to all those random fluctuations of the
     system that cannot be controlled, the sounds that are not part of the message.
     The striking thing about the child is that along with his "messages about
     spelling" he learns all the *noise* in the system also. But—and mark this well
     —it is not primarily the message (the spelling) that constitutes the most im-
     portant subject to be learned, but the noise! The most significant cultural
     learnings—primarily the cultural drives—are communicated as noise.[6]

     JULES HENRY

[6]By permission of Jules Henry, "American Schoolrooms: Learning the Nightmare," *Columbia University
Forum,* vol. VI, p. 26, Spring, 1963.

3   *WEATHER NEWS FROM HOME*
. . . People in Binghamton, New York, looked out of their windows and found the ground covered with snowballs, rolling along without visible means of propulsion, and increasing in size as they rolled. The Weather Bureau explained that this was a phenomenon, rare in the East, resulting from a peculiar combination of soft, wet snow, a high wind and a temperature of about 36 degrees.

What kind of news is that for a homesick man to read in a batch of papers fresh off the boat?

ROBERT BENCHLEY, from *News from Home*

4   *THE BEGINNINGS OF SPEECH*
Before the child has any active vocabulary of true words, however, he does try to speak, pointing to something he wants and working his mouth strenuously as though in search of words. Further, the child may give evidence of building a vocabulary prior to speaking. He may point at an object, making an interrogatory sound (in one child, "Bah? Bah?") and when supplied with a name, point to something else.[7]

JOSEPH CHURCH

QUOTATIONS TO STIMULATE IMPROMPTU TALKS OR CONVERSATION
1   Seeing is better than hearing.   [*African Proverb*]
2   Long roads test the horse. Long dealings, the friend.   [*Chinese Proverb*]
3   You say there is nothing to write about. Then write to me that there is nothing to write about.   [PLINY THE YOUNGER]
4   As long as there are postmen, life will have zest.   [WILLIAM JAMES]
5   Whatever is worth doing is worth doing well.   [EARL OF CHESTERFIELD]
6   He who loses his temper is in the wrong.   [*French Proverb*]
7   I am nothing, but truth is everything.   [ABRAHAM LINCOLN]
8   A long tongue shortens life.   [*Persian Proverb*]
9   Like all strong stuff, music is capable of becoming a principle of evil as well as of good.   [PAUL ROSENFELD]
10   There is certainly something in angling . . . that tends to produce a gentleness of spirit, and a pure serenity of mind.   [WASHINGTON IRVING]
11   A harbor, even if it is a little harbor, is a good thing, since adventures come into it as well as go out, and the life in it grows strong, because it takes something from the world and has something to give in return.

[SARA ORNE JEWETT]

[7]From *Language and the Discovery of Reality*, Random House, Inc., New York, 1961, p. 61.

12 Questioning is not the mode of conversation among gentlemen.
[SAMUEL JOHNSON]

13 He has left off reading altogether to the great improvement of his origi-
nality. [CHARLES LAMB]

14 Nothing prevents our being natural so much as the desire to appear so.
[LA ROCHEFOUCAULD]

15 Take any streetful of people buying clothes and groceries, cheering a hero
or throwing confetti and blowing tin horns . . . tell me if the lovers are losers
. . . tell me if any get more than the lover . . . in the dust . . . in the cool
tombs. [CARL SANDBURG]

16 There's something so beautiful in coming on one's very own inmost
thoughts in another. In one way it's one of the greatest pleasures one has.
[OLIVE SCHREINER]

17 Whether I am on the winning or losing side is not the point with me; it is
being on the side where my sympathies lie that matters and I am ready to
see it through to the end. Success in life means doing that thing than which
nothing else conceivable seems more noble or satisfying or remunerative.
[ALAN SEEGER]

18 It is a foolish thing to make a long prologue and to be short in the story
itself. [*Bible*]

LATERAL

/l/ AS IN *LAKE*

/l/ is a lateral lingua-alveolar semivowel. The tip of the tongue is placed lightly
against the alveolar ridge with one or both sides down so that air escapes over
the side or sides. There is little or no escape of air through the nose. The teeth
are apart.

As in other sounds, phonetic context makes for variations or allophones of /l/.
Two that are distinguishable acoustically are sometimes called *light l* and *dark l*.
The dark quality results from the raising of the back of the tongue. The light (or
clear) /l/ occurs in words such as *leap* and *lace*. The dark /l/ occurs in words
such as *role*, *law* and *able*.

Other allophones of /l/ exist. In words like *million* and *billiard* and in phrases
like *will you*, a palatal /l/ frequently occurs because of the difficulty of the shift
from /l/ to /j/. The tip of the tongue remains in contact with the alveolar ridge,
but the blade rises toward the palate until /j/ is uttered. /l/ becomes dental,
made with the tip of the tongue on the teeth, before /θ/ or /ð/, as in the word
wealth or in the phrase *bill the customer*. Like /m/ and /n/, /l/ may fulfill the
function of a syllable. Examples include *little* /'lɪtl̩/, *bottle* /'bɑtl̩/, and *ladle*
/'ledl̩/. As just noted, the syllabic /l̩/ is a dark /l/.

/l/ is unacceptably articulated in several ways: You may retract and elevate the back of your tongue to such a degree that a sound somewhat like /ʊ/ results. Or you may make a dental /l/. Or it may have a weak sound. Or you may substitute a light /l/ for a dark /l/.

DRILL MATERIAL FOR /l/

DIRECTIONS FOR DRILL

1   In the following phrases containing dark /l/'s, make sure that you do not substitute a light for a dark /l/. Listen to other speakers say words with dark and light /l/'s to distinguish the difference. Say words which require a dark /l/ and those which require a light /l/. For the light /l/, make sure that the tongue tip is in contact with the alveolar ridge and that the back of the tongue does not rise.

2   Make certain that you do not articulate dark /l/ carelessly so that a word like /mɪlk/ sounds somewhat like /mɪʊk/, that is, so that the /l/ seems to be omitted and a kind of /ʊ/ substituted.

PHRASES

LIGHT /l/	DARK /l/
A big leap.	Evading the law.
The latecomer.	Another look.
The right lane.	Losing one's friend.
Lead the way.	The lost horizon.
Least of all.	A big log.
A bad leak.	Spending time loafing.
A swim in the lake.	A lonely man.
The relay race.	Longing to go.
Odd belief.	The lord of the manor.
Delete the error.	Rollaway cot.
Value of it.	Rule of thumb.
In the milieu.	A hard ball.
A true failure.	A tall tale.
A million dollars.	A dull book.
Billions in debt.	The Lawson sofa.

DARK SYLLABIC /l/	
A little boy.	A purple cow.
A bottle of ink.	A horrible example.
A tattletale.	A maple tree.
An able leader.	A marble table.

DARK /l/ FOLLOWED BY A LABIAL OR VELAR
In these words, be sure that your tongue tip maintains contact with the alveolar ridge. Do not substitute a vowel for /l/, as /sɪuk/ for /sɪlk/.

A silk dress.	A selfish man.
Bulbs from New York.	Involve your fortune.
The bulk of the magazines.	The milkman.

DARK /l/—DENTAL /l/ BEFORE /θ/ OR /ð/
Remember that this /l/ is usually assimilated into the dental position.

/l/ BETWEEN VOWELS
Make sure that you maintain strong tip-of-the-tongue contact in these /l/'s.

A great wealth.	Molly Brown.
A stealthy walk.	The bridge tally.
A healthy respect.	The folly of it all.
Call them soon.	Follow the leader.
Bell the cow.	Ballyhoo of the circus.

/l/ CLUSTERS
Again—make sure that the tongue tip is in contact with the alveolar ridge.

The Scottish Highland fling.	A good sleep.
A flash of fire.	A slip of the tongue.
A flock of sheep.	Slow moving.
Glad you could come.	The slain murderer.
A glass of water.	Bidding a slam.
A clap of thunder.	Snowflakes.
An interesting class.	A gleam of understanding.
The clatter of dishes.	An American flag.

/pl/ AND /bl/ CLUSTERS
Be sure that you do not carry too much of the labial quality of /p/ and /b/ into the /l/. In these words, observe whether you tend to use a labial /l/.

A pleasant place.	A complete set.
Plenty of blackberries.	Explaining the appliance.
Blaming your parents.	Fill in the blanks.
Blow by blow.	The blast of air.
Black and blue.	A blessing in disguise.
A platter of beef.	The plague of your life.

QUOTATIONS TO STIMULATE IMPROMPTU TALKS OR CONVERSATION
1   Be civil to all; sociable to many; familiar with few.   [BENJAMIN FRANKLIN]
2   Justifying a fault doubles it.   [*French Proverb*]

3   Do not delay; the golden moments fly.   [HENRY WADSWORTH LONGFELLOW]
4   I fear explanations explanatory of things explained.   [ABRAHAM LINCOLN]
5   One may smile and smile and be a villain.   [WILLIAM SHAKESPEARE]
6   One of the pleasures of reading old letters is the knowledge that they need no answer.   [LORD BYRON]
7   I love my music because it is most important to love something in life; to be in love with something. . . . This is most important: people who have nothing in their insides, in their souls, they are poor. But a man or a woman who has a conviction that something is beautiful and something is profound, it helps him to overcome his grief. And we have plenty of very sad hours in our lives.   [WANDA LANDOWSKA]
8   How pleasant it is for a father to sit at his child's board. It is like an aged man reclining under the shadow of an oak which he has planted.

[SIR WALTER SCOTT]

9   My children return tomorrow, probably having quarreled all the way. They have reached that embarrassing moment in their lives when it is no longer possible to settle things with the fists.   [W. B. YEATS]
10   They that can give up essential liberty to obtain a little temporary safety deserve neither liberty nor safety.   [BENJAMIN FRANKLIN]
11   I have always regarded that Constitution as the most remarkable work known to me in modern times to have been produced by the human intellect, at a single stroke (so to speak), in its application to political affairs.

[WILLIAM EWART GLADSTONE]

12   Who rules by cruelty must sleep lightly or sleep long.   [*Chinese Proverb*]
13   Learn to live and live to learn.   [BAYARD TAYLOR]
14   Old men love to give good advice; it consoles them for being able no longer to set a bad example.   [LA ROCHEFOUCAULD]
15   To establish their position in the world, men go to any length to appear established already.   [LA ROCHEFOUCAULD]
16   In our relations with men we please more by our faults than by our virtues.

[LA ROCHEFOUCAULD]

17   Knowledge is like a garden; if it is not cultivated, it cannot be harvested.

[*African Proverb*]

18   He who loves money must labor.   [*African Proverb*]

VERSE
1   Some ladies smoke too much and some ladies drink too much
       and some ladies pray too much.
   But all ladies think that they weigh too much.

OGDEN NASH, from *Curl Up and Diet*

2   When the lamp is shattered
   The light in the dust lies dead—

When the cloud is scattered,
The rainbow's glory is shed.
When the lute is broken,
Sweet tones are remembered not;
When the lips have spoken,
Love accents are soon forgot.

>   PERCY BYSSHE SHELLEY, from
>   *When The Lamp Is Shattered*

3   *THE TOM-CAT*[8]

At midnight in the alley
    A Tom-Cat comes to wail,
And he chants the hate of a million years
    As he swings his snaky tail.

Malevolent, bony, brindled,
    Tiger and devil and bard,
His eyes are coals from the middle of Hell
    And his heart is black and hard.

He twists and crouches and capers
    And bares his curved sharp claws,
And he sings to the stars of the jungle nights
    Ere cities were, or laws.

Beast from a world primeval,
    He and his leaping clan,
When the blotched red moon leers over the roofs,
    Give voice to their scorn of man.

He will lie on a rug tomorrow
    And lick his silky fur,
And veil the brute in his yellow eyes
    And play he's tame, and purr.

But at midnight in the alley
    He will crouch again and wail,
And beat the time for his demon's song
    With the swing of his demon's tail.

>   DON MARQUIS

---

[8] From *The Awakening & Other Poems*, by Don Marquis. Copyright 1917 by Sun Printing and Publishing Association. Reprinted by permission of Doubleday & Company, Inc., Garden City, N.Y.

4   *THE CITY OF FALLING LEAVES*[9]
Leaves fall, Brown leaves,
Yellow leaves streaked with brown.
They fall,
Flutter, Fall again.
The brown leaves,
And the streaked yellow leaves,
Loosen on their branches
And drift slowly downwards.
One,
One, two, three,
One, two, give.
All Venice is a falling of Autumn leaves—
Brown,
And yellow streaked with brown.

AMY LOWELL, from *1777*

5   Left, left, I had a good home and I left,
Left, left, I had a good home and I left,
Left my wife and four fat babies, left 'em—
Right, right, right in the middle of the kitchen floor.

ANONYMOUS

PROSE

1   Rochester is a temperate city, satisfiedly walking the middle of the road, always circumspect, prudent, discreet. It has never had much of that quality which for want of a better name is called color. Its one picturesque citizen was Rattlesnake Pete; Pete with his big hat and his twin St. Bernards and his saloon with all its snakes and guns and games of chance and rough male atmosphere. But Pete is dead and his place is gone and he left no influence behind.[10]

CARL CRAMER

2   Sleep at a late hour in the morning is not half so pleasant as the more timely one. It is sometimes, however, excusable, especially to a watchful or over-worked head; neither can we deny the seducing merits of "t'other doze,"— the pleasing wilfulness of nestling in a new posture, when you know you ought to be up, like the rest of the house. But then you cut up the day, and your sleep the next night.

LEIGH HUNT, from *A Few Thoughts on Sleep*

[9] By permission from Amy Lowell, *Men, Women & Ghost*, from *The Collected Poems of Amy Lowell*, Houghton Mifflin Company, Boston.

[10] From *Listen for a Lonesome Drum*, Holt, Rinehart and Winston, Inc., New York, 1936, p. 41.

3   I once knew a man who was inordinately greedy. He was also inordinately rich. The combination of these two qualities had rendered him fussy and asthmatic. . . . Lonely and expectant, he lived in a large untenanted house, and the pleasures which graced his solitary life were in their nature transitory: a spring chicken, the first asparagus, a new salad—but, then, how quickly do such things pass out of our lives! Love, politics even, afford more durable stimulants.

HAROLD NICOLSON, from *Good*

GLIDES

/r/ AS IN *RAT*

Authorities do not always agree on the nature of /r/. Indeed, C. K. Thomas, noting that its history has been "long, complicated, and controversial," gives an interesting account of the variety of *r*'s used in Scotland, England, and America.[11]

Generally, the American /r/ is either a voiced lingua-alveolar glide or a lingua-palatal glide. In both instances, the nasal port is closed; little or no vocalized air is directed through the nose. Like all glides, its sound results from the rapid change of resonance produced by the continuing movement of the articulatory agents. The lingua-alveolar /r/ is made by the tip of the tongue moving up close behind the alveolar ridge and turning back toward the hard palate. The lingua-palatal /r/ is made by raising the middle of the tongue toward the line between the hard palate and the velum while the tip of the tongue remains low. /r/ made in either of these two ways occurs before a vowel, as in *rain* and *inroad*. When the /r/ is between vowels, as in *Mary*, or before an unstressed vowel, as in *Africa*, the /r/ is of short duration. In such words, the tongue glides rapidly from the alveolar ridge position to the position of the unstressed vowel or humps toward the palate and glides to the position of the unstressed vowel.

The authors have not, so far, been concerned with the /r/ that occurs at the end of a word or a syllable or with the one that precedes a consonant. This /r/ occurs in such words as *far, car, learn, board, turn, pear,* and *fierce.* Some phoneticians regard this /r/ as a vocalic (vowel-like) element, and others as a consonantal glide. If you are interested in the evidence supporting these points of view, your teacher will supply you with references. In some sections of the country, a lengthened vowel replaces the vowel with the /r/ sound, as in /fɑːm/ for *farm.* In these same sections of our country, the last syllable of *better* may be pronounced as the schwa /ə/ /'bɛtə/. In a recent study, William Labov points out that the inclusion of /r/ in such words as *farm* and *better* in New York City

---

[11] C. K. Thomas, *Phonetics of American English,* 2d ed., The Ronald Press Company, New York, 1958, p. 87.

is one of the chief characteristics of a new prestige pattern being superimposed upon native New York City patterns.[12]

The sounds /ɝ/ as in *learn* and /ɚ/ as in *better* will be discussed in the section dealing with vowels. Since these /r/-colored vowels are varieties or allophones of /r/, the authors are referring to them here.

In the phrase *far away,* the /r/ is pronounced even by those who normally omit the /r/ in *far*. This /r/ is called a *linking* /r/. Persons who habitually use the linking /r/ often extend its use to phrases where it does not appear in the spelling. They say "the idear of her going." This /r/, labeled an *intrusive* /r/, has become widespread in many sections. Both President Kennedy and President Roosevelt used *idear*.

/r/ is one of the most troublesome of sounds. The foreign student may have difficulty with it. He may make a fricative /r/ or a trill. If you make an /r/ habitually in such a way, remember that it should be a glide when speaking English. Some authorities suggest thinking of /r/ as a vowel-like sound. For instance, in the word *road,* start with the sound in *bird* /ɝ/, then glide into *road*. For foreign students, this procedure usually brings about the necessary vowel-like quality. A second nonstandard /r/ is the weak /r/, frequently called the *labialized* /r/. This sound seems to some to be near /w/; to others, near /ʊ/. The back of the tongue is frequently high. It occurs most often in words where the /r/ follows /b/ or /p/, but it may also be found in other contexts. Some speakers for whom English is a second language do not distinguish between /l/ and /r/.

DRILL MATERIAL FOR /r/

DIRECTIONS FOR DRILL

1   If you use a trilled /r/, follow the directions for making an /r/ with a vowel-like quality suggested in the paragraph which deals with /r/ difficulties.

2   If your /r/ is weak, if it has some of the characteristics of /w/ or /ʊ/, check the position of the back of your tongue. Make sure that it is lower than for /ʊ/. Place your tongue with the tip and blade turned up toward the hard palate and with the tip reaching toward the alveolar ridge. Although you may make /r/ acceptably with the midportion of the tongue bunched and raised toward the back section of the hard palate, raising the tip is probably more successful when you make a weak /r/, for this position contrasts more sharply with your inaccurate position than does raising the central portion of the tongue.

   a.   Distinguish carefully between /r/ and /w/ in these pairs of words and in these phrases:

[12] William Labov, *The Social Stratification of English in New York City,* Center for Applied Linguistics, Washington, D.C., 1966, p. 82.

rake	wake	rise	wise
raid	wade	writ	wit
rage	wage	rig	wig
rail	wail	rage	wage
rain	wane	rate	wait
read	weed	rude	wooed
reap	weep	ride	wide

The railroad worker.   Weeding in the rain.
Raging at waiting.   Sunset red in the West.
Winning a new rate.   A wide runway.
Wearing a ring.   A red wing.

b.   Pay particular attention to pronouncing the /r/ in words in the lists where /p/ and /b/ precede /r/. Since /p/ and /b/ are bilabial sounds, you may tend to carry over the lip movement to the following /r/. Be sure that the tongue is in the position for the production of /r/ before the /p/ or /b/ is released.

3   If you confuse /l/ and /r/, you may do better to make the /r/ by raising the middle of the tongue toward the line between the hard palate and the soft palate, with the tongue's tip remaining low, than you would by raising the tip toward the alveolar ridge. Do not hold onto the /r/ too long. Distinguish between /l/ and /r/ in the following pairs of words and phrases:

lead	read	laid	raid
leaf	reef	lap	rap
leech	reach	look	rook
lid	rid	law	raw
limb	rim	load	rode
lip	rip	lie	rye
lend	rend	loud	rowdy
lest	rest	light	right

A lot of rules.   The loud, rowdy students.
A leaking roof.   Rode a lamb.
A weak limb.   Arrested for breaking the law.
Laid to rest.   Raking the lawn.

4   Read the words; then use each word in a sentence. Read the phrases, paying particular attention to phrases where the /r/ occurs in words which are difficult for you. Use the phrases in sentences. Make sure that you incorporate changes already made on plosives, fricatives, nasals, and /l/. Finally, carry over the changes into reading and into conversation or impromptu speeches based on the quotations.

WORDS

/r/ BEFORE A VOWEL	/r/ BETWEEN VOWELS	/r/ PRECEDED BY /p/ OR /b/	/r/ PRECEDED BY A CONSONANT
rapidly	barren	present	fragment
rate	embarrass	price	fresh
realize	error	approximate	grew
ring	ferry	provoke	grow
rise	irregular	deprive	concrete
rock	merrily	pray	confront
rode	miracle	profound	grab
rule	operate	Britain	grind
run	tarry	brought	shrug
write	ceremony	embrace	thrice
radio	corridor	brim	credit
random	borrow	broke	incredible

/r/ PRECEDED BY /t/ OR /d/

trade	tribute	drawn
trip	try	dread
trouble	trim	dreary
true	dream	drift
trust	drive	drum

PHRASES

/r/ BEFORE A VOWEL

A good race.
The Susquehanna Railroad.
A substantial raise.
A real dog.
A good reply.
The Mississippi River.
A roadblock.
Roll away.
A blue room.
A football rally.
An idle refrain.
Rhyming words.

/r/ BEFORE A CONSONANT[13]

A large arm.
Expensive art.
Articles for sale.
Board and room.
Fort Knox.
Artificial fruit.
A horse of a different color.
Coarse cloth.
A black beard.
Tarred and feathered.
The lord of the manor.
Playing cards.

---

[13] In eastern New England, in the South, and sometimes in New York City, the /r/ is acceptably omitted.

/r/ BETWEEN VOWELS

In a big hurry.
Marry in haste.
America the Beautiful.
Going to Europe.
A black berry.
The golden era.
A horrid example.
Irish wit.
A jury trial.
A narrative style.

FINAL /r/[14]

The fear of a lifetime.
Chicago fire.
Floor covering.
A hair style.
Do you hear?
Keep in order.
Hot air.
Dear friend.
An open door.
Explore the cave.

/r/ PRECEDED BY A CONSONANT

This week Friday.
Frail Fred.
Concrete evidence.
A new shrub.
A graceful entrance.
A subtle threat.
Throne for the king.
Orange crush.

/r/ PRECEDED BY /p/ OR /b/

Daily practice.
A look of approval.
A foolish compromise.
Promote your product.
The club's program.
The branch office.
Broke the glass.
A bad bruise.

/r/ PRECEDED BY /t/ OR /d/

A late train.
Many travels.
A treat in store.
An oak tree.

Tried and true.
A bad dream.
A new dress.
A drink of water.

/r/ PRECEDED BY /st/

Straighten your tie.
A strand of hair.
The last straw.
A streak of lightning.

The stricken child.
Stars and stripes.
Strive to do well.
A broken strap.

LINKING /r/

A sore arm.
Tear away.
The car of a friend.
The care of a child.
Don't pare it all away.

PHRASES WHERE INTRUSIVE /r/
MAY OCCUR

Banana oil.
Elsa Owen.
The idea of her going.
The law of the land.
A raw onion.

[14] In eastern New England, in the South, and sometimes in New York City, the /r/ is acceptably omitted.

LINKING /r/	PHRASES WHERE INTRUSIVE /r/
	MAY OCCUR
A rare old pitcher.	I saw her yesterday.
Stare at him hard.	Emma Eaton.
Far away.	Calla lily.
Wear out the jacket.	The data of the experiment.
Air it out.	The paw of the cat.

VERSE

1 *FOUR DUCKS ON A POND*
   Four ducks on a pond,
   A grass bank beyond,
   A blue sky of spring,
   White clouds on the wing;
   What a little thing
   To remember for years—
   To remember with tears.

   WILLIAM ALLINGHAM

2 *THE CATERPILLAR*
   Brown and furry
   Caterpillar in a hurry;
   Take your walk
   To the shady leaf, or stalk,
      Or what not,
   Which may be the chosen spot.
      No toad spy you,
   Hovering bird of prey pass by you;
   Spin and die,
   To live again as butterfly.

   CHRISTINA ROSSETTI

3 *THE RIDE*
   As I ride, as I ride,
   Ne'er has spur my swift horse plied,
   Yet his hide, streaked and pied,
   As I ride, as I ride,
   Shows where sweat has sprung and dried,
   —Zebra-footed, ostrich-thighed—
   How has vied stride with stride
   As I ride, as I ride.

   ROBERT BROWNING, from *Through the Metidja to Abd-el-Kadr*

4   Does the road wind up-hill all the way?
         Yes to the very end.
     Will the day's journey take the whole long day?
         From morn to night, my friend.

                    CHRISTINA ROSSETTI, from *Up-Hill*

5   Round and round the rugged rock
     The ragged rascal ran,
     How many *r*'s are there in that?
     Now tell me if you can.

                    ANONYMOUS

6   *PSALM 147*
     Praise ye the Lord:
     For it is good to sing praises unto our God;
     For it is pleasant; and praise is comely.
     Great is our Lord, and of great power:
     Who covereth the heaven with clouds,
     Who prepareth rain for the earth.
     Who maketh grass to grow upon the mountains.
     He giveth to the beast his food,
     And to the young ravens which cry.
     He giveth snow like wool;
     He scattereth the hoarfrost like ashes.
     He casteth forth his ice like morsels;
     Who can stand before his cold:
     He sendeth out his word, and melteth them:
     He causeth his wind to blow, and the waters flow.
     Sing unto the Lord with thanksgiving;
     Praise ye the Lord.

                         Bible

PROSE

1   *CHANGES*
     And in this way many suburbans have seen the paradise of their boyhood
     effaced. The building rises during some long farewell, and steals away a
     fraction of the very sky in which once we beheld Orion sink down like a fall-
     ing sword into the west and its line of battlemented woods. Only here and
     there a coppice will survive, blockaded by houses a-row.

                    EDWARD THOMAS, from *Broken Memories*

2   *IDLENESS AS A VIRTUE*

The idea that laziness is the primary sin and the accompanying doctrine of the strenuous life are very prevalent in America, and we cannot escape the fact that America is an amazingly prosperous country. But neither can we escape the fact that society there is in such a condition that all its best contemporary writers are satirists. Curiously enough, most of the great American writers have not hesitated to praise idleness, and it has often been their faculty for doing nothing and praising themselves for doing it, that has been their salvation.

J. B. PRIESTLEY, from *On Doing Nothing*

3   I have sometimes wondered whether tragedy, as a form of art, may not be doomed. But the fact that we are still profoundly moved by the tragic masterpieces of the past—that we can be moved, against our better judgment, even by the bad tragedies of the contemporary stage and film—makes me think that the day of chemically pure art is not over. Tragedy happens to be passing through a period of eclipse, because all of the significant writers of courage are too busy exploring the newly discovered, or re-discovered world of the Whole Truth to be able to pay any attention to it.

ALDOUS HUXLEY, from *Tragedy and the Whole Truth*

4   *STOPPING FOR HAMBURGERS*

It had been raining for a long time, a slow, cold rain falling out of iron-colored clouds. They had been driving since morning and they still had a hundred and thirty miles to go. It was about three o'clock in the afternoon. "I'm getting hungry," she said. He took his eyes off the wet, winding road for a fraction of a second and said, "We'll stop at a dog wagon." She shifted her position irritably, "I wish you wouldn't call them *dog*-wagons," she said. . . . "That's what they are," he said, "Dog-wagons."

JAMES THURBER, from *A Couple of Hamburgers*

QUOTATIONS TO STIMULATE IMPROMPTU TALKS OR CONVERSATION

1   Write injuries in sand, but benefits in marble.   [*French Proverb*]

2   Even in Paradise, it's not good to be alone.   [*Yiddish Proverb*]

3   It is a grand mistake to think of being grand without goodness.
[BENJAMIN FRANKLIN]

4   The object of oratory is not truth, but persuasion.   [THOMAS B. MACAULAY]

5   Pride is at the bottom of all great mistakes.   [JOHN RUSKIN]

6   Important principles may and must be flexible.   [ABRAHAM LINCOLN]

7   He who does not advance recedes.   [*Latin Proverb*]

8   Why has my motley diary no jokes? Because it is a soliloquy and every man is grave alone.   [RALPH WALDO EMERSON]

9   Many years ago I learned to discount the hurry and flurry of New York. We are no busier than Bridgeport or Jersey City, but we pretend we are. It is necessary for our municipal vanity to squeeze and jam and rush and crush.
                                                                                        [JAMES HUNEKER]

10   Born writers make their own rule, or, rather, they have none. They change style at every moment, at the dictation of inspiration.   [ANATOLE FRANCE]

11   Thy friend has a friend, and thy friend's friend has a friend: be discreet.
                                                                                        [*Talmud*]

12   Our impressions of Bach, or any music, change continuously. We find a beauty in a certain place that we didn't get to before. This is why everything is new—everything is new. There are always new satisfactions and new joys because it is new; and it must be new.   [PABLO CASALS]

13   Few fathers care much for their sons, or at least, most of them care more for their money. . . . Of those who really love their sons, few know how to do it.   [EARL OF CHESTERFIELD]

14   Dictionaries are like watches; the worst is better than none, and the best cannot be expected to go quite true.   [SAMUEL JOHNSON]

15   All modern American literatures comes from one book by Mark Twain called *Huckleberry Finn*. . . . There was nothing before. There has been nothing as good since.   [ERNEST HEMINGWAY]

16   Papa, potatoes, poultry, prunes, and prism, are all very good words for the lips; especially prunes and prism.   [CHARLES DICKENS]

17   Regrets are the natural property of gray hairs.   [CHARLES DICKENS]

18   Arrogance, pedantry, and dogmatism are the occupational diseases of those who spend their lives directing the intellects of the young.
                                                                                        [HENRY SEIDEL CANBY]

FOR DISCUSSION
1   What further uses can be made of the nuclear power program?
2   How can the United States do more to encourage tourism?
3   How can racial tensions be alleviated in this area?

/j/ AS IN *YOU*
/j/ is a voiced linguapalatal glide. The nasal port is closed; as /j/ is emitted, little or no vocalized air comes through the nose. The sound begins very near the vowel /i/ as in e*at,* with the front of the tongue arched high near the hard

palate, and then moves to the position of the next vowel. The sound occurs only before vowels and does not occur finally or before consonants.

Phonetic context influences /j/. For instance, when preceded by an unvoiced plosive in a stressed syllable, it is partially devoiced except where /s/ precedes the plosive. It is also devoiced when preceded by the other unvoiced consonants.

In many words, whether to use /u/ alone or to precede it with a *y* sound /j/ or the short *i* sound /ɪ/ puzzles some speakers. If you do not regularly use /ju/ or /ɪu/ in words like *tune* and *new,* the authors advise that you do not attempt to introduce this pronunciation, because you may have difficulty in deciding where to use /ju/ and where to use /u/.

If you are interested in finding out more about the usage of /ju/, /ɪu/, and /u/, consult one of the phonetics texts listed in the Bibliography.

DRILL MATERIAL FOR /j/

DIRECTIONS FOR DRILL
1   Review on page 146 the material on /h/.
2   Be aware of inserting a /j/ in the last set of phrases where italicized. This excrescent sound can occur easily, for as you move from /i/ or /ɪ/ to the following vowel, you can economize effort by inserting /j/. This excrescent sound is not ordinarily heard in formal educated speech.

PHRASES

INITIAL /j/

A yellow dress.	Bright youngsters.
A trip to Europe.	Yearly taxes.
Universal appeal.	Younger of the two.
Unique approach.	Youth of today.
Useless work.	Yesterday's children.

PHRASES WHERE AN EXCRESCENT /j/ IS LIKELY TO OCCUR

He *is* a good boy.	Bea *is* a nonreader.
Tea *is* served.	He *eats* beans daily.
My only son.	Lee *is* an architect.

QUOTATIONS TO STIMULATE IMPROMPTU TALKS OR CONVERSATION[15]
1   Oh, it is so beautiful here. I feel as if my heart would jump out of my chest like a hare at night—it is such a lovely spring.   [D. H. LAWRENCE]

[15] These include words with /ju/, /ɪu/, and /u/.

2   I've watched my duty straight and true,
And tried to do it well.

WILL CARLETON

3   Music is well said to be the speech of angels.   [THOMAS CARLYLE]

4   Beware the fury of a patient man.   [JOHN DRYDEN]

5   Genius will live and thrive without training, but it does not the less reward the watering-pot and pruning knife.   [MARGARET FULLER]

6   If you do not think about the future, you cannot have one.

[JOHN GALSWORTHY]

7   A little credulity helps one on through life very smoothly.

[ELIZABETH GASKE]

8   No human feeling can ever be so appalling as joy.   [VICTOR HUGO]

9   The loveliest tune imaginable becomes vulgar and insupportable as soon as the public begins to hum it and the hurdy-gurdies make it their own.

[JORIS HUYSMANS]

10   His wife "ruled the roost," and in governing the governor, governed the province, which might thus be said to be under petticoat rule.

[WASHINGTON IRVING]

/w/ AS IN WON

/w/ is a voiced bilabial glide. The velum is raised; little or no vocalized air comes through the nose. The lips are rounded. Initially, the back of the tongue is raised toward the soft palate, but then the articulatory agents move to the position of the following vowel. Because the tongue is raised toward the soft palate, /w/ is sometimes labeled a *bilabial velar glide.* The sound is similar to the vowels /u/ in *true* and /ʊ/ in *good.*

Context again plays a role: When the following vowel is rounded, the lips in the production of /w/ are more rounded than when the following vowel is not rounded. The tongue is higher in /w/ when the following vowel is a high vowel such as /i/ and is lower when the following vowel is a low vowel such as /ɑ/. When /w/ follows a voiceless consonant, it is somewhat devoiced. This devoicing occurs in words like *twit, quick, swim,* and *catchwords* and in phrases like *fat worms, half water,* and *class wit.* /w/ may occasionally be inserted in words such as *blowing* /'blowɪŋ/ and *blueing* /'bluwɪŋ/ and in phrases like *you are, go away,* and *row on* (/juwɑr/, /'gowəwe/, and /'rowɑn/). If you consistently insert /w/ in such words and phrases, be aware that this pronunciation is not often heard in educated speech.

Difficulties with this sound, although rare, do occur. The overuse of an excrescent /w/ has already been noted. Some foreign speakers confuse /v/ and /w/. Such speakers should think of /w/ as a shortened version of /ʊ/.

DRILL MATERIAL FOR /w/

WORDS AND PHRASES

For those who tend to confuse /w/ and /v/, the authors provide the following list. Make sure that you use the upper teeth and the lower lip in /v/ and the lips in /w/.

Walt	vault	My friend Walt.
wail	vale	A wail of torture.
ways	vase	Ways to try.
wane	vain	The sun wanes.
worse	verse	Worse yet.
wall	vault	A huge wall.
west	vest	Going west.

PHRASES WHERE /w/ IS LIKELY TO BE INSERTED

Observe whether you consistently insert /w/ in these phrases where italicized:

You *a*re the most.	Mowing the lawn.
You *a*re too beautiful.	Sowing seeds.
The w*i*nd is blowing.	The cro*w*ing of the bird.
Going *a*way too soon.	Queu*i*ng in.

VERSE

Practice the changes you have made in /w/ and in all other sounds with the following:

1   With fingers weary and worn,
    With eyelids heavy and red,
    A woman sat in her unwomanly rags plying her needle and thread.

THOMAS HOOD, from *The Song of the Shirt*

2   I knock unbidden once at every gate!
    If sleeping, wake; if feasting, rise before
    I turn away. It is the hour of fate.

JOHN JAMES INGALLS, from *Opportunity*

3   *THE LARK IN THE MORN*
    As I was a-walking
    One morning in the Spring,
    I met a pretty maiden
    So sweetly she did sing
    And as we were a-walking
    These words she did say,

"There's no life like the ploughboy's
All in the month of May."

Folk Song

4   *CHILD'S TALK IN APRIL*
I wish you were a pleasant wren,
   And I your accepted mate;
How we'd look down on the toilsome men!
   We'd rise and go to bed at eight
   Or it may not be quite so late.

CHRISTINA ROSSETTI

QUOTATIONS TO STIMULATE IMPROMPTU TALKS OR CONVERSATION

1   More men are killed by overwork than the importance of the world justifies.

[RUDYARD KIPLING]

2   Women never seem to realize that the poet is first of all a word-lover.

[LEBARON COOKE]

3   The reason women always blush when you hand them back a stolen handbag
is that their whole life is in there—letters, bonds, hair curlers, old check stubs,
etc.   [A Washington, D.C., detective]

CHAPTER THIRTEEN

Front Vowels

/i/ **AS IN** *BEAT,* /ɪ/ **AS IN** *HIT,* /e/ **AS IN** *SAY,* /ɛ/ **AS IN** *BET,* /æ/ **AS IN** *BAT.*
(See Charts 3 and 4 and Figure 10.)

/i/ AS IN *BEAT*

In /i/—a high, front, tense vowel,—the tongue is higher than for any of the other
front vowels. The front part of the tongue is raised so that it nearly touches the
alveolar ridge or the front part of the hard palate. The teeth are almost closed;
the lower jaw is raised to make this closing possible. The lips are unrounded and
slightly spread.

This sound frequently becomes diphthongized as /ɪi/, with the utterance
gliding from the lax, lower /ɪ/ to the tense, higher /i/. If you prolong the /i/ in
see, you can hear this diphthongization, which occurs frequently when /i/ is a
final sound, infrequently before voiced stops.

Some alternate pronunciations of this sound occur. The final sound in a word
like *city* may be either /i/ or /ɪ/ or a sound between these two. Students tend to
argue that the final sound in *city* is always /i/, for as they pronounce the word
alone, they elongate the final sound. When spoken in a phrase such as *a city
mouse,* the final *y* frequently more nearly approaches /ɪ/. Another alternate pronunciation is the use of either /i/ or /ɪ/ in words like *hero* and *zero,* where /r/
is immediately followed by another vowel. Thomas indicates that if you are a
Northerner, you place /r/ at the end of the first syllable and pronounce *zero*

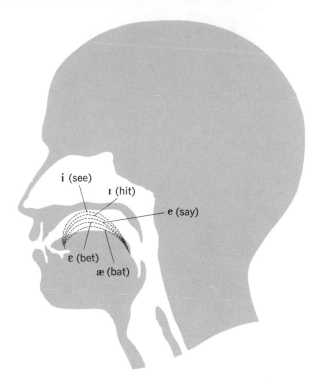

FIGURE 10.   Tongue positions for front vowels.

/zɪr-o/. If you are a Southerner, you place /r/ at the beginning of the second syllable, /zi-ro/. He notes that the pronunciation /ɪ/ is more frequent in the United States as a whole than /i/.[1] /i/ or /ɪ/ is also used in some few words such as *creek* or *breeches*. When /i/ appears before /l/, it is frequently diphthongized or lowered, as /riəl/ or /rɪəl/ for *reel*. When /i/ appears before /r/, similar changes may occur, as /riɚ/ or /rɪɚ/ for *rear*.

DRILL MATERIAL FOR /i/

PHRASES

Equal to it.	Even division.
Easing it into the space.	Agree with the child.
Easy does it.	A B.A. degree.
Eager beaver.	A plea for mercy.

[1] C. K. Thomas, *Phonetics of American English*, 2d ed., The Ronald Press Company, New York, 1958, p. 63.

Eat it all.

Meet my friend.

Leave it to the leader.

A clean room.

Teach her to take defeat.

An agreeable belief.

A sheet of music.

A previous marriage.

An oak tree.

A bumblebee.

The letter B.

See her now.

A free land.

A bruised knee.

The wrong key.

Black tea.

POETRY

WHEN I HAVE FEARS THAT I MAY CEASE TO BE
When I have fears that I may cease to be
Before my pen has gleaned my teeming brain,
Before high-piled books, in charactery,
Hold like rich garners the full ripened grain;
When I behold, upon the night's starred face,
Huge cloudy symbols of a high romance,
And think that I may never live to trace
Their shadows, with the magic hand of chance;
And when I feel, fair creature of an hour,
That I shall never look upon thee more,
Never have relish in the faery power
Of unreflecting love;—then on the shore
Of the wide world I stand alone, and think
Till love and fame to nothingness do sink.

JOHN KEATS

QUOTATIONS TO STIMULATE IMPROMPTU TALK OR CONVERSATION

1   Sweet is a grief well ended.   [AESCHYLUS]

2   Better beans and bacon in peace than cakes and ale in fear.   [AESOP]

3   Doing easily what others find difficult is talent; doing what is impossible for talent is genius.   [HENRI-FRÉDÉRIC AMIEL]

4   Economic distress will teach men, if anything can, that realities are less dangerous than fancies, that fact finding is more effective than fault finding.
[CARL BECKER]

5   Peace and tranquility . . . a thousand gold pieces.   [*Chinese Proverb*]

6   Seeing is different from being told.   [*African Proverb*]

7   Men will confess to treason, murder, arson, false teeth, or a wig. How many of them will own up to a lack of humor?   [FRANK MOORE COLBY]

8   Every reform, however necessary, will by weak minds be carried to an excess, that itself will need reforming.   [SAMUEL COLERIDGE]

9   Frequently we do good so that later we may do evil with impunity.
[LA ROCHEFOUCAULD]

10   We easily forget those faults that are known to ourselves alone.
[LA ROCHEFOUCAULD]

/ɪ/ AS IN *HIT*

/ɪ/ is a high, front, lax vowel. The front of the tongue is raised so that it approaches the alveolar ridge or hard palate; it is somewhat lower and slightly further back than for /i/. In other words, the jaw moves slightly down from /i/. Another difference between /i/ and /ɪ/ is that /i/ is tense whereas /ɪ/ is lax. In /ɪ/, the lips are not rounded.

/ɪ/ is almost always pronounced acceptably. Some persons, however, whose speech has a foreign influence may substitute /i/ for /ɪ/. And two other non-standard pronunciations may occur. The first is the substitution of /i/ for /ɪ/ in words like *ambition, condition, beautiful, decision, revision,* and *Patricia.* The second occurs in stressed syllables where /ɪ/ precedes /r/, /l/, /m/, /p/, or /b/, as in such words as *spirit, milk, limb, rip,* and *rib.* In these cases, a shift toward a back vowel occurs. Thus /mɪlk/ tends to a pronunciation somewhat similar to /mʊlk/.

DRILL MATERIAL FOR /ɪ/

In the following words with final /ɪʃən/ or /ɪʃ/, note whether in your pronunciation the /ɪ/ becomes /i/.

Overwhelming ambition.	Fighting the opposition.
Excellent condition.	An odd superstition.
A keen competition.	Adequate supervision.
An exciting musical composition.	Suspicious characters.
The wrong decision.	A tasty dish of fish.
Signing the petition.	A wish on the stars.

In the following pairs of words, be sure to distinguish between /i/ and /ɪ/. If you do substitute /i/ for /ɪ/, make sure that you are using the lax vowel. As you utter /i/ and then /ɪ/, you should feel a bulge under your chin on /i/ but little on /ɪ/.

meat	mitt	beat	bit
leave	live	cheap	chip
queen	Quinn	deep	dip
lead	lid	speak	spick and span
least	list	each	itch

reach	rich	seen	sin
seek	sick	peak	pick
sheep	ship	scheme	skim

In the following phrases, make sure that you do not pull the /ɪ/ toward a central or back position.

A wide brim.	Skimmed milk.
A million dollars.	Tripped across.
Build a house.	A broad rip.
Still and quiet.	A red ribbon.
Unusual ability.	Read *The Trib.*
A smoking chimney.	Noisy children.

Carry over all changes as you read the following phrases. After reading each phrase, use it in a sentence. Then incorporate all changes into conversation or impromptu talk based on the quotations.

PHRASES WITH /ɪ/

The ill child.	Singing to his sister.
The impatient teacher.	Sitting still.
The initial run.	A foolish difficulty [2]
Insuring yourself.	A distinct greeting.
Good intentions.	A busy city.[2]
An exciting invitation.	Entering the ministry.[2]
An immense breakfast.	Lily-white.[2]
Complete indifference.	A pretty kitty.[2]
A luxury building.[2]	Pleasant hospitality.[2]
Delivering milk.	A jury trial.[2]
Visiting the village.	Living in luxury.[2]
The Lucy show.[2]	A seedy-looking individual.[2]

QUOTATIONS TO STIMULATE IMPROMPTU TALK OR CONVERSATION

1   I charge thee, fling away ambition; by that sin fell the angels.
[WILLIAM SHAKESPEARE]

2   Simplicity is the most deceitful mistress that ever betrayed men.
[HENRY BROOKS ADAMS]

3   Pessimism when you get used to it is just as agreeable as optimism.
[ARNOLD BENNETT]

4   Adversity is sometimes hard upon a man; but for one man who can stand prosperity, there are a hundred that will stand adversity.   [THOMAS CARLYLE]

[2] In words ending in the letter *y*, you may use /i/, or /ɪ/ or a vowel in between the two.

5   Sincerity is an open heart. Few people show it; usually what we see is an imitation put on to snare the confidence of others.   [LA ROCHEFOUCAULD]
6   Vanity, shame, and disposition above all, make men brave and women chaste.   [LA ROCHEFOUCAULD]
7   A house is infinitely communicative and tells many things besides the figure of its master's income. There are houses that confess intellectual penury and houses that reek of enlightenment.   [ROBERT CHAPMAN]
8   The only guide to a man is his conscience; the only shield to his memory is the rectitude and sincerity of his actions.   [WINSTON CHURCHILL]
9   Nothing is more difficult than to speak about music. The attempt is very arduous for musicians themselves and nearly impossible for others.

[CAMILLE SAINT-SAENS]
10   A letter is an unannounced visit, and the postman thus the agent of impolite surprises.   [FRIEDRICH NIETZSCHE]

/e/ AS IN *MAY*

/e/, a midfront, tense vowel, is a step lower than /ɪ/, and the jaw drops some-what from /ɪ/. The lips are slightly spread. The tongue is bunched in the front part of the mouth, and the tongue muscles are tense. /e/ is frequently diphthongized to /eɪ/. For example, in the word *vacation*, as noted earlier, the first /e/ is short and is transcribed /e/ whereas the second /e/ develops a diphthongal off-glide and may be transcribed as /eɪ/. Whether or not /e/ is diphthongized depends upon the degree of stress and upon the phonetic con-text generally. Sometimes, however, the unstressed /e/ becomes /ɪ/, as in the days of the week: /ˈmʌndɪ/, /ˈtjuzdɪ/, and /ˈwɛnzdɪ/. When /e/ appears before /l/, as in *fail*, it is frequently diphthongized to /feəl/ or lowered to /fɛəl/. When /e/ appears before /r/, similar changes may occur, as /feɚ/ or /fɛɚ/ for *fair*.

Most speakers have little or no difficulty with this sound. Speakers with a foreign influence, however, may tend not to use the diphthongized /eɪ/ and to substitute /e/. A kind of staccato rhythm often goes along with the consistent use of /e/ rather than /eɪ/.

DRILL MATERIAL FOR /e/

DIRECTIONS FOR DRILL
1   In the following words which contain the /eɪ/ diphthong, discover whether, as you stress the syllable with /eɪ/, you triphthongize it—in other words, whether /eɪ/ becomes /eɪə/.
2   If you tend not to diphthongize /e/, be sure that in stressed positions you begin with /e/ and glide into /ɪ/.
3   After reading each phrase, use it in a sentence.

4   Incorporate your changes into conversation based on the quotations.
5   Be sure to incorporate all articulatory changes you have made so far.

PHRASES

She's an angel.	The late Major.
Agency for the aged.	Raise the rate.
A drink of ale.	Change your base.
An able lawyer.	A May morn.
Good air.	Kay came.
Aid to the enemy.	Made of clay.
Explain the arrangement.	Stay for the affair.
Amazed at his brain.	A way of life.
Maintain attention to details.	The Hudson Bay.
A fatal wait.	A lay preacher.

QUOTATIONS TO STIMULATE IMPROMPTU TALK OR CONVERSATION

1   There is no appreciation of my books that is so precious to me as appreciation from my children. Theirs Is the praise we want, and the praise we are least likely to get.   [MARK TWAIN]

2   God save me from a bad neighbor and a beginner on the fiddle.
                                                        [*Italian Proverb*]

3   You may share the labors of the great, but you will not share the spoil.
                                                        [AESOP]

4   It is easy to be brave from a safe distance.   [AESOP]

5   Ordinary saints grow faint to posterity; whilst quite ordinary sinners pass vividly down the ages.   [MAX BEERBOHM]

6   Men of genius do not excel in any profession because they labor in it, but they labor in it, because they excel.   [WILLIAM HAZLITT]

7   More brawn than brain.   [CORNELIUS NEPOS]

8   Many a dangerous temptation comes to us in fine gay colours that are but skin deep.   [MATTHEW HENRY]

9   Haste maketh waste.   [JOHN HEYWOOD]

10   When we heartily praise good deeds, we seem to share in the credit for them.   [LA ROCHEFOUCAULD]

/ɛ/ AS IN *MET*

/ɛ/ is a midfront, lax vowel. The tongue is in a similar but somewhat lower position than for /e/; the muscles, however, are relaxed, in contrast to /e/. /ɛ/ is a variable sound: although in the South /ɛ/ often replaces /e/ in *great, snake,* and *naked,* many educated Southerners retain /e/ in these words. Furthermore, in the South /pɛn/ frequently becomes /pɪn/. The shift occurs where /ɛ/ precedes an alveolar consonant. A similar shift occurs in the pronunciation of *get* in many sections of the country. Sometimes /ɛ/ becomes /e/, as in *head* or *egg*. These two particular pronunciations are not commonly heard in educated speech. The tongue may be pulled back in words like *very* or *merry*, where /ɛ/ is followed by /r/, /l/, or a labial consonant. A kind of midvowel somewhat similar to /ɝ/ appears to replace the /ɛ/. This pronunciation is usually labeled nonstandard. For example, the pronunciation of *American* as /ə'mɝɪkɪn/ tends to sound uneducated.

DRILL MATERIAL FOR /ɛ/

DIRECTIONS FOR DRILL
1   In the following phrases, scan your speech to discover whether you use any of the variants described in the preceding paragraph. Make changes as necessary.
2   Carry over the changes in articulation that you have already made.
3   Use each phrase in a sentence.

PHRASES

Ezra Stone.	Good attendance.
Make an effort.	Avenging the arrest.
The ethics of the man.	Contest to win a blender.
An edge on the gem.	A ferryboat.
A dozen eggs.	The generation of relics.
A good head.	Relish the menace.
The elbow of the elder.	A kettle of lettuce.
An elegant elevator.	The last leg.
Emphasize the message.	Settle the debt.
A reckless error.	A special step.
An embarrassing celebration.	Find the berries.
Went west.	A dented fender.
A bad check.	Lending an ear.
Many pens.	Promotion by merit.

/æ/ AS IN CAT

/æ/, a low, front vowel, is usually labeled a lax vowel, although in the United States a tense /æ/ occurs frequently. In fact, in most areas and in many phonetic contexts, /æ/ is raised and fronted, with the result that /æ/ approaches /ɛ/. It is also frequently diphthongized so that it approaches /ɛə/. This change exists particularly before final voiced plosives and affricates, before final nasals, and before voiced and unvoiced fricatives, as in *tab, badge, tan, salve,* and *half.* Before /r/ in words like *Barry, carry, Garry, Harry, marry,* and *tarried,* the /æ/ often becomes a long /ɛ/. This pronunciation occurs in those areas where /r/ is regularly pronounced in words like *card* and *further.*

In words like *dance* and *calf,* where the *a* precedes /s/, /f/, /θ/, /m/, or /n/ and when the *n* is followed by a stop or voiceless fricative, the pronunciation /æ/ is heard in most of our country. In many sections of England, these words are pronounced with /a/, a vowel halfway between /æ/ and /ɑ/ as in *father.* Since the largest area of our country derived its dialect from seventeenth-century British English, which included the pronunciation of /æ/ in such words, most persons in the United States do use /æ/ in these words. But in certain sections of Eastern United States, the /a/ sound is used. If you do not ordinarily use /a/, the authors recommend that you avoid its usage. This sound is discussed later.

You may in certain words habitually pronounce /æ/ as a too high, too tense, and diphthongized /ɛə/. Listeners from some areas regard this variant as unpleasant, while those in other areas use it themselves and expect to hear it. With the help of your instructor, discover whether this variant is standard in your region. It may appear in words like *man, cat, personality,* and *camp.* /æ/ is relaxed and shorter than /ɛ/. Consistent use of raised, tense, and nasalized /æ/ produces an unpleasant vocal quality. But be sure that you do not overcorrect this sound so that it approaches /a/, for then you will sound affected.

Some of you with a foreign influence in your speech may substitute /a/, /e/, /ɛ/, or /ɑ/ for /æ/ in words like *hat, cat, rat, cap,* and *match.* Most foreign languages do not possess a vowel phoneme acoustically close to /æ/.

DRILL MATERIAL FOR /æ/

DIRECTIONS FOR DRILL
1   Listen to how you say /æ/ in these words: *tap, wrap, sat, fat, tag, nag, latch, tan, ran, can, laugh, wrath,* and *calf.* If you wish to avoid substituting /ɛə/ for /æ/ in such words as these, try making /æ/ with tongue and jaw in a lower position and with the muscles relaxed. Feel the difference between a tense /æ/ and a lax /æ/ by placing your hand under your chin. If you feel your muscles bulge on /æ/, relax them so that the bulging exists to a small degree or not at all.
2   If you substitute /a/, /e/, /ɛ/, or /ɑ/ for /æ/, listen to other speakers pronounce /æ/ and learn to differentiate /æ/ from /ɛ/, /ɑ/, /e/, or /a/. Then practice the phrases with /æ/. Use a tape recorder during this exercise.
3   Practice /æ/ first in the following phrases; then read the poetry and prose. Finally, carry over changes in /æ/ and in other sounds you have worked on.

PHRASES

Apt to go.	Plenty of cash.
All aspects of the problem.	Carriage or a camel?
Ambassador to England.	A flattering bit of chatter.
Accept the offer.	Grabbing the gang.
Anxiety-producing drugs.	Battle of the animals.
Act your age.	Captain of the brigade.
Answer the phone.	Dan's cat.
A red apple.	Down in the valley.
Bang away.	Going traveling.
An old ballad.	Back of the cabin.
Damp weather.	A can of raspberries.

The following words may be pronounced with /æ/ or /a/. If you habitually use /æ/, do not change to /a/.

The last opening.	French class.
Laugh out loud.	Demand your right.
Ask again.	The path in the woods.
Advance your cause.	Forget the past.
Dance with me.	Take a chance.

VERSE

1 Mistress Anne,
    I am your man,
    As you may well espy.
    If you will be
    Content with me,
    I am your man.
        JOHN SKELTON, from
        To Mistress Anne

2 So many pointed caps
    Laced with double flaps,
    And so gay felted hats,
      Saw I never:
    JOHN SKELTON, from
    The Manner of the World Nowadays

3 Of all the girls that are so smart,
    There's none like pretty Sally;
  She is the darling of my heart,
    And she lives in our alley.
  There is no lady in the land.
    Is half so sweet as Sally;

She is the darling of my heart,
And she lives in our alley.

HENRY CAREY, from
Sally in Our Alley

4   Rats!
They fought the dogs and killed the cats,
   And bit the babies in the cradles,
And ate the cheeses out of the vats,
   And licked the soup from the cook's own ladles,
Split open the kegs of salted sprats,
Made nests inside men's Sunday hats,
And even spoiled the women's chats,
   By drowning their speaking
   With shrieking and squeaking
In fifty different sharps and flats.

ROBERT BROWNING, from *The Pied Piper of Hamelin*

5   "Why do you wear your hair like a man,
      Sister Helen?
This week is the third since you began."
"I'm writing a ballad; be still if you can,
   Little brother."

HENRY DUFF TRAILL, from
After Dilettante Concetti

6   There was a young lady of station,
   "I love man," was her sole exclamation;
      But when men cried: "You flatter,"
      She replied: "Oh! no matter,
   Isle of Man is the true explanation!"

LEWIS CARROLL

7   Hippety hop to the barber shop,
      To get a stick of candy,
One for you and one for me,
      And one for Sister Mandy.

MOTHER GOOSE

8   *THE BAT AND THE SCIENTIST*[3]
   A bat of rather uncertain age
   Was caught by a scientific sage

---

[3] By permission from J. S. Bigelow, *The Atlantic Monthly*, vol. 211, p. 112, June, 1963.

Who, unaware that the creature's ears
Were weakened by advancing years,
Set it to fly through the crooked spaces
Between wires strung in strategic places.

The bat, aware of its incapacity,
Clung to the savant with tenacity;
Indeed, as the struggle increased its fears,
It sank its teeth in one of his ears.
The man, with a loud and angry shout,
Started to wave his arms about.

So three or four pieces of copper wire
Fell on a fuse and started a fire.
They perished together in awful fear.
Let go of a bat if he bites your ear.

J. S. BIGELOW

PROSE
1   *THE FAN*

"Mr. Spectator, Women are armed with fans as men with swords, and sometimes do more execution with them. To the end, therefore, that ladies may
be entire mistresses of the weapon which they bear, I have erected an
academy for the training up of young women in the exercise of the Fan,
according to the most fashionable airs and motions that are now practised
at court. The ladies who carry fans under me are . . . exercised by the following words of command:

Handle your fans,
Unfurl your fans,
Discharge your fans,
Ground your fans,
Recover your fans,
Flutter your fans.

By the right observation of these few plain words of command, a woman of
tolerable genius . . . shall be able to give her fan all the graces that can possibly enter into that little modish machine."

JOSEPH ADDISON, from *The Exercise of the Fan*

2   The men on Madison Avenue are a mixed lot. The Madison Avenue man can be
Mr. John, who makes ladies' hats just a step from The Street, or Cardinal
Spellman, who enjoys a good brisk constitutional up Madison. Stick around
57th and Madison long enough and you'll see Thomas J. Watson of IBM,
whose salary check is probably the biggest on Madison Avenue—or any

other avenue. The Madison Avenue man is also the television actor standing in front of the Columbia Broadcasting Building. . . .

SIDNEY CARROLL, from *Madison Ave. The New York Manner*

QUOTATIONS TO STIMULATE IMPROMPTU TALK OR CONVERSATION

1   Go, sir, gallop, and don't forget that the world was made in six days. You can ask me for anything you like, except time.   [NAPOLEON BONAPARTE]

2   I think that if I get into the habit of writing a bit about what happens, or rather doesn't happen, I may lose a little of the sense of loneliness and desolation which abides with me.   [ALICE JAMES]

3   Imitation is the sincerest flattery.   [CHARLES CALEB COLTON]

4   Some of mankind's most terrible misdeeds have been committed under the spell of certain magic words or phrases.   [JAMES BRYANT CONANT]

5   France has lost a battle. But France has not lost the war.   [CHARLES DEGAULLE]

6   Tyranny is a habit capable of being developed, and at last becomes a disease. . .   The man and the citizen disappear forever in the tyrant.
[FEDOR DOSTOEVSKI]

7   Healing is a matter of time, but it is sometimes also a matter of opportunity.
[HIPPOCRATES]

8   What people say behind your back is your standing in the community.
[EDGAR WATSON HOWE]

9   A man travels the world over in search of what he needs and returns home to find it.   [GEORGE MOORE]

10   Practice is the best of all instructors.   [PUBILIUS SYRUS]

11   Perhaps the only true dignity of man is his capacity to despise himself.
[GEORGE SANTAYANA]

12   Every why hath a wherefore.   [WILLIAM SHAKESPEARE]

13   The best prophet of the future is the past.   [LORD BYRON]

14   I would rather make my name than inherit it.   [WILLIAM M. THACKERAY]

15   Bad men excuse their faults; good men leave them.   [BEN JONSON]

16   A man is not better than his conversation.   [*German Proverb*]

17   The grandest ambition looks least like it when faced with the impossible.
[LA ROCHEFOUCAULD]

18   Men and their actions must be seen in proper perspective; some are judged best close at hand, some at a distance.   [LA ROCHEFOUCAULD]

19   One camel does not make fun of the other camel's hump.   [*African Proverb*]

20   Change clothes you can; you cannot change the man.   [*Chinese Proverb*]

FOR DISCUSSION

1   Is the phrase "a kind of verbal dandy" applicable to Jean Anouilh?

2   Why were the framers of the Constitution reluctant to define the relationships among the three branches of the government?

/a/ AS IN *PATH* IN SOME SPEECH PATTERNS

/a/ is the lowest front vowel in our language. The tongue, however, is not bunched as far forward for /a/ as for /æ/. It moves to a central position. This sound is midway between the low front /æ/ of *cat* and the low back /ɑ/ of *ah*. As noted on page 201, only in eastern New England is /a/ heard in such words as *dance, path,* and *half*. Its use in other areas in these words is uncommon except as a learned pronunciation. It is, however, used as the first half of the diphthong /aʊ/ in *cow* and /aɪ/ in *my*. These are discussed in the chapter on diphthongs. Southerners sometimes use a lengthened /a/ as a substitute for /aɪ/ in words like *mind* and *pie.*

/a/ is sometimes heard in affected speech in words where /æ/ should be heard. For example, in *Summer and Smoke,* Nellie, home from finishing school, says:

> They're teaching me diction, Miss Alma. I'm learning to talk like you, long A's and every-thing, such as "cahnt" and "bahth" and "lahf" instead of "laugh." Yesterday I slipped. I said I "lahfed and lahfed till I nearly died laughing."

DRILL MATERIAL FOR /a/

Since most of you do not use /a/ as a pure vowel but only as part of a diphthong, the list of phrases is short. Other phrases with /a/ are included on page 202.

Ask your mother.	The advancing dilemma.
Pass the butter.	Going to the dance.
A task well done.	Demanding payment.
A newborn calf.	A hot bath.
The last laugh.	Walking down the path.

CHAPTER FOURTEEN

Central Vowels

/ɝ/ **OR** /ɜ/ **AS IN** *FERN,* /ɚ/ **OR** /ə/ **AS IN** *BUTTER,* /ʌ/ **AS IN** *CUP*
(See Figure 11.)
In the central vowels, stress and /r/ coloring or its absence are important. Stress
plays a decided role. The *er* /ɝ/ or /ɜ/ sound in *fern* is stressed, whereas the
er /ɚ/ or /ə/ sound in *finer* is not. The schwa /ə/ always occurs in an unstressed
position. The /ʌ/ sound, as in *cup,* always occurs in a stressed position. The
Bostonian may omit the /r/ coloring in both *fern* and *finer;* the Philadelphian
will include it.

The tongue height of /ɝ/, /ɜ/, /ɚ/, and /ə/ are about the same as for /ɛ/,
which has already been discussed, but the center rather than the front of the
tongue is raised. /ʌ/ is included as the last of the central vowels by many
phoneticians. Others, like C. K. Thomas, include it among the back vowels. The
height of the tongue varies from the level of /o/ to that of /ɑ/; the bunching of
the tongue occurs toward the middle or back of the palate. As just indicated, however, all these sounds do not have as definite positions as do the front and back
vowels.

GALVESTON COMMUNITY COLLEGE LIBRARY

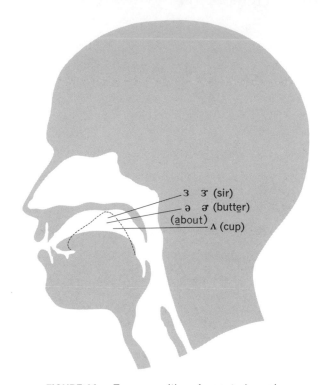

FIGURE 11. Tongue positions for central vowels.

/ɝ/ OR /ɜ/ AS IN *FERN*

/ɝ/ and /ɜ/ are midcentral, stressed vowels. They have little or no lip-rounding, and the lips remain open. /ɝ/ has /r/ coloring, whereas /ɜ/ does not. The large majority of Americans use /ɝ/, but those in areas such as eastern New England and the Southern coastal states use /ɜ/. In /ɜ/, although the tongue is fairly flat, the middle part is arched. In /ɝ/, the vowel sound /ɜ/ is blended with /r/. The /r/ blend is made either by curling the tip of the tongue back or by a greater retraction of the tongue muscles, or by a combination of both. Both /ɝ/ and /ɜ/ occur only in stressed syllables.

Variants of /ɝ/ include:

1 Some speakers substitute a labialized vowel in pronouncing /ɝ/. This sound has some of the qualities of /w/.
2 The /ɝ/ sound may become the diphthong /ɜɪ/, /ʌɪ/, or even /ɔɪ/ or /ʊɪ/ in some persons. While this diphthongized variant is accepted in some sections of the South, in New York City comedians use it for humorous effects. The younger generation of New Yorkers rarely uses this variant.
3 The substitution of /ʌ/ for the final /ɜ/ or /ɝ/ in words like *cur, fur, purr,* and *sir* is used by some educated persons, while others avoid it.

DRILL MATERIAL FOR /ɝ/ **AND** /ɜ/

DIRECTIONS FOR DRILL

1   If you substitute a labialized vowel for /ɝ/, make sure that you do not round the lips excessively on /ɝ/. In addition, make sure that the midsection of the tongue is raised.

2   If you substitute /ɜɪ/, /ʌɪ/, /ɔɪ/, or /ʊɪ/ for /ɝ/, determine whether you wish to use /ɝ/ instead. Say the sound /r/ alone; then say /r/ lengthening the sound. The result is a sound approaching /ɝ/.

3   Incorporate your changes in this sound and in other sounds while reading the phrases and while engaging in conversation based on the quotations.

PHRASES

An earnest researcher.	A purchase of a birch tree.
An earthly inhabitant.	Berlin and Persia.
The Earl of Kent.	Turnip and perch.
An early riser.	The interne in the hospital.
Urbana, Illinois.	Finding the germ.
Ernest Hemingway.	I said *her*, not *him*.
An ermine cape.	The burr of the Scotsman.
The name Irwin.	Infer what you please.
A gentle urging.	Continue to stir.

QUOTATIONS TO STIMULATE AN IMPROMPTU TALK OR CONVERSATION

1   Some disgust us with their virtues; others attract us even in their faults.
[LA ROCHEFOUCAULD]

2   No one is injured save by himself.   [ERASMUS]

3   The best mirror is an old friend.   [GEORGE HERBERT]

4   It is as right to boast to ourselves as it is wrong to do so to the world.
[LA ROCHEFOUCAULD]

5   To tell of disappointment and misery, to thicken the darkness of futurity, and perplex the labyrinth of uncertainty, has been always a delicious employment of the poets.   [SAMUEL JOHNSON]

/ə/ AS IN *ABOUT, SOFA, MENTION*

/ə/ is a short, lax, midcentral vowel that occurs in unstressed syllables, as in *about, sofa,* and *mention.* The schwa is called a neutral, indeterminate, unstressed, indefinite, or weak vowel. These terms suggest that this vowel plays an important role in the stress patterns of our language. They also suggest that no particular position exists for it, that it is unstressed or weak, and that it has little distinctive vowel quality. The variations depend upon the phonetic context of the vowel.

As noted later, /ə/ is found frequently—in the articles *the* and *a*; in prepositions such as *for, from,* and *to;* in conjunctions such as *and* and *but;* in auxiliary verbs such as *will* and *shall;* in unstressed syllables of many words like about, offend, select, soda, system, circus, resolution, attention, lariat, syringa, talisman, talus, and tangerine. In addition, the use of weak forms, such as /tə/ for *to,* gives a natural sound to speech. On the other hand, the consistent use of stressed forms, such as /tu/ for *to* and /ænd/ for *and,* gives speech a pedantic, overly careful sound. Stress on such words detracts from the words which need stress to carry meaning.

/ɪ/ is also used frequently in unstressed syllables. Whether you use /ɪ/ or /ə/ depends on your own speech habits and on phonetic context. For example, you usually use /ə/ before final labials /p/, /b/, and /m/, as in *system.* But you probably use /ɪ/ before a final /k/, as in *rustic.* In both of these instances, the vowel you use may be one with the characteristics of both /ɪ/ and /ə/. Phonetic texts will furnish you with more information if you are interested. See the references at the end of the book.

/ə/ OR /ɚ/

Both /ə/ and /ɚ/ occur in unstressed syllables where a vowel, usually *e, a,* or *u,* is followed by *r.* /ɚ/ is the *r*-colored, lax, unrounded central vowel heard in such words as learner, lizard, and measure in most sections of our country. /ə/, discussed in the two previous paragraphs, is the lax, central, unrounded vowel heard in unstressed syllables of such words in sections of the South, in New England, and sometimes in New York City.

DRILL MATERIAL FOR /ə/

If you consistently use strong forms such as /ði/ for /ðə/, be careful to use /ə/ in unstressed positions of articles, conjunctions, prepositions, pronouns, and auxiliary verbs.

PHRASES WITH /ə/

Attract the able.	A remote Polish village.
An advocate of the law.	Postage on the magazine.
From the apartment.	Australia and the Pacific.
Wait for an accurate description.	The Monroe Doctrine.
An ambitious ambassador to Spain.	A remedy for retirement.
A delicate but delightful bit of lace.	The privilege of being prejudiced.
She will reside at home.	An owl and a bat.
Can you manage the bandage?	Pay attention to Alice.
Refrain from stressing the successful result.	The boy and the girl.

PHRASES WITH /ə/ OR /ɚ/

The character enters.	Glittering silver.
A bitter beggar.	Miserable traitor.
The cowardly bachelor.	Transfer the younger man.
The explorer of cellars.	The porter ponders.
Roger, the teacher.	Further and further.
Eager to find errors.	The flicker of light.

/ʌ/ AS IN *CUP*

/ʌ/ is a central or back, mid or low, lax vowel. As noted earlier, phoneticians do not agree on what portion of the tongue is bunched or on its height. Some speakers bunch the central part of the tongue, whereas others tend to bunch the tongue further back than the middle. The height of the tongue varies from mid-high to low in the mouth. /ʌ/ is never diphthongized and is short in duration. The region that you come from influences your use of /ʌ/. In some regions, such as Boston, *courage, curry,* and *worry* are pronounced with /ʌ/, whereas in other regions, such as Cleveland, the sound /ɚ/ is used.

/ʌ/ is generally pronounced acceptably. But one substitution, that of /ɪ/ or /ɛ/ for /ʌ/ in *such* and *just,* is questionable. Most speakers, however, probably do use in these words a vowel midway between /ʌ/ and /ɪ/ which is heard as /ʌ/. The use of /ʌ/ for /ɑ/ in the stressed forms of words like *of, from,* and *was* appears in the speech of some educated persons, although many educated speakers in formal conversation do not use this pronunciation. On the other hand, /ʌ/ does present problems to the person with foreign speech influences, since most languages do not contain this sound. As a result, such persons tend to substitute /u/, /ʊ/, /ɔ/, or /ɑ/ for /ʌ/. For instance, /bɑt/ may be substituted for /bʌt/ or /pɑp/ for /pʌp/. These persons must listen to learn that /ʌ/ is a short, unrounded vowel and then must reproduce it as such.

DRILL MATERIAL FOR /ʌ/

WORDS

Be sure to distinguish between /ʌ/ and /ɑ/. In /ʌ/, the tongue is higher and is bunched further forward than for /ɑ/. In /ɑ/, the mouth is more open than in /ʌ/. After you have differentiated the sounds in the following pairs of words, use the words in phrases or sentences.

some	psalm	bum	balm
clutch	Klotch	plum	palm
comely	calmly	run	Ron

In the following list, be sure to distinguish between /ʌ/ and /ʊ/. In /ʌ/, the tongue is slightly lower and is bunched further forward than for /ʊ/. In /ʊ/, the lips are more rounded.

luck	look	knuckle	nook
shudder	should	tuck	took
crux	crook	cud	could
buck	book	putt	put
Huck	hook	stud	stood

In the following, distinguish between /ʌ/ and /ɔ/. For /ɔ/, the tongue is bunched further back, the mouth is open wider, and the lips are much more rounded. In addition, the tongue is somewhat lower for /ɔ/.

cut	caught	nut	nought
huck	hawk	mud	Maud
cull	call	done	dawn
London	lawn	run	wrong
but	bought	sun	song

PHRASES

Incorporate your changes of this sound and of other sounds in reading the following phrases. Use each phrase in a sentence.

Muttering about Blue Monday.
Punishing the monkey.
An uncomfortably ugly shoe.
Understanding the unusual circumstance.
Unwilling to undertake the plunge.
Unlike a sponge.
Another brother.
Loving her son.

Study the touch system.
Adjust to his humble beginnings.
Clutching his luggage.
Hungry for lunch.
Substitute study for fun.
Running off to London.
Just don't be so clumsy.
Among the unjust.

People in certain areas of our country use /ʌr/ rather than /ɝ/ in some words. The following phrases include these words. If you live in an area where /ʌr/ is seldom used and you do use this substitution, you may wish to use /ɝ/.

A worry wart.
In a great hurry.
Unusual courage.

Encourage the gifted.
A discouraging project.
Stirring his coffee.

CHAPTER FIFTEEN

Back Vowels

/u/ **AS IN** BOOT, /ʊ/ **AS IN** BOOK, /o/ **AS IN** OBEY, /ɔ/ **AS IN** LAW,
/ɒ/ **AS SOMETIMES IN** COD, /ɑ/ **AS IN** FATHER   (See Figure 12.)

Back vowels are distinguished from central or front vowels by the bunching of the tongue toward the velum. As in front vowels, the height of the tongue goes from high to low. In the back vowels, the lips are generally rounded, except for /ɑ/, but the degree of rounding varies. The high back vowels have a greater degree of rounding than the low back vowels.

/u/ AS IN BOOT

/u/ is the highest, roundest, and most tense of the back vowels. The teeth and jaws are parted somewhat. With its diphthongal quality in some situations, /u/ can be accurately transcribed as /ʊu/, just as /i/ can be accurately transcribed as /ɪi/. The authors, however, will transcribe the sound as /u/.

The phonetic context in which /u/ occurs plays an important role. In certain words, as noted on page 189, the /u/ is always pronounced with a /j/ as /ju/. In another series of words, alternate pronunciations of /ʊ/ or /u/ occur. These words include *room, broom, roof,* and *soot*. In function words, the pronunciation /u/ occurs in stressed positions whereas /ʊ/ and /ə/ occur in unstressed positions. For example, if you are reading *to* in a list of spelling words, you are likely

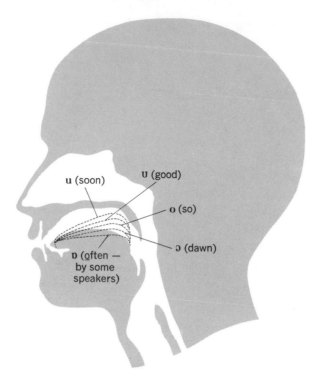

FIGURE 12.   Tongue positions for back vowels.

to hear /tʊu/. At the other extreme, *to* is usually /tə/ in the sentence *I went to see her.* /tə/ usually occurs before a consonant; /tu/ or /tʊ/ before a vowel.
   /u/ is seldom made inaccurately.

DRILL MATERIAL FOR /u/

PHRASES

Approve and don't argue.
Remove your shoe.
Chew your food.
A crusade against jewelry.
The schooner from Massachusetts.
Ruth's mule.
A mood to be entirely truthful.

Refuse to go this afternoon.
A blue shoe.
A true statement.
Group rule.
Prove that the move makes sense.
A unit of local government.
Moonlight ride.

/ʊ/ AS IN *BOOK*

The vowel /ʊ/, a high, back, lax vowel with some lip-rounding, is somewhat lower and possesses less lip-rounding than /u/; while /u/ is tense, /ʊ/ is lax.

/ʊ/ is never diphthongized, but it does play an important role in the diphthongs /aʊ/ as in *cow* and /oʊ/ as in *loan,* as noted in the chapter on diphthongs.

As already indicated, the variant pronunciations /ruf/ and /rʊf/ for *roof* are both acceptable. /ʊ/ and not /u/ occurs where /r/ follows in the same syllable, as in *poor* /pʊr/, *moor* /mʊr/, *lure* /lʊr/, *manure* /mə'nʊr/, and *sure* /ʃʊr/. Both /u/ and /ʊ/ occur in *tourist* /tʊrɪst/, /tʊrɪst/; in *manual* /'mænjuəl/, /'mænjʊəl/; and in *ruin* /rʊɪn/, /rʊɪn/.

Speakers who have been under a foreign-language influence frequently confuse /u/ and /ʊ/, for in most foreign languages /u/ and /ʊ/ are not distinguished from one another. Consequently, speakers who substitute /u/ for /ʊ/ or confuse them must listen to the two sounds and make obvious the differences in lip-rounding, tension, and length.

DRILL MATERIAL FOR /u/
In the following pairs of words, distinguish /ʊ/ from /u/. The /u/ is a higher, longer vowel than /ʊ/; /u/ is tense, whereas /ʊ/ is lax.

look	Luke	would	wooed
should	shooed	could	cooed
pull	pool	foot	flood

PHRASES
Incorporate your changes in this sound and in other sounds in reading the following phrases.

Should you look?	Chocolate cookie.
Her good foot.	A woolen dress.
The mad bull.	The good cook.
A bullet through the crook.	A nook in the woods.
Look at the hood.	The Siamese pussy.
She stood still.	She forsook the gay life.
Would you go?	She took the train.

/o/ AS IN *OBEY*
/o/ is a tense, midback, lip-rounded vowel. The tongue's height is between that for /ʊ/ and that for /ɔ/. As /o/ is stressed and lengthened, it becomes diphthongized /oʊ/. In the word *obey,* the /o/ sound is usually not diphthongized, but in *bow* it usually is. Since /o/ and /oʊ/ are not considered phonemically distinct, the authors will broadly transcribe this family of sounds as /o/. In most words, however, the off-glide /ʊ/ does occur after /o/. The presence of the off-

glide is particularly noticeable as the sound occurs finally or before a voiced consonant, as in *low* or *moan*.

Before /r/, the /o/ is often lowered to /ɔ/. *Horse* and *mourning* may be pronounced as either /hors/ or /hɔrs/ and /'mornɪŋ/ or /'mɔrnɪŋ/. Consequently, the distinction between *mourning* and *morning* no longer exists in some Eastern sections of our country. According to Bronstein, this use is increasing in Middle Atlantic areas and sporadically through the country.[1]

Native-born speakers normally find little difficulty with this sound. But some speakers do substitute /ʊ/ or /ə/ for the final /o/ in words like *follow, fellow, potato, tomato, tomorrow, bureau,* and *yellow.* The authors believe that when these words are used in phrases like *tomato salad, the fellow in the laundry, tomorrow morning, bureau drawer,* and *yellow dress,* /o/ is commonly replaced by /ə/ because of the influence of the stress patterns. These words frequently retain /o/ when spoken singly or when stressed in phrases like *the color yellow, the ripe tomato, the old bureau.* Two clearly nonstandard pronunciations are the use of /'jɛlɚ/ for *yellow,* /tə'metɚ/ for *tomato,* and /tə'marɚ/ for *tomorrow* and the use of /ʌ/ for /o/ in a phrase like /gʌ'naʊ/ for /go'naʊ/.

Those with foreign speech influences often use only /o/ and never /oʊ/. They would do well to learn to diphthongize the /o/ sound, for, as noted earlier, Americans generally use the diphthongized /oʊ/.

DRILL MATERIAL FOR /o/

If you use a monothongal /o/ for diphthongal /oʊ/, make sure that you use /oʊ/ in the following italicized words:

Blow your horn.	A *moaning* sound.
Sew up the rip.	*Global* impact.
As the *crow* flies.	*Rogues'* gallery.
Mow the lawn.	The *roaming* child.
Her best *beau.*	*Rover* boy.
Flown away.	A pure *tone.*

In the following, pay special attention to where the final /o/ becomes /ə/ and to where it may not.

A mellow old man.	A pillow behind his shoulder.
A radio program.	A tomato aspic.
A tobacco auction.	The black crow.
Below deck.	Yellow flowers.

---

[1] Arthur J. Bronstein, *The Pronunciation of American English,* Appleton-Century-Crofts, Inc., New York, 1958, p. 169.

OTHER PHRASES

Incorporate your changes in this sound and in other sounds in reading the following phrases. Use each phrase in a sentence.

Oatmeal cookies.	Joan the joker.
An old-fashioned girl.	The lonely boat.
Omit the soda.	An automatic snow cleaner.
Overhead expense.	Coax him to compose.
The ownership of the program.	Toast the rogue.
Overthrowing the government.	The Pacific Ocean.
An old hat.	Gold on his shoulder.
A cloak for the ceremony.	The echo of the ghost.

/ɔ/ AS IN *LAW*

/ɔ/ as in *law* is a low, back, somewhat rounded, somewhat tense vowel. The tongue is not quite as low as for /ɑ/ in *father*. /ɔ/ is frequently used interchangeably with /u/. For example, in words like *orange, log, gong, God,* and *laundry,* both /ɑ/ and /ɔ/ and the vowel between these two, /ʊ/, are heard in different areas. In some words, the particular region of the United States does have a bearing on the preference for one sound over another. In other words, all three variations are heard in the same region of the United States. Thomas gives an interesting analysis of the usage of these three sounds in the various sections of our country.[2]

A regional variation of this sound, more frequent as you go further west, occurs when /ɑ/ or /ʊ/ replaces the /ɔ/ in the *wa* of such words as *wash* and *water*. In other regions, a clearly nonstandard variation of /ɔ/ is one with excessive rounding and tension and noticeable retraction of the back part of the tongue. To correct this sound, open your mouth wider toward the /ɑ/ to make sure that the excessive rounding is eliminated. To avoid the retraction of the back of the tongue, try touching your tongue tip to the back of your lower teeth as you make the sound.

/ʊ/ AS HEARD IN *COD* IN SOME AREAS

/ʊ/ is a low, back, lax vowel with more rounding and less lip opening than /ɑ/ but with less rounding and more lip opening than for /ɔ/. This sound, like /a/, is found in particular words in particular areas. Often it varies slightly from /ɑ/ or from /ɔ/. But listeners hear it as /ɑ/ or /ɔ/. Since some persons in certain areas do make use of it, it is for them a phoneme distinct from /ɑ/ or /ɔ/. It occurs in words like *horrid, torrid, often, Ross, cloth, watch, dodge, cod,* and *mop*.

---

[2] See C. K. Thomas, *Pronunciation of American English,* The Ronald Press Company, New York, 1958, pp. 117–122.

DRILL MATERIAL FOR /ɔ/ **AND** /ɑ/ **OR** /ɒ/

According to Kenyon and Knott in their *Pronouncing Dictionary of American English,* the following words are pronounced with /ɔ/. Make sure you do not make /ɔ/ with excessive rounding and tension and noticeable retraction of the tongue. Be especially careful in italicized words.

Caution at dawn.	In broad daylight.
All of you.	A mortal enemy.
The author of the best seller.	A normal stormy day.
An awful bore.	The warmth in the orchard.
August moon.	The gorgeous hawk.
The new automobile.	A good law.
Nought and three equals three.	A worn-out saw.
Cordial applause.	A broken jaw.
The corner lawn.	He tortured his daughter.
George's jaw.	*Salt* in the sauce.
Crawl down.	A *tall* man.

In the following words spelled with *or* or *oar,* either /ɔ/ or /o/ is used, depending to a large extent on the section in which you live.

Afford a car.	Hoard your gold.
Before noon.	A gored skirt.
Open the door.	Adore the picture.
Fort Totten.	In the doorway.

Either /ɑ/ or /ɒ/ is used in the following italicized words:

Feeding the *opposition.*	*Drop* the *holiday.*
The outstanding *scholar.*	Beyond the *mailbox.*
Respond to the goblin.	*Stockings* for the blonde.
Homage to *democracies.*	*Approximately blossom* time.

Either /ɒ/ or /ɔ/ is used in the following italicized words:

Cross the street.	The *Frosh* ralley.
The *cost* of it all.	

Either /ɑ/ or /ɔ/ or /ɒ/ is used in the following italicized words:

An *authority* on *coffee.*	A *horrible correspondent.*
Offer for the *dog.*	The *origin* of *sausage.*
The *Chicago office.*	A *strong hog.*
Launching a *catalogue.*	A big *frog.*

In reading the following verse, carry over your correction of /ɔ/. Incorporate corrections you have made of any other sounds. Finally carry over all corrections into conversation based on the quotations.

VERSE

1   *SPRING*
"My dear," said Mrs. Wren," if Mrs. Cuckoo comes to call,
I really think it would be best to see her in the hall,
Explaining that our house it is so very, very small
We have no room for paying guests, or any guests at all."

E. LUCIA TURNBULL

2   *UP IN THE NORTH*
Up in the North, a long way off,
The donkey's got the whooping-cough.

ANONYMOUS

3   *AN OLD MAN OF BOULOGNE*
There was an old man of Boulogne
Who sang a most topical song.
   It wasn't the words
   Which frightened the birds,
But the horrible double entendre.

ANONYMOUS

4   I saw Esau sawing wood,
And Esau saw I saw him:
Though Esau saw I saw him saw
Still Esau went on sawing.

ANONYMOUS

5   I come from the city of Boston,
The home of the bean and the cod,
Where the Cabots speak only to Lowells,
And the Lowells speak only to God.

ANONYMOUS

PROSE
And then a scholar said, Speak of Talking. And he answered, saying: You talk
when you cease to be at peace with your thoughts. . . . And in much of your talking, thinking is half murdered.

KAHLIL GIBRAN, from *The Prophet*

QUOTATIONS TO STIMULATE AN IMPROMPTU TALK OR CONVERSATION
1   One falsehood spoils a thousand truths.   [*African Proverb*]
2   Money is sharper than a sword.   [*African Proverb*]

3   Philosophy is lord of past and future ills; the slave of present ones.
[LA ROCHEFOUCAULD]

4   I do not love him because he is good, but because he is my little child.
[RABINDRANATH TAGORE]

5   A lawyer without history or literature is a mechanic, a mere working mason; if he possesses some knowledge of these, he may venture to call himself an architect.   [SIR WALTER SCOTT]

6   Mind is the great lever of all things; human thought is the process by which human ends are ultimately achieved.   [DANIEL WEBSTER]

7   Rigorous law is often rigorous injustice.   [TERENCE]

8   Women have, commonly, a very positive moral sense; that which they will is right; that which they reject, is wrong; and their will, in most cases, ends by settling the moral.   [HENRY BROOKS ADAMS]

9   United we stand, divided we fall.   [AESOP]

10   Choose an author as you choose a friend.   [ROSCOMMON]

11   Take the world as it is, not as it ought to be.   [German Proverb]

12   Whatever advice you give, be short.   [HORACE]

13   Words without thoughts never to heaven go.   [WILLIAM SHAKESPEARE]

14   The primary cause of an individual's failure in business is not lack of brains, but lack of ability to get along with other people.
[AMERICAN FIRE AND CASUALTY COMPANY]

15   The gallery in which the reporters sit has become a fourth estate of the realm.   [LORD MACAULAY]

16   The general idea, of course, in any first class laundry, is to see that no shirt or collar ever comes back twice.   [STEPHEN LEACOCK]

17   Our faults are generally more excusable than the means we take to hide them.   [LA ROCHEFOUCAULD]

18   Of all the diversions of life, there is none so proper to fill up its empty spaces as the reading of useful and entertaining authors.   [JOSEPH ADDISON]

FOR DISCUSSION

1   Is baseball or football the better sport to watch?

2   What subjects are generally the best taught in college?

3   Are daughters more compliant than sons?

/ɑ/ AS IN *FATHER*

In /ɑ/ as in *father*, the tongue is in the lowest position of all the back vowels. It is the only back vowel made with the mouth open wide. The vowel is lax and is relatively undiphthongized. According to Thomas, since the exact quality of /ɑ/ varies greatly, there are many regional allophones.[3]

[3]C. K. Thomas, *Phonetics of American English*, 2d ed., The Ronald Press Company, New York, 1958, p. 90.

There are few unacceptable variations of this sound. On occasion, /æ/ is substituted for it in words like *calm* and *palm*. But the pronunciation of /dræmə/ for /'drɑmə/ has become so widespread that most authorities consider it acceptable. At times, in *ar* words such as *card, barn,* and *far,* a sound approaching /ɔr/ is substituted. The authors suggest that you consider avoiding this substitution.

DRILL MATERIAL FOR /ɑ/
Observe whether your /ɑr/ approaches /ɔr/.

PHRASES

Arthur the artist.	A charming comedy.
The architect designed the lodge.	A red mark.
Artistic commodity.	A bag of charcoal.
Arguing about money.	A pair of socks.
Enlisted in the army.	Solid furniture.
A party in March.	Count the stars.
The stain darkened the carpet.	A stiff arm.
The Doctor of Philosophy.	A hearty meal.

   Carry over all the changes you have made into the reading of the following verse and prose. Finally, carry over all the changes into conversation based on the quotations.

VERSE

1   A man to whom illness was chronic,
    When told that he needed a tonic,
        Said, "Oh, doctor, dear,
        Won't you please make it beer?"
    "No, no," said the Doc, "that's Teutonic."
                    ANONYMOUS

2   *OSCAR WILDE*
    When Oscar came to join his God,
    Not earth to earth, but sod to sod,
    It was for sinners such as this
    Hell was created bottomless.
        Attributed to ALGERNON CHARLES SWINBURNE

3   A diller, a dollar,
    A ten o'clock scholar,
    What makes you come so soon?

You used to come at ten o'clock,
But now you come at noon.

MOTHER GOOSE

4   *TO SIT IN SOLEMN SILENCE*
To sit in solemn silence in a dull, dark dock,
In a pestilential prison, with a life-long lock,
Awaiting the sensation of a short, sharp shock,
From a cheap and chippy chopper on a big black block!

W. S. GILBERT

5   *DUST OF SNOW*[4]
The way a crow
Shoo, down on me
The dust of snow
From a hemlock tree

Has given my heart
A change of mood
And saved some part
Of a day I rued.

ROBERT FROST

PROSE
1   A poor Relation—is the most irrelevant thing in nature—a piece of impertinent
    correspondency,—an odious approximation,—a haunting conscience,—a
    preposterous shadow, lengthening in the noontide of our prosperity,—an un-
    welcome remembrancer,—a perpetually recurring mortification,—a drain on
    your purse,—a more intolerable dun upon your pride,—a drawback upon
    success, . . . an apology to your friends,—the one thing not needful,—the
    hail in harvest,—the ounce of sour in a pound of sweet.

CHARLES LAMB, from *Poor Relations*

2   THESE ARE MY LIKINGS
    An old park in our middle England, dripping trees, undergrowth, decay, a
    lady many years disconsolate; bleak pinches, moors and winding roads; old

[4]From *Complete Poems of Robert Frost*. Copyright 1923 by Holt, Rinehart and Winston, Inc., New York. Copyright renewed 1951 by Robert Frost. Reprinted by permission of Holt, Rinehart and Winston, Inc.

inns, coffee rooms, and faded prints; high noon in market squares, the roguery of dealers, Hodge's reverence to parson and bank manager; all that England which lies between Hogarth and Trollope; . . . the apple-sense of Somerset; the mothy coombes of Devon.

JAMES AGATE, from *Likes and Dislikes*

QUOTATIONS TO STIMULATE AN IMPROMPTU TALK OR CONVERSATION

1   Birds have trouble keeping warm at night. Sometimes they shiver from dark till dawn.   [A zoologist of the University of Rhode Island]

2   No man was ever yet a great poet, without being at the same time a profound philosopher. For poetry is the blossom and the fragrance of all human knowledge, human thoughts, human passions, emotions, language.

[SAMUEL TAYLOR COLERIDGE]

3   Language is as much an art and as sure a refuge as painting or music or literature.   [JANE ELLEN HARRISON]

4   My argument is that war makes rattling good history; but peace is poor reading.   [THOMAS HARDY]

5   Sorrow is the child of too much joy.   [*Chinese Proverb*]

6   A man who has once been tossed by a buffalo, when he sees a black ox, thinks it's another buffalo.   [*African Proverb*]

7   Fate laughs at probabilities   [EDWARD BULWER LYTTON]

8   Responsibility's like a string we can only see the middle of. Both ends are out of sight.   [WILLIAM MCFEE]

9   Poverty is the parent of revolution and crime.   [ARISTOTLE]

10   So many people have an unconquerable instinct to help an underdog. . . . Many people have a snobbish instinct to deal only with top dogs. There are these two kinds of people in the world, as unlike as male and female.

[TOM TREANOR]

11   I come from a State that raises corn and cotton and cockleburs and Democrats, and frothy eloquence neither convinces me nor satisfies me. I am from Missouri. You have got to show me.   [WILLARD DUNCAN VANDIVER]

12   Optimism is the madness of maintaining that everything is right when it is wrong.   [VOLTAIRE]

13   The world is a comedy to those that think, a tragedy to those who feel.

[HORACE WALPOLE]

14   History is merely gossip.   [OSCAR WILDE]

15   Knowledge of human nature is the beginning and end of political education.

[HENRY BROOKS ADAMS]

CHAPTER SIXTEEN

Diphthongs

/aɪ/ **AS IN** *RIDE;* /au/ **AS IN** *HOW;* /ɔɪ/ **AS IN** *BOY*

/aɪ/ AS IN *RIDE*

The movement of the diphthong /aɪ/ proceeds from a position which varies between /ɑ/ and /a/ forward to /ɪ/. The low front /a/ is frequently heard in eastern New England or western Pennsylvania, whereas the somewhat back vowel /ɑ/ is heard in many other areas. In still other areas, this diphthong is replaced by /aə/, a lengthened /a/, /a:/, or a lengthened /ɑ/ /ɑ:/. Kenneth Goodman relates the story of a child who asked his teacher how to spell *rat.* "R-a-t," she said. "No," he responded, "I don't mean rat mouse, I mean right now."[1] A variant pronunciation of this diphthong is one which retracts it to /ɔɪ/ or /ʊɪ/. In New York City, this variant is frequently regarded as nonstandard. Speakers using this variant may utter /ˈraɪt anˈtʊɪm/ and /əˈfʊɪn ˈŋaɪt/, using the two variants of /aɪ/ in the same phrase.

---

[1] Kenneth Goodman, "Dialect Barriers to Reading Comprehension," in Eldonna L. Evertts (ed.), *Dimensions of Dialect,* National Council of Teachers of English, Champaign, Ill., 1967, p. 42.

DRILL MATERIAL FOR /aɪ/

If you retract /aɪ/ to /ɔɪ/ or /ɒɪ/, separate the diphthong, saying /a/ and then /ɪ/. Then start with /a/ and glide into /ɪ/. Practice first in words, then in phrases, then in reading, and finally in conversation. Carry over all the changes you have already made.

PHRASES

Idle delight.	The bride sang in the choir.
Any icy dessert.	A quiet Friday.
Island in the Pacific.	Frightened of lightning.
The Irish wit.	A red lining.
I'm a student.	Fine wine.
Iron your own clothes.	Precisely on time.
The Ides of March.	A sign of delight.
I'll go now.	A kind child.
Identification card.	A typewritten note.
Anxiety kills the appetite.	A rival site.

VERSE

1   Jennie, come tie my,
          Jennie, come tie my,
      Jennie, come tie my bonnie cravat;
          I've tied it behind,
          I've tied it before,
      I've tied it so often, I'll tie it no more.

                              MOTHER GOOSE

2   There's no need to light a night-light
     On a light night like tonight.
     For a night-light's a slight light
     On a light night like tonight.

                              ANONYMOUS

3   There was an old woman who swallowed a fly;
     I wonder why she swallowed a fly.
     Poor old woman, she's sure to die.

     There was an old woman who swallowed a spider,
     That went oops-oops right down inside her;
     She swallowed the spider to catch the fly,
     I wonder why
     She swallowed a fly.
     Poor old woman, she's sure to die . . .

                              ANONYMOUS

4   She walks in beauty, like the night
        Of cloudless climes and starry skies;
    And all that's best of dark and bright
        Meet in her aspect and her eyes;
    Thus mellowed to that tender light
        Which heaven to gaudy day denies.

    LORD BYRON, from *She Walks in Beauty*

5   Where the bee sucks, there suck I:
    In a cowslips's bell I lie;
    There I couch when owls do cry.
    On the bat's back I do fly
    After summer merrily.
    Merrily, merrily shall I live now
    Under the blossom that hangs on the bough.

        WILLIAM SHAKESPEARE, from *The Tempest*

6   *LINES ON A CLOCK IN CHESTER CATHEDRAL*
    When as a child, I laughed and wept,
        Time crept.
    When as a youth, I dreamt and talked.
        Time walked.
    When I became a full-grown man,
        Time ran.
    When older still I daily grew,
        Time flew.
    Soon I shall find on travelling on—
        Time gone.
    O Christ, wilt Thou have saved me then?
        Amen.

                    HENRY TWELLS

PROSE

1   The Cries of London may be divided into vocal and instrumental. As for the
    latter, they are at present under a very great disorder. A fireman of London
    has the privilege of disturbing a whole street for an hour together, with a
    twanking of a brass kettle or frying-pan. The watchman's thump at midnight
    startles us in our beds as much as the breaking in of a thief. . . . I would
    therefore propose, that no instrument of this nature should be made use of,
    which I have not tuned and licensed, after having carefully examined in what
    manner it may affect the ears of her majesty's liege subjects.

                    JOSEPH ADDISON, from *On the Cries of London*

2   It is not easy to write a familiar style. Many people mistake a familiar for a vulgar style, and suppose that to write without affectation is to write at random. On the contrary, there is nothing that requires more precision, and, if I may so say, purity of expression, than the style I am speaking of. It utterly rejects not only all unmeaning pomp, but all low, cant phrases, and loose, unconnected, *slipshod* allusions.

WILLIAM HAZLITT, from *On Familiar Style*

3   I then tried to explain the rather delicate logical shade, that I not only liked brown paper, but liked the quality of brownness in papers, just as I liked the quality of brownness in October woods, or in beer, or in the peat-streams of the North. Brown paper represents the primal twilight of the first toil of creation, and with a bright-colored chalk or two you can pick out points of fire in it, sparks of gold, and blood-red, and sea-green, like the first fierce stars that sprang out of divine darkness. All this I said (in an off-hand way) to the old woman; and I put the brown paper in my pocket along with the chalks, and possibly other things.

G. K. CHESTERTON, from *A Piece of Chalk*

QUOTATIONS TO STIMULATE IMPROMPTU TALKS OR CONVERSATION

1   Every baby born into the world is finer than the last.   [CHARLES DICKENS]
2   Nothing is so much worth as a mind well instructed.   [*Bible*]
3   Kind hearts are more than coronets.   [ALFRED, LORD TENNYSON]
4   There is a time to fish and a time to dry nets.   [*Chinese Proverb*]
5   The sense of sight is indeed the highest bodily privilege, the purest physical pleasure, which man has derived from his Creator.   [SYDNEY SMITH]
6   The Republican form of government is the highest form of government; but because of this it requires the highest type of human nature—a type nowhere at present existing.   [HERBERT SPENCER]
7   Pride is therefore pleasure arising from a man's thinking too highly of himself.   [BARUCH SPINOZA]
8   Women are wiser than men because they know less and understand more.
[JAMES STEPHENS]
9   Mankind was never so happily inspired as when it made a cathedral.
[ROBERT LOUIS STEVENSON]
10   In the choice of a horse and a wife, a man must please himself, ignoring the opinion and advice of friends.   [GEORGE WHYTE MELVILLE]
11   They wrote in the old days that it is sweet and fitting to die for one's country. But in modern war there is nothing sweet and fitting in your dying. You will die like a dog for no good reason.   [ERNEST HEMINGWAY]
12   Life is made up of marble and mud.   [NATHANIEL HAWTHORNE]
13   We admit of no government by divine right . . . the only legitimate right to govern is an express grant of power from the governed.
[WILLIAM HENRY HARRISON]

14   An Englishman is a man who lives on an island in the North Sea governed by Scotsmen.   [PHILIP GUEDALLA]
15   The illusion that times that were are better than those that are, has probably pervaded all ages.   [HORACE GREELEY]

FOR DISCUSSION
1   Is accuracy the basis of style in writing?
2   Are there signs that the romance between psychoanalysis and literature of the twentieth century is subsiding?
3   Does regular reading of *Time, Life,* and the *New York Times* produce a well-informed citizen?

/aʊ/ AS IN *HOW*
This diphthong begins with /ɑ/ or /a/ and proceeds to a position near /ʊ/. Both /aʊ/ and /ɑʊ/ are common in this country. A third allophone is /æʊ/—strongly fronted, raised, and overtense. If you live in the South, you will hear this pronunciation more frequently than in the North. But listen to the speech of the educated in your region to determine who does say /æʊ/. Perhaps many will say /æʊ/; you yourself, however, may prefer to say /aʊ/. In some few sections, /ɜʊ/ as in /mɜʊs/ for *mouse* is heard; in these instances, the diphthong procedes a voiceless consonant.

DRILL MATERIAL FOR /aʊ/
If you discover that most of the educated in your region say /aʊ/ rather than /æʊ/, you can imitate the production by saying /a/ and then gliding into /ʊ/. Listen to the difference between /aʊ/ and /æʊ/ on a tape recorder. Practice the phrases, using them in sentences; then practice reading and finally conversing. Carry over all the changes that you have made so far.

PHRASES

An ounce of prevention.   Count out loud.
Our college.   Monthly allowance.
Outside our jurisdiction.   The downstairs hall.
Outward Bound.   The story of the ploughman.
An hour ago.   The Boy Scout drive.
Outboard motor.   Highbrow literature.
An outstanding novel.   Allow her to go.
Abound in riches.   A Jersey cow.

A cloudy day.

The cowardly hound.

The proud housekeeper.

The flowers by the side of the house.

How about it?

An angry row.

Go right now.

An arched eyebrow.

VERSE

1   *NOTTAMUN TOWN*
    In Nottamun Town not a soul would look up,
    Not a soul would look up, not a soul would look down,
    Not a soul would look up, not a soul would look down,
    To tell me the way to Nottamun Town.

                                             ANONYMOUS

2   *CORN-RIGGS ARE BONNY*
    There was a piper had a cow
        And had no hay to give her.
    He played a tune upon his pipes,
        "Consider, old cow, consider!"

    The old cow considered well
        And promised her master money,
    Only to play that other tune,
        "Corn-riggs are bonny!"

                                             ANONYMOUS

3   Her life was turning, turning,
        In mazes of heat and sound
    But for peace her soul was yearning.
        And now peace laps her round.

        MATTHEW ARNOLD, from *Requiescat*

4   *PARTING AT MORNING*
    Round the cape of a sudden came the sea,
    And the sun looked over the mountain's rim:
    And straight was a path of gold for him,
    And the need of a world of men for me.

                                        ROBERT BROWNING

5   The grand old Duke of York,
        He had ten thousand men,
    He marched them up a very high hill
        And he marched them down again.

And when he was up he was up,
  And when he was down he was down,
And when he was only halfway up
  He was neither up nor down.

MOTHER GOOSE

PROSE

1   Only the sea and the mountain forest brook are pure; all between is contami-
nated more or less by the work of man. An ideal trout brook is this, now
hurrying, now loitering, now deepening around a great boulder, now gliding
evenly over a pavement of green-gray stone and pebbles.

JOHN BURROUGHS, from *A Mountain Brook*

2   In noting that Washington did not like new people, Schlesinger quotes:

"A plague of young lawyers settled on Washington," one observer had said of the New
Dealers. . . . "They floated airily into offices, took desks, asked for papers and found
no end of things to be busy about. I never found out why they came, what they did or
why they left."

ARTHUR SCHLESINGER, from *A Thousand Days*

3   When they had gone round the knoll, the lodge which now contained the
heaven-derived Majesty of Japan came to view. It stands five feet above the
ground, is one story high, and consists of four square rooms of equal size,
with sliding partitions, the ceilings six feet high and the whole building surrounded by a veranda. All the rooms were thrown open and were without
furniture. The visitors entered . . . saw only Ishtabashi surrounded by a crowd
of official persons, all crouched on the floor.

WILLIAM SEWARD, from *The Mikado Grants an Audience*

QUOTATIONS TO STIMULATE IMPROMPTU TALKS OR CONVERSATION

1   To be proud of knowledge is to be blind with light.   [BENJAMIN FRANKLIN]
2   We often feel sad in the presence of music without words; and often more
than that in the presence of music without music.   [MARK TWAIN]
3   A huge gap appeared in the side of the mountains. At last a tiny mouse
poked its little head out of the gap. . . . Much outcry, little outcome.   [AESOP]
4   Knowledge is power.   [FRANCIS BACON]
5   Any well-established village in New England or the Northern Middle West
could afford a town drunkard, a town atheist, and a few Democrats.

[DENNIS WILLIAM BROGAN]

6   An empty house is like a stray dog or a body from which life has departed.

[SAMUEL BUTLER]

7   No matter how stout . . . one beam cannot support a house.
[*Chinese Proverb*]

8   Fortune and flowers do not last forever.   [*Chinese Proverb*]

9   Advise and counsel him; if he does not listen, let adversity teach him.
[*African Proverb*]

10 Even over cold pudding, the coward says: "It will burn my mouth."
[*African Proverb*]

11 We do not count a man's years until he has nothing else to count.
[RALPH WALDO EMERSON]

12 I have a profound respect for the sea as a moral teacher. No man can be tossed about upon it without feeling his impotence and insignificance.
[CHARLES B. FAIRBANKS]

13 There's just one rule for politicians all over the world: Don't say in Power what you say in Opposition; if you do, you only have to carry out what the other fellows have found impossible.   [JOHN GALSWORTHY]

14 A man is so in the way in the house.   [ELIZABETH GASKELL]

15 A teacher who can arouse a feeling for one single good action, for one single good poem, accomplishes more than he who fills our memory with rows on rows of natural objects, classified with name and form.
[JOHANN W. VON GOETHE]

16 I never found the companion that was so companionable as solitude.
[HENRY DAVID THOREAU]

17 No house should ever be on any hill or on anything. It should be of the hill, belonging to it, so hill and house could live together each the happier for the other.   [FRANK LLOYD WRIGHT]

18 One day in the country.
Is worth a month in town.
CHRISTINA ROSSETTI

19 A land without ruins is a land without memories . . .
A land without memories is a land without history.   [ABRAM JOSEPH RYAN]

20 One hour of life, crowded to the full with glorious action, and filled with noble risks, is worth whole years of the mean observances of petty decorum.
[SIR WALTER SCOTT]

/ɔɪ/ AS IN *BOY*

This diphthong proceeds from /ɔ/ to /ɪ/. In some areas, it approaches /oɪ/. In the South, it is often simplified to /ɔ/ when it precedes /l/, as /brɔːl ðə mit/ for /brɔɪl ðə mit/. A recent television show pointed up this similarity when a Southern child pronounced *oil* and *all* identically. Although television also portrays the New Yorker as saying, "Ersters will sperl if you berl them in erl," such pronunciations are more frequently heard on television programs than on the streets of New York or Brooklyn. This substitution is that of /ɜɪ/ or /ɝ/ for /ɔɪ/.

Earlier, the retraction of /ɔ/ was discussed. This same type of retraction can occur in /ɔɪ/, when in the first part of the diphthong, the lips are too rounded and the back part of the tongue is retracted. As a result, there is increased tension in the sound. The excessive retraction of /ɔɪ/ is seldom heard in educated speech.

DRILL MATERIAL FOR /ɔɪ/

DIRECTIONS FOR DRILL
1   If you worked on not retracting /ɔ/, make sure that in the first element of the diphthong you do not protrude your lips; open your mouth wider toward the /a/ sound. This movement will keep the tongue from being excessively retracted.
2   If you wish not to substitute /ɜɪ/ for /ɔɪ/, start your diphthong with the position for the vowel /ɔ/ rather than with the position for /ɜ/.
3   Practice the sound in phrases. Then use the phrases in sentences. Carry over all the changes you have already made. Finally, carry over all changes in reading the verse and prose and in impromptu speaking.

PHRASES

An oily substance.	Gain poise.
Yellow oilskin.	A moist surface.
Oyster stew.	Rejoice in his good fortune.
Table oilcloth.	The spoiled cheese.
Keep your appointment.	Broil the fish.
A noisy engine.	Helen of Troy.
Join the club.	An educational toy.
A voice class.	Enjoy the play.
The void ticket.	A boy and a girl.
Poison, beware.	Roy, the brilliant student.

VERSE
1   There was an old widower Doyle,
     Who wrapped his wife up in tin foil;
          He thought it would please her
          To stay in the freezer,
     And anyway, outside she'd spoil.
                              ANONYMOUS

2   *TO MINERVA*

My temples throb, my pulses boil,
   I'm sick of Song, and Ode, and Ballad—
So, Thyrsis, take the Midnight Oil,
   And put it on a lobster salad.

My brain is dull, my sight is foul,
   I cannot write a verse, or read,—
Then Pallas, take away thine Owl,
   And let us have a lark instead.

THOMAS HOOD

3   A fine strong gentle cat is prowling
As in his bedroom, in my brain;
So soft his voice, so smooth its train
That you can scarcely hear him meowing.

   CHARLES BAUDELAIRE, from *The Cat and I*
   (translated by ROY CAMPBELL)

PROSE

1   A parent buys a toy anticipating its meaning to his boy. But the young boy's first joy is often not in playing with the toy but rather in taking it apart and putting it together again. And when he no longer finds joy in this pursuit, he finds joy in destroying the toy.

2   You will enjoy meeting my boy friend Roy. He's just back from Saudi, Arabia. You know that he's employed as a geologist by Shell Oil. When we're married, my life will be one voyage after another!

QUOTATIONS TO STIMULATE AN IMPROMPTU TALK OR CONVERSATION

1   Nothing spoils a romance so much as a sense of humor in the woman.
[OSCAR WILDE]

2   The voice of the people needs a whole art of harmonic transcription to be understood.   [WOODROW WILSON]

3   There are all kinds of employers wanting all sorts of servants and all sorts of servants wanting all kinds of employers, and they never seem to get together.   [CHARLES DICKENS]

4   There's some small choice in rotten apples.   [WILLIAM SHAKESPEARE]

5   Our hope is ever livelier than despair, our joy livelier and more abiding than our sorrows are.   [ROBERT BRIDGES]

6   Young men entering life should seem either shy or bold; for poise and self-possession in those so young soon turn into impertinence.
[LA ROCHEFOUCAULD]

7   Often we conceal venom in the arrow of our praise, to poison reputation in the guise of pointing to it.   [LA ROCHEFOUCAULD]

8   If you like your eggs hardboiled, you are persistent, dynamic, sincere; soft-boiled, gentle, patient, kind; medium boiled, calm, cool, collected; poached, speedy, peppy, intelligent; scrambled, artistic, nervous, passionate; shirred, fastidious, romantic, sensitive; raw, overbearing, conceited.

[A restaurant in Washington, D.C.]

9   The real joy of a woman in spring cleaning is that she suddenly feels that she is a tremendous power in the house, and the fact that she is upsetting everyone's convenience only increases her pleasure.   [ARTHUR PENDENYS]

10   For many years I was self appointed inspector of snow-storms and rain-storms, and did my duty faithfully.   [HENRY DAVID THOREAU]

CENTERING DIPHTHONGAL GLIDES

Front and back vowels may glide into /ə/ or /ɚ/. The glide moves from a reso-nance such as /ɪ/ or /ɛ/ toward a central position /ə/ or /ɚ/. These glides occur usually in words where the vowel is followed by r in the same syllable. Examples are beard and fear as /bɪəd/ or /bɪɚd/ and /fɪə/ or /fɪɚ/. Most such pronunciations occur in the speech of the educated. The pronunciation of /ɛə/ for /æ/ has already been discussed in the chapter on front vowels. Centering diphthongs are also heard in words where the vowel is not followed by r. They occur, for example, when you say really! /rɪəlɪ/ or study law /stʌdɪ lɔə/. In fact, in American English a tendency exists to diphthongize all long vowels by adding a kind of /ə/.

PART FOUR

Using Effective Voice and Pronunciation in Communicative Situations

CHAPTER SEVENTEEN

Pronunciation of Words

In earlier chapters, the authors have indicated what the standards of voice and pronunciation are in our society. And they have made clear their concept of acceptability—that speech which is spoken by the cultured, educated leaders of a community—those men and women who by their positions of leadership and responsibility set standards of behavior in social, business, and professional situations. The authors have noted that specific regions, particular cultures, types of speaking situations, and assimilative changes all leave their imprint on the pronunciations you use. Furthermore, they have said that for everyday words your best guide to pronunciation is your own ear used for listening to the educated speakers in your area but that for unusual words your best guide is a recent authoritative dictionary. They have suggested that dictionaries vary in their recording of pronunciations: in the level of language usage (informal or formal), in markings and symbols, and in the listing of alternate or variant pronunciations.

In addition, the authors have completed their discussion of the consonant and vowel sounds of American English and have described the production of these sounds. However, as indicated earlier, speech involves not only individual sounds but also the combination of these sounds into words. The acceptable and unacceptable ways in which you combine sounds into words, then, are the subject of this chapter. Since in the discussion of consonants and vowels, the authors found separating sounds from words and phrases difficult, material relevant to this chapter is often included elsewhere. Consequently, the substitution of one sound for another sound has already been covered. The pronunciation problems which remain may be placed in five categories: (1) addition of a sound or sounds in a syllable, (2) omission of a sound or sounds in a syllable, (3) transposition of sounds in a syllable, (4) spelling pronunciation, and (5) misplaced syllabic stress. Syllabic stress will be treated in the chapter which follows.

ADDITION OF A SOUND OR SOUNDS

Sounds are frequently added or inserted. Some additions and insertions are used by educated speakers; others are not. That the excrescent /t/ in *mince* and the excrescent /p/ in *empty* are widely used by the educated was indicated earlier. But some additions and insertions are less common in the speech of the educated. Some of these have already been noted in the section on *ng* /ŋ/ in the chapter dealing with nasal consonants.

In the following words, sounds are sometimes added or inserted, usually by less educated speakers.

WORD	PRONUNCIATION WITH ADDED SYLLABLE	PRONUNCIATION WITHOUT ADDED SYLLABLE
athletic	/æθə'lɛtɪk/	/æθ'lɛtɪk/
elm	/'ɛləm/	/ɛlm/
film	/'fɪləm/	/fɪlm/
grievous	/'grivɪəs/	/'grivəs/
cry	/kəraɪ/	/kraɪ/
please	/pə'liz/	/pliz/
series	/'sirɪəz/	/'siriz/ or /'sɪriz/

In the following words, sounds are unacceptably added or inserted:

WORD	PRONUNCIATION WITH ADDITION OR INSERTION	PRONUNCIATION WITHOUT ADDITION OR INSERTION
Addition of /s/		
anywhere	/'ɛnɪˌʌɛrs/	/'ɛnɪˌʌɛr/
nowhere	/'noˌʌɛrs/	/'noˌʌɛr/
somewhere	/'sʌmˌʌɛrs/	/'sʌmˌʌɛr/
Insertion of /b/		
chimney	/'tʃɪmblɪ/	/'tʃɪmnɪ/
family	/'fæmblɪ/	/'fæmlɪ/ or /'fæməlɪ/
Insertion of /t/		
across	/ə'krɔst/	/ə'krɔs/
closer	/'klostɚ/	/'klosɚ/
twice	/twaɪst/	/twaɪs/
once	/wʌnst/	/wʌns/

WORD	PRONUNCIATION WITH ADDITION OR INSERTION	PRONUNCIATION WITHOUT ADDITION OR INSERTION
Insertion of /j/		
good	/gjud/	/gʊd/
card	/kjɑrd/	/kɑrd/
cow	/kjaʊ/	/kaʊ/
catch	/kjætʃ/	/kætʃ/
Insertion of /ʒ/		
duty	/dʒjutɪ/	/djutɪ/ or /dutɪ/
Insertion of /r/		
wash	/wɔrʃ/	/wɔʃ/
push	/pʊrʃ/	/pʊʃ/

As noted earlier, some educated persons object to the intrusive /r/, as in /aɪdir/ for *idea* and /lɔr/ for *law*. The educated in certain northeastern areas of our country use the intrusive /r/ widely. Surely, in these areas, the intrusive /ɪ/ is not undesirable; however, in some sections of our country, your speech may draw less attention if you delete the intrusive /r/. Chapter 12 lists phrases and words where it is likely to occur.

OMISSION OF SOUNDS
All of you omit sounds as you speak rapidly in informal situations. But in formal situations, educated speakers usually speak slowly enough to include most sounds. The following are examples of assimilations which occur only in the most informal situations:

OMISSION OF SYLLABLES

WORD	PRONUNCIATION WITH OMISSION	PRONUNCIATION WITHOUT OMISSION
accurate	/ˈækrət/	/ˈækjərət/
about	/baʊt/	/əˈbaʊt/
believe	/bliv/	/bəˈliv/ or /bɪˈliv/
belong	/blɔŋ/	/bəˈlɔŋ -ˈlɒŋ -ˈlɑŋ/
Buffalo	/ˈbʌˌflo/	/ˈbʌfəlo/
didn't	/dɪnt/	/dɪdn̩t/
explanation	/spləˈneʃən/	/ˈɛkspləˈneʃən/
extension	/ˈstɛnʃən/	/ɪkˈstɛnʃən/
geography	/ˈdʒɑgrəfɪ/	/dʒiˈɑgrəfɪ/
across	/krɔs/	/əˈkrɔs/
curiously	/ˈkjʊrəslɪ/	/ˈkjʊrɪəslɪ/

WORD	PRONUNCIATION WITH OMISSION	PRONUNCIATION WITHOUT OMISSION
couldn't	/kʊnt/	/kʊdn̩t/
poem	/poʊm/	/'poəm, -ɪm/
suppose	/spoz/	/sə'poz/
wouldn't	/wʊnt/	/wʊdn̩t/

OMISSION OF SOUNDS

WORD	PRONUNCIATION WITH OMISSION	PRONUNCIATION WITHOUT OMISSION
Omission of /k/		
asked	/æst/	/æskt/
Omission of /g/		
recognize	/'rɛkəˌnaɪz/	/'rɛkəgˌnaɪz, -ɪg/
Omission of /t/		
asked	/æsk/	/æskt/
backed	/bæk/	/bækt/
didn't	/dɪdn̩/	/dɪdn̩t/
lists	/lɪs/	/lɪsts/
grasped	/græsp/	/græspt/
kept	/kɛp/	/kɛpt/
crisped	/krɪsp/	/krɪspt/
leaped	/lip/	/lipt/
mostly	/moslɪ/	/mostlɪ/
Omission of /d/		
breadth	/brɛθ/	/brɛdθ/
hugged	/hʌg/	/hʌgd/
old	/ol/	/old/
slaved	/slev/	/slevd/
width	/wɪθ/	/wɪdθ, wɪtθ/
Omission of /l/		
all right	/ɔ'raɪt/	/ɔl'raɪt/
already	/ɔ'rɛdɪ/	/ɔl'rɛdɪ/
billion	/'bɪjən/	/'bɪljən/
million	/'mɪjən/	/mɪljən/
William	/'wɪjəm/	/'wɪljəm/
Omission of /θ/		
eighths	/ets/	/etθs/
depths	/dɛps/	/dɛpθs/

WORD	PRONUNCIATION WITH OMISSION	PRONUNCIATION WITHOUT OMISSION
Omission of /s/		
asks	/æsk/	/æsks/
grasps	/græsp/	/græsps/
ghosts	/gost/	/gosts/
masks	/mæsk/	/mæsks/
nests	/nɛst/	/nɛsts/

Omission of /h/[1]

TRANSPOSITION OF SOUNDS

Sounds sometimes are transposed; phoneticians call this transposition *metathesis*. Three common examples are /æks/ for *ask,* /ˈhʌndəd/ for *hundred,* and /prəˈspair/ for *perspire.* The following are transpositions rarely used in educated speech.

WORD	PRONUNCIATION WITH TRANSPOSITION	PRONUNCIATION WITHOUT TRANSPOSITION
bronchial	/ˈbrɑnɪkəl/	/ˈbrɑŋkɪəl/
hundred	/ˈhʌndəd/[2]	/ˈhʌndrɪd, -əd/
introduce	/ɪntɚˈdus/	/ˌɪntɹəˈdus, -ˈdɪus, -djus/
larynx	/ˈlarnɪks/	/ˈlæɪɪŋks/
modern	/ˈmɑdrɪn/	/ˈmɑdɚn/
officer	/ˈɔsəfɚ/	/ˈɔfəsɚ, ˈɒf, ˈɑf/
pattern	/ˈpætrɪn/	/ˈpætən/
patronize	/ˈpetɚˌnaɪz/	/ˈpetrəˌnaɪz/
predicament	/pɚˈdɪkəmɪnt/	/prɪˈdɪkəmɪnt/
presume	/pɚˈzum/	/prɪˈzum, -ɪum, -jum/
pretty	/ˈpɝtɪ/	/ˈprɪtɪ/
prevent	/pɚˈvɛnt/	/prɪˈvɛnt/
perspire	/prəsˈpair/	/pɚˈspair/
relevant	/ˈrɛvələnt/	/ˈrɛləvənt/
secretary	/ˈsɛkɚˌtɛrɪ/	/ˈsɛkrəˌtɛrɪ/
tragedy	/ˈtrædədʒɪ/	/ˈtrædʒədɪ/

SPELLING PRONUNCIATIONS

As noted in Chapter 8, people tend to pronounce words the way they are spelled. For example, *chasm* /ˈkæzm̩/ is frequently mispronounced /ˈtʃæzm̩/. But *forehead*

---

[1] In the chapter on fricatives, you will find practice material on /h/.

[2] Kenyon and Knott accept this pronunciation.

as /ˈfɔrhɛd/ is an acceptable variant pronunciation for *forehead* /ˈfɔrɛd/. Some of the other spelling pronunciations are:

WORD	SPELLING PRONUNCIATION	WIDELY USED PRONUNCIATION
bade	/bed/	/bæd/
draught	/drɔt/	/dræft/
forbade	/fɚˈbed/	/fɚˈbæd/
frigate	/frɪˈget/	/ˈfrɪgɪt/
gesture	/ˈgɛstʃɚ/	/ˈdʒɛstʃɚ/
corps	/korps/ or /kɔrps/	/kɔr/ or /kor/
quay	/kwe/	/ki/
salmon	/ˈsælmən/	/ˈsæmən/
salve	/sælv/	/sæv/ or /sɑv/
schism	/skɪzm/	/sɪzm/
subtle	/ˈsʌbtl̩/	/ˈsʌtl̩/
victuals	/ˈvɪktʃuəlz/	/ˈvɪtl̩z/
worsted	/ˈwɝˈstəd/	/ˈwʊstəd/

LISTENING AND OBSERVING EXERCISES

1   Listen to a newscaster. List five words which you ordinarily pronounce differently from the way he pronounces them. Look them up in a recent dictionary to find out whether two or more alternate pronunciations of the words exist.

2   Spelling pronunciations occur frequently in words that you see in print but seldom hear or use. List spelling pronunciations that may occur in the following words: *clapboard, challis, chamois, grimace, gingham, gibbet, brooch, blackguard, breeches, Worcester.*

3   Listen to a group of young children. Do they use transpositions of sound (metatheses) more often than adults? What are the transpositions children commonly use for *spaghetti* and *hospital?* List any others that you hear in children's speech.

4   What insertions or omissions may occur in the following words: *escape, particularly, obvious, probably, calm, postman, burglar, compulsory, flaw, drawing, realm, ticklish, translate?*

CHAPTER EIGHTEEN

Integrating the Factors
of Voice and Pronunciation
in Communication

The preceding chapters treat both the vocal variables of pitch, loudness, quality, and time and the speech sounds of our language. You have learned how physiological, psychological, and cultural determinants affect these variables and sounds. Because speakers use vocal features such as pitch or a speech sound such as the vowel /u/ in combination with other vocal features and other sounds, it was often difficult to discuss each factor singly. Your familiarity with these factors, however, now makes possible and profitable the consideration of their interrelationships in spoken language.

You have already noted that audible features other than the sounds of speech carry elements of the speaker's message. Earlier examples indicate that such factors as the speaker's loudness and rhythm affect the understanding of spoken words. As a listener, you have probably been less aware of the effect of vocal variables on communication than of the effect of speech sounds. Similarly, linguistic scientists have in the past spent far more time and effort studying and classifying the articulated sounds of spoken languages than the vocal features accompanying these sounds.

In recent years, however, students of linguistics have attempted to analyze and describe the use of the audible features other than articulated speech sounds and to show their systematic contribution to the spoken form of the language. To distinguish between the types of significant sound features emerging from their analysis, linguists use the term *segmental phonemes* to refer to the articulated sounds of speech that follow one another in time and are transcribed with written symbols in space across the page and the term *suprasegmental* or *nonsegmental phonemes* to refer to those essential audible features that accompany one or more speech sounds and are indicated in superscript in the phonemic transcription. The suprasegmental phonemes are phonemes of pitch, stress, and juncture; together, they constitute the elements of what is sometimes called *intonation.*

The suprasegmental phonemes do not account for all the vocal features that linguistic analysts observe in spoken language. They do account for those vocal features that are conventional to the language and cannot be altered to any great degree within a given utterance without a concurrent alteration in meaning. They do not account for those optional vocal features deriving from the speaker's habits, style, and attitudes. This second group of vocal features, the *vocal qualifiers* (sometimes called *paralinguistic factors*), includes extremes of pitch and loudness, unusual rate patterns, deviations in vocal quality such as breathiness and hoarseness, and patterns combining several of these features, such as whining and whispering.

In contrast to the suprasegmental phonemes, the contribution of the vocal qualifiers to the speaker's message, far more subtle and complex, still has not been adequately analyzed and described. You recall having read about the vocal qualifiers in earlier sections which deal with the expression of feelings through the manipulation of vocal variables. The purpose of this chapter, however, is to show how the essential vocal features of the spoken language (suprasegmental phonemes) interrelate systematically with speech sounds (segmental phonemes) to communicate the speaker's message.

A brief overview of the structural levels of the spoken language will show the function of these phonemic elements. When the speaker combines phonemes in meaningful ways, he produces what the linguist calls *morphemes.* A morpheme has sometimes been defined as a minimal unit that carries meaning, and it may consist of one or more phonemes. Lloyd and Warfel point out that "Written sentences break up into words, but spoken sentences break up into morphemes."[1] When the speaker combines morphemes in meaningful ways, he produces phrases and sentences, or what the linguist more objectively calls *utterances.* The following example may illustrate these distinctions: The word *student* is a combination of the segmental phonemes /s/, /t/, /u/, /d/, /ɪ/, /n/, and /t/. This combination of phonemes constitutes a morpheme. The combination cannot be broken into smaller forms with meaning, for neither of the syllables /stu/, or

[1] D. J. Lloyd and H. R. Warfel, *American English in Its Cultural Setting,* Alfred A. Knopf, Inc., New York, 1956, p. 61.

/dɪnt/ carry meaning; the syllables within the word cannot be combined with other morphemes to produce new forms. In the plural form *students*, however, the added /s/ is a morpheme in itself, for it is a minimal unit that carries meaning. When you describe the student as *lively*, /laɪv/ and /lɪ/ are both morphemes.

If you expand the phrase to *brilliant lively student*, the larger unit carries more meaning than *student*. You can further add to this structure: The *brilliant lively student denounced the policy of the administration*. You can then add a substructure: The *brilliant lively student, who worked with Professor Smith, denounced the policy of the administration*. You may follow this sentence with another one contrasting the *brilliant lively student* with the *mediocre passive student*.

As you speak or read aloud these sentences, your listener attends to the combinations of speech sounds and to their order. But in addition, he attends to your signaling of the relative importance of these units and to the relationships among them. This signaling occurs through the use of loudness, pitch, and time patterns. In the language of phonemics, these factors are the suprasegmental phonemes of *stress*, *pitch*, and *juncture* (elements of intonation, as noted on page 244).

LISTENING AND OBSERVING: THE EFFECT OF VOCAL FEATURES ON MEANING

1   Spend some time with a child learning to talk. If his desire for expression outstrips his mastery of vocabulary and syntactical development, you may hear a vocal output consisting of a few recognizable words among much unintelligible jargon. By contrast, the child's intonation patterns may be so well developed that you recognize immediately whether he is asking a question, making a statement, or issuing a command.

2   Elementary school teachers sometimes instruct their pupils to read "with expression." What phonemes does the reader use poorly when his reading lacks "expression"? What is the relationship of "expression" to the communication of meaning?

3   A singer who had learned the sound values of numerous foreign languages once joined a class to study Russian. The professor called on the student, who proceeded to read aloud a passage, confidently thinking that his ability to pronounce Russian words would mask his lack of preparation. The professor permitted him to finish reading and then commented, "That might as well have been Greek." What vocal inaccuracies revealed that the student did not comprehend the passage?

4   Recently, a group of housewives volunteered to record for blind students textbooks too technical to be available in braille. The housewives read the textbooks aloud into inexpensive recording equipment and then donated the records to the blind students. The charitable venture was a failure, however, because the students could not understand what the well-intentioned

readers did not themselves understand. Of what factors in communication were these volunteers unaware?

5   When addressing an audience, some speakers read aloud from a manuscript while others prefer to speak extemporaneously from a prepared outline. Can you, by listening only, determine whether the speaker is reading aloud or speaking extemporaneously? What audible features may reveal to the listener the type of delivery the speaker is using?

ANALYSIS OF SUPRASEGMENTAL PHONEMES

Perhaps linguistic scientists were slow to identify the suprasegmental phonemes because they are difficult to "hear"; being so integral a part of the spoken language, these very obvious vocal features are easy to overlook. Another obstacle to satisfactory analysis of these factors is that they function interdependently and are difficult to treat in isolation. As you read the following discussion, which will begin with the phonemes of pitch and go on to their relationships with the phonemes of stress and juncture, keep these problems of analysis in mind.

PHONEMES OF PITCH

The listener hears the speaker's voice through the vowels and through the voiced continuant consonants such as nasals and semivowels. As the speaker of English utters these sounds, he uses four relative levels of pitch. The pivotal level, that which is most frequent in any utterance, was referred to earlier as the speaker's habitual pitch. You recall that the speaker varies his pitch around that level according to the conventions of his language and according to his feelings about what he is saying. These variations consist of three more levels of pitch, one level below the habitual pitch and two levels above it. If the lowest level is labeled 1, the habitual pitch level becomes 2. Level 3 is that level above the habitual level to which the pitch rises most frequently, and level 4 is a still higher level to which the pitch rises infrequently under emotional stress. Three phonemes of pitch result from this analysis, numbered 1, 2, 3 in order from the lowest to the highest pitch levels used in ordinary speaking. A fourth, 4, is used infrequently —under decided emotional stress.

The following illustrations show the uses of these pitch phonemes:

1   When you count aloud or recite some other familiar series, your pitch level remains generally at 2, or your habitual pitch.

One, two, three, four, five, six, seven, eight, . . . A, B, C, D, E, F, G, H, I, J, K, L, . . .

2   When you speak calmly and unemotionally, you use pitch levels 1, 2, and 3, as in the following examples. (The pitch remains more or less steady until the syllable with the next number is reached.)

```
2                    3   1
```
This student speaks Spanish.

```
2                  3  1
```
I've just finished my paper.

```
   2                 3  1
```
Professor Jones is retiring.

```
 3    2     3  1
```
Please pass the salt.

```
2      3     3
```
Did the mail come?

3   When you speak to convey strong feeling, you may use four pitch levels, as in these examples:

```
2       4   1
```
He's been killed. (when spoken with extreme emotion)

```
2                    4
```
Do you call that a hat? (spoken with extreme anger by an irate husband)

4   In some instances, the pitch pattern alone signals the statement or question, as In these alternatives:

```
2      3   1
```
He's been killed.

```
2             4
```
He's been killed?

In an abbreviated sentence, the pitch pattern may signal the meaning that would otherwise be implied by the missing words.

```
          2  3      1
```
(Some people) Call that a hat.

```
      2           3
```
(Do you) Call that a hat?

Observe that these pitch levels are relative. Although speakers vary in habitual pitch level, each native speaker of English uses one level below and two levels above his habitual pitch, combining the four levels systematically to produce the familiar patterns of the above examples. When he temporarily raises his habitual pitch to express an emotion such as surprise, he raises the other levels proportionately. When the speaker uses the levels at intervals that are unusually small, he sounds monotonous. When he uses the levels inappropriately, his pitch pattern may be singsong, unmeaningful, or foreign. These problems and approaches to dealing with them appear in Chapter 4.

PHONEMES OF STRESS

You are already accustomed to the concept of stress in pronunciation when you look in your dictionary to find which syllable or syllables of a polysyllabic word are ordinarily stressed. You correctly associate these stressed syllables with loudness, for you pronounce them louder than the others. But dictionaries provide pronunciation guides for words spoken singly, while you are now concerned with the stress as words are spoken in connected speech. Linguistic analysis of the stress patterns of a sample of connected speech take into account the levels of stress of one-syllable words as well as those of polysyllabic words. Analysis yields four distinctive levels of stress to signal meaning. These four distinctive phonemes of stress complete the description of how relative loudness can serve as a signal in spoken language. These phonemes, varying from loudest or strongest to softest or weakest, are heavy stress / ´ /, medium stress / ^ /, light stress / ` /, and weak stress / ˘ /. In physiological terms, stress appears to result from increased muscular effort accompanying the production of stressed syllables.[2]

In words of more than one syllable, characteristic patterns of stress occur. These may vary somewhat from speaker to speaker and from context to context.

ánў	édĭblĕ	ùndĕrstándĭng
áblĕ	Sátŭrdày	ìntrŏdúctĭon
fáthĕr	óppŏsĭte	ĭncrédĭblĕ
árròw	tŏmátŏ	sìgnífĭcănce
ábseǹce	sŭggéstĭon	élĕvàtŏr
béehìve	pótĕntàte	úndĕrtàkĕr
bĕháve	álĭbì	ĭngénùoŭsnĕss
ălóne	gréasemònkĕy	ĭmpôssĭbílĭtў
ŭntíl	grándfàthĕr	ìncăpácĭtàtĕd

In some cases, the pronunciation of a word changes as its function in the sentence changes:[3]

áffèct	(noun)	ăfféct	(verb)
récŏrd	(noun)	rĕcórd	(verb)
prótèst	(noun)	prŏtést	(verb)
cónvìct	(noun)	cŏnvíct	(verb)
cóntènt	(noun)	cŏntént	(adjective)

---

[2] See I. Fónagy, "Electrophysiological and Acoustical Correlates of Stress and Stress Perception," *Journal of Speech and Hearing Research*, vol. IX, pp. 231–244, June, 1966.

[3] In the first five words, whereas the stress does change, the vowel phoneme also changes. In the last two, the vowel phonemes do not normally change.

impòrt	(noun)	impórt	(verb)
pérmìt	(noun)	pèrmít	(verb)

Patterns of stress also help to distinguish meaning between two identical phrases:

stéel mìll (a mill producing steel)	steèl míll (a mill made of steel)
hòt dóg (a frankfurter on roll)	hòt dóg (a dog affected by the heat)
rédheàd (a girl with red hair)	rèd héad (a head that is red)
hárdtòp (a kind of car)	hard tóp (a top that is not soft)

When words are combined into phrases and sentences, patterns of stress shift and all four levels of stress appear.

pápĕr

wállpàpĕr

wállpàpĕr pâste

Don't fŏrgèt thĕ wállpâpĕr ănd thĕ wâllpàpĕr páste.

rólling

ă rôllĭng stóne

Ă rôllĭng stóne gàthĕrs nô móss.

Some words usually spoken with weak stress receive heavy or medium stress in certain contexts. Chief among words having strong (accented) forms and weak (unaccented) forms are auxiliary verbs, articles, prepositions, conjunctions, and pronouns. Whatever the vowel of the strong form of the word, the vowel in the weak form usually weakens to the schwa /ə/, to another neutral vowel such as /ɪ/, or to a vowel between the two. For example, the strong form of *and* is /ænd/; the weak form may be /ənd/ or /ən/, or even /n/, as in *head and toe* /hɛdn̩to/.

	WEAK FORM	STRONG FORM
am	Î ăm thĕ leádĕr.	Yês Î ám!
could	Ì coŭld gô látĕr.	Ĭ coûld só!
a	Brĭng mè ă péncĭl.	Á pèncĭl, nòt áll thĕ pèncĭls.
to	Hĕ's on hĭs wây tŏ wórk.	Hĕ's òn hĭs wây tó wôrk, nòt frŏm wôrk.
from	Hĕ's on hĭs wây frŏm wŏrk.	
and	Ă wômăn ănd chĭld.	Ă wòmăn ánd chîld ĭs nót thĕ sâme ăs ă wòmăn wĭth chîld.
with	Ă wômăn wĭth chĭld.	
he, me	Hĕ kĭcked mĕ.	Nó, hê kĭcked mé.

As in the case of pitch, the levels of stress are relative. When you speak louder than usual, you increase your over-all loudness while maintaining the pattern of four distinct levels of stress. Similarly, your classmate may speak too softly to be heard at a distance, but when you are close enough to hear him, you note that he uses the same four levels of stress as do the other students. Chapter 5 covers problems of loudness in the speaking voice.

PHONEMES OF JUNCTURE

Four phonemes of juncture complete the group of vocal features known as the suprasegmental phonemes. Junctures are ways of setting apart words or syllables and of terminating phrases or sentences. The phonemes of juncture involve characteristic pitch contours combined with breaks or gaps in onflowing speech (except the internal pitch juncture, which does not involve change in pitch). Like the phonemes of pitch and stress, the phonemes of juncture are inadequately represented in the written version of the language; conventional syllabification and punctuation offer incomplete and misleading indications of how speakers use juncture to signal meaning.

The juncture phoneme that may set apart syllables or words within phrases is the *internal open juncture,* marked $/+/$. This juncture is a small but significant break within the utterance; without the internal open juncture, the sound of neighboring syllables run together and may bring about changes in each other. The presence of an internal open juncture distinguishes *some thing* from *something* and *cup full* from *cupful;* it appears between *a noodle* but also between *an oodle;* it appears between the syllables of *baseball* but not between the syllables of *basin.* Internal open juncture usually occurs more frequently in slow, careful speaking than in rapid, informal speaking.

Three other phonemes of juncture exist for terminating or setting off phrases and sentences; they are rising juncture (↑), falling juncture (↓), and level juncture (→).[4] For rising juncture, the phrase (including a one-word phrase) or sentence terminates with a rise in pitch. Falling juncture occurs when a drop in pitch accompanies the termination of a phrase or sentence. Level juncture occurs when the pitch remains at the same level throughout the termination of the phrase or sentence. Occasionally, authorities talk of a fifth juncture, the closed juncture, which refers to the lack of a break within an utterance. For instance, /sɪdaun/ for *sit down* represents closed juncture. No break occurs in this particular pronunciation from the beginning to the end of the phrase.

The following examples illustrate the three terminal junctures.

1   When you complete a phrase but anticipate another phrase, you may use rising juncture.

When he plays football, ↑ he eats at the training table. ↓

[4]The traditional symbols for phonemes of rising, falling, and level juncture are $/\parallel/$, $/\#/$, and $/\mid/$. These symbols have been replaced by the arrows, which for the purpose of this text are more useful and meaningful.

2   When you ask a question requiring a *yes* or *no* response, you use rising juncture.

Did you go to the game? ↑
He took Mary to the dance? ↑

3   When you ask a question requiring a lengthy answer, you terminate the question with falling juncture.

How do I get to Chicago? ↓
What time is breakfast? ↓

4   When you make a statement or issue a command, you terminate the sentence with falling juncture.

Go at once. ↓
I must see you alone. ↓

5   When you read or recite a list of single words or unconnected phrases, you use falling juncture.

elephant ↓   at home ↓
hotel ↓   brother and sister ↓
Pittsburgh ↓   sad story ↓
psychology ↓   end of the line ↓

6   When you speak a sentence with more than one phrase, you may use level juncture.

By eight o'clock → I'll be finished. ↓
John's cousin Jack → is coming to town. ↓

7   When you speak a sentence and follow it with another that seems to complete the idea, you may use level juncture.

Go into the house. → I'll be there in a minute. ↓
Harold couldn't make it. → His car broke down. ↓

8   When you speak a sentence containing a series, you may use level juncture or rising juncture for each item except the last.

The tour includes England, → Scotland, → France, → and Italy. ↓
Mary is taking French, ↑ education, ↑ speech, ↑ and anthropology. ↓

Although juncture involves breaks between syllables or word groups, the break alone does not fully describe juncture. As indicated earlier, each type of terminal juncture has its own pattern of pitch. The pitch contour contributes more heavily to the listener's perception of juncture than does the break; a speaker may sometimes perceive that he is using pauses when no pauses really exist, and yet the meaning remains clear, while if he uses the pitch contours inappropriately, he alters or distorts meaning.

ACHIEVING SKILL IN THE USE OF VOCAL FEATURES

USING STRESS AND PITCH

You have already observed that the vocal features of stress and pitch vary together. In the accenting of syllables and words, an increase in force or loudness is normally accompanied by a rise in pitch.

1 Read aloud the following examples, using the pitch and stress patterns to achieve the accents indicated.

```
                    4
                    3   phó
    photograph      2
                    1           tŏ    gràph

                    4
                    3                tóg
    photographer    2   phŏ
                    1                ră       phĕr

                    4
    photographic    3                gráph
                    2   phò   tŏ
                    1                      ĭc

                    4
    photographic    3                gráph            p
        display     2   phô   tŏ                ĭc  dĭs   l
                    1                                     a
                                                          y
```

2 Analyze the following words and phrases, marking the patterns of pitch and stress as in the above examples. Read them aloud as you have marked them.

electric	system
electricity	systematic
electrical	systematize
electromagnetic	systematically
electromagnetic field	systematically covered
music	certify
musical	certificate
musician	certification
musicology	certifiable
a musical evening	teaching certificate

3 Pronunciation of words involves appropriate shifts in both stress and pitch. Analyze and mark the stress and pitch patterns of the following words, which contain a varying number of syllables. If you are uncertain about their pro-

nunciation, look them up in the dictionary.[5] Some of these words have more than one acceptable pronunciation.

a.   Two-syllable words:

blatant	facade	lilacs
bouquet	faucet	Mozart
brigand	fragile	orgy
comely	Gloucester	pleasure
coupon	gratis	piquant
credence	grievous	regime
debris	grimace	ribald
despot	heinous	status
direct	hostile	Worcester
escape	khaki	

b.   Words of three syllables:

acumen	decorous	Italian
atrophy	diffidence	myriad
cerebral	dolorous	phlegmatic
clandestine	errata	posthumous
comptroller	gondola	sonorous
credulous	impious	tangential
debonair	impotent	verbatim
apropos	inclement	labyrinth
attaché	deprecate	masquerade
cavalier	epaulet	repartee

c.   Words of four or more syllables:

amenable	exigency	irreparable
applicable	equitable	irrevocable
autocracy	euphonious	lamentable
bureaucracy	formidable	peremptory
chiropodist	Herculean	precedence
comparable	incomparable	revocable
diaresis	impiety	superfluous
epitome	inexorable	esoteric
additional	genealogy	pharmaceutical
catastrophic	incognito	qualitatively
civilization	machination	sacrilegious
culinary	malefactor	solecism

---

[5] A list of acceptable desk dictionaries appears at the end of the Bibliography.

deprecation	panegyric	soporific
detestation	predatory	spontaneity
Edinburgh	perspiration	transmutation

4   In phrases, some words receive more emphasis than others. When the word has more than one syllable, accent falls on the syllable that normally has the heaviest stress. In the following phrases, decide which word or words must stand out because of the intent of your thought. Analyze the phrases for patterns of stress and pitch and indicate your intent, noting the status of the weakly stressed syllables of the words selected for emphasis. Read the phrases aloud.

a.   Under the table.
b.   Over it, not under it.
c.   A book of matches.
d.   Consider it.
e.   Another one.
f.   Inside the house.
g.   Tobacco leaves.
h.   An enlightening book.
i.   An inconspicuous hat.
j.   An overwhelming experience.

5   The following sentences contain numerous examples of words having both strong and weak forms. Identify where the strong or weak form is needed in the sentences that follow, and analyze the sentences in appropriate patterns of stress and pitch. Again indicate your thought intent. Read the sentences aloud, noting the changes in vowels.

a.   She eats no more than a mouse's earful.
b.   Don't ask me!
c.   You can't see her today.
d.   But I told him to bring it, not you.
e.   Who says so? I say so.
f.   John wrote the letter, but he didn't mail it.
g.   A fool and his money are soon parted.
h.   They were waiting, but they finally had to leave.
i.   I said coffee and tea, not coffee or tea.
j.   Harold and Jay are meeting us in town.

6   Accent is often strongest when words present ideas in contrast to one another. Find the contrasting ideas in the following sentences, analyze them for appropriate patterns of stress and pitch, and read them aloud accordingly. Note that sometimes contrast is implied rather than explicit.

a.   I have no money, but plenty of time.
b.   Bring the lady in, and ask the gentlemen to wait.
c.   I prefer my steak well done.
d.   The third little pig made his house of bricks.
e.   Linda wanted a new dress but had to settle for her old one.
f.   I'm certain that the accident took place last year.
g.   It's better to be lucky than to be rich, smart, or good-looking.
h.   What he lacks in brains he more than makes up in ignorance.

i.   Don't tell me that.

j.   It's news when man bites dog.

7   As meaning changes, patterns of accent change accordingly. Read the following sentences, accenting the word or the stressed syllable above the line. Observe the effect on meaning of the shifts in accent.

a.   JOHN   MARY.

       loves

       LOVES

John   Mary.

JOHN

       loves   Mary.

               MARY.

John   loves

b.   JOE!

Why,

WHY,

       Joe?

c.   In this exercise, phrase the question for which each sentence as marked is an answer.

I

saw him walking down Main Street.

  SAW

I   him walking down Main Street.

       HIM

I saw   walking down Main Street.

               WALKING

I saw him   down Main Street.

                   DOWN

I saw him walking   Main Street.

                   MAIN

I saw him walking down   Street.

8   Analyze the following passages, indicating levels of stress and pitch. Make note of instances of strong and weak forms, ideas in contrast, and the effect of accent on meaning. Where you are uncertain of syllable stress, use the dictionary. Read aloud.

a.   Americans are people who prefer the continent to their own country, but refuse to learn its language.   [EDWARD V. LUCAS]

b.   Woman is the last thing which will be civilized by man.   [GEORGE MEREDITH]

c.   There is only one thing in the world worse than being talked about, and that is not being talked about.   [OSCAR WILDE]

d.   Every man is as Heaven made him, and sometimes a great deal more.

[MIGUEL DE CERVANTES]

e.   Decision by majorities is as much an expedient as lighting by gas.

[WILLIAM GLADSTONE]

f.   Labor disgraces no man; unfortunately you occasionally find men disgrace labor.   [ULYSSES S. GRANT]

g.   I wish the Bald Eagle had not been chosen as the Representative of our Country; he is a bird of bad moral character; like those among men who live by sharping and robbery, he is generally poor, and often very lousy.

The Turkey is a much more respectable bird, and withal a true original native of America.   [BENJAMIN FRANKLIN]

h.   Father declared he was going to buy a new plot in the cemetery, a plot all for himself. "And I'll buy one on a corner," he added triumphantly, "where I can get out!"

Mother looked at him, startled but admiring, and whispered to me, "I almost believe he could do it."   [CLARENCE DAY]

i.   Work is love made visible.

And if you cannot work with love but only with distaste, it is better that you should leave your work and sit at the gate of the temple and take alms of those who work with joy.   [KAHLIL GIBRAN, from *The Prophet*]

USING JUNCTURE AND PITCH CONTOURS

1   Many spoken sentences proceed through a 2-3-1 pitch pattern and terminate with a drop in pitch (falling juncture). The stressed syllable of the accented word receives the highest pitch level, 3; preceding words or syllables are on level 2, and the final syllable is on level 1 before dropping to a still lower pitch at the terminal level. The following example illustrates this pattern:

```
4
3                        full
2   The woods are
1                             of them.
```

Analyze, then read aloud, the following sentences:

a.   Statements.

(1) I gave him another one.

(2) There is more than one way to skin a cat.

(3) A stitch in time saves nine.

(4) There are Sally and Joe.

(5) The box is open.

      b.   Commands.
          (1) Please pay the cashier.
          (2) Open this end first.
          (3) Put it on the shelf.
          (4) Give everybody one.
          (5) See America first.
      c.   Questions requiring other than *yes* or *no* response.
          (1) Who goes there?
          (2) What's your name?
          (3) Where are the scissors?
          (4) Which color do you prefer?
          (5) How much does it cost?

2   Some utterances spoken with strong emotion are especially emphatic. When this happens in statements or commands, the accented syllable may rise to level 4, as in the following illustration:

```
4            out
3
2   Get
1                of here.
```

Read the following phrases and sentences with similar contour.
   a.   Come here this minute!
   b.   I said *milk!*
   c.   Let me in!
   d.   How stupid!
   e.   Get it off me!

3   Some questions require only a *yes* or *no* response. These sentences generally follow a 2-3-3 pattern and terminate with a rise in pitch (rising juncture), as in the following example:

```
4
3                mother home?
2   Is your
1
```

Read the following questions with similar contour and rising juncture.
   a.   Were John and Jim there?
   b.   Was it the black one?
   c.   Did you ever live on a farm?
   d.   Did someone ring the bell?
   e.   Do they always talk that way?

4   When a sentence presents ideas in a series, each item in the series generally rises or remains level. The rise is not a phonemic rise but merely a juncture rise. In other words, there is a double-bar rising or level juncture. Use rising or level juncture for each item in the series except the last, where it concludes the sentence.

a. The store is open late on Monday, Thursday, and Friday.
b. Rats, mice, rabbits, squirrels, and chipmunks are all members of the rodent family.
c. Penicillin, sulfa, terramycin, and other wonder drugs were unknown in the last century.
d. The library circulates books, periodicals, pamphlets, and records.
e. At her shower Mary received four toasters, two can openers, one table-cloth, and three icebuckets.

5   In a complex sentence, each phrase before the last may follow the 2-3-1 pitch pattern or a variant. The pitch may rise or remain level at the final syllable of the phrase. Read these sentences aloud, using rising or level junc-ture for each phrase except the last.
a. When you say that,   smile.
b. I'm laughing on the outside,   but crying on the inside.
c. When she was good,   she was very, very good, but when she was bad she was horrid.
d. While you're up,   get me a drink.

6   When a sentence expresses an incomplete thought, another sentence may follow or merely be implied. Such a sentence may follow the 2-3-1 pitch pat-tern; level juncture commonly signals the incompleteness of meaning. Read the following sentences with level juncture ending the first of each pair.
a. I called you three times this morning. There was no answer.
b. He said he'd be back early. I can't imagine what's keeping him.
c. The university has changed so! It's much bigger than I remember.
d. I'd like to lend you five dollars.
    (*Implied:* But I'm broke myself.)
e. She was right here a minute ago.
    (*Implied:* She must have left when my back was turned.)

7   Examine the following passages, noting and marking the pitch contours and junctures that terminate the sentences and those that set off parts of sen-tences. Read them aloud accordingly.
a. A university should be a place of right, of liberty, and of learning.
                                        [BENJAMIN DISRAELI]
b. Any man more right than his neighbors, constitutes a body of one.
                                        [HENRY DAVID THOREAU]
c. Girls marry to please parents; widows, to please themselves.
                                        [*Chinese Proverb*]
d. A Daniel come to judgment! Yea, a Daniel!   [WILLIAM SHAKESPEARE]
e. Tell me where is fancy bred,
        Or in the heart, or in the head?
    How begot, how nourished,
        Reply, reply.
    WILLIAM SHAKESPEARE

f.   Is life so dear, or peace so sweet, as to be purchased at the price of chains and slavery? Forbid it, Almighty God! I know not what course others may take, but as for me, give me liberty, or give me death.

[PATRICK HENRY]

g.   "When I was alive and had a human heart," answered the statue, "I did not know what tears were, for I lived in the Palace of Sans-Souci, where sorrow is not allowed to enter. In the daytime I played with my companions in the garden, and in the evening I led the dance in the Great Hall. Round the garden ran a very lofty wall, but I never cared to ask what lay beyond it, everything about me was so beautiful. My courtiers called me the Happy Prince, and happy indeed I was, if pleasure be happiness. So I lived, and so I died. And now that I am dead they have left me up here so high that I can see all the ugliness and all the misery of my city, and though my heart is made of lead yet I cannot choose but weep."

OSCAR WILDE, from *The Happy Prince*

INTEGRATING THE SEGMENTAL AND SUPRASEGMENTAL PHONEMES

It is possible to analyze a portion of spoken language showing the segmental and suprasegmental phonemes. The following example illustrates such a phonemic analysis. Read the quotation aloud as marked.

```
    2                    3               2
/wɛ̀n mǽn ənd wûmĭn dáɪ → ǽz pôŭts sʌ̀ŋ →
```

```
  2  3                    1   3  2    2    1
hîz hárts ðə lǽst pûrt múvz ↓ hɝ̆ lǽst → ðɔ̄ tʌ́ɲ ↓ /
```

One speaker read this dialogue as marked below.

Jane:	Mary, come down.
Mary:	What do you want?
Jane:	Answer the phone.
Mary:	Why don't you?
Jane:	Because it never rings for me.
Mary:	Oh? No? Except when Tom, Harry, John, and Joe call.
Jane:	All right. Makes no difference. Oh, it's for you.

```
        3      2   3 1
Jane:   /mɛ́ə̆ɪ → kʌ̀m dáun↓/
```

```
        2       3 1
Mary:   /ʍât dəjŭ wánt↓/
```

```
        2       3 1
Jane:   /ǽnsɝ̆ ðɔ̄ fóun↓/
```

       2   31
Mary: /ʍâɪ dòntjú↓/

       2   3 2   31
Jane: /bĭkɔ̀z ĭt ńɛvə̆ rîŋz fə̆ mí↓/

       3   4   2   3   3   3   2 3 1
Mary: /óʊ ↑ nóʊ ↑ ĕksɛ̂pt ʍə̆n tɑ́m ↑ hǽrĭ ↑ dʒɑ́n ↑ ə̆n dʒóʊ kɔ̀l↓/

       2 21   3 2 2   31 2   41
Jane: /ɔ̂l râɪt ↓ méks nò dîfrĭnts → óʊ ↓ ìts fə̆ jú↓/

Other speakers may interpret these lines quite differently. Indicate the meaning and feelings implied by the above markings. Show how other meanings and feelings would be reflected by different markings. Using similar phonemic analyses, mark the passages that follow in the same way. Read aloud.

1 John: I'm thinking of buying a car.
Jo: How are you going to pay for it?
John: I've saved a couple hundred bucks. I can get something on the old jalopy. And my folks have promised to help.
Jo: Are you planning on a new or used car?
John: New.
Jo: What make?
John: Oh. A Ford, Plymouth, Chevrolet, Volvo, or Volkswagen. I'd really like a fancy sports car, but I don't have that kind of money.
Jo: Well, you can't buy champagne on a beer pocket.

2 Traffic Officer: Pull over, lady.
Lady: Why, officer, did I do something wrong?
Traffic Officer: Didn't you see that stop sign?
Lady: Lived here for twenty years. Never been one there before.
Traffic Officer: Tell it to the Judge.

3 His mother was in the yard, throwing feed to the chickens. She watched the boy trip and fall and get up and skip again. He came quickly and quietly and stood beside her, then went to the hen nest to look for eggs. He found one. He looked at it a moment, picked it up, brought it to his mother and very carefully handed it to her, by which he meant what no man can guess and no child can remember to tell.[6]

WILLIAM SAROYAN

4 "I can't get over you!" Ralph exclaimed. "You're so tiny!"
"Oh I know! And I hate it. Why I wear size eleven." "You could look taller,"

[6]From *The Human Comedy*, Harcourt, Brace & World, Inc., New York, 1943, p. 5.

Louise Matson said. "If you wanted to, you could wear high heels, rather than flats."

Penny surveyed her shoes, saying, "It's all very well for you to talk. Your feet are a decent size. You have nice big feet."

SALLY BENSON, from *Little Woman* (adapted)

5   When a bird flips his tail in getting his balance on a tree he feels much gayer than if somebody has left him a fortune or than if he's just built himself a nest with a bathroom—Why can't people be gay like that?

D. H. LAWRENCE, from *Many Mansions*

Bibliography

Abercombie, D.: "Paralanguage," *British Journal of Disorders of Communication*, vol. III, pp. 55–59, April 1968.

Allen, H. B.: *Readings in Applied English Linguistics*, Appleton-Century-Crofts, Inc., New York, 1958. (Contains an excellent discussion of the standards of pronunciation and grammar.)

———— et al.: "Webster's Third New International Dictionary: A Symposium," *Quarterly Journal of Speech*, vol. XLVIII, pp. 431–440, December, 1962. (Evaluates this dictionary from a linguistic point of view.)

Aronson, A. E., H. W. Peterson, Jr., and E. M. Litin: "Psychiatric Symptomatology in Functional Dysphonia and Aphonia," *Journal of Speech and Hearing Disorders*, vol. XXXI, pp. 115–127, May, 1966. (Reports a study showing a causal relationship between situational conflicts and voice disorders.)

Brodnitz, F. S.: *Keep Your Voice Healthy*, Harper & Row, Publishers, Incorporated, New York, 1953. (Discusses the human voice and the origins and treatment of voice disorders.)

————: "The Holistic Study of the Voice," *Quarterly Journal of Speech*, vol. XLVII, pp. 280–284, October, 1962. (Points out the need for a thorough understanding of the human voice through a broad study of materials from varied sources.)

Bronstein, A. J.: *The Pronunciation of American English*, Appleton-Century-Crofts, Inc., New York, 1958. (Chapter 1 gives the nature of standard speech and explains levels of speech. Chapter 3 talks about regional variations. On pages 250 to 256, there is a discussion of pitch, stress, and juncture in relation to meaning.)

Bronstein, A. J., and B. F. Jacoby: *Your Speech and Voice,* Random House, Inc., New York, 1967. (Discusses pitch, stress, and juncture as related to meaning.)

Carrell, J., and W. R. Tiffany: *Phonetics: Theory and Application to Speech Improvement,* McGraw-Hill Book Company, New York, 1960, chaps. 1 and 13. (Give characteristics of good speech form and discusses "speech styles." Notes the relationship of acoustic variables of speech to phonetics.)

Denes, P. B., and E. N. Pinson, *The Speech Chain,* Bell Telephone Laboratories, New York, 1963. (Chapter 3 discusses the physics of sound. Chapter 4 outlines the anatomy and physiology of speech production. Chapters 7 and 8 discuss the acoustic characteristics of human and artificial speech.)

Diehl, C. F., and E. T. McDonald: "Effect of Voice Quality on Communication," *Journal of Speech and Hearing Disorders,* vol. XXI, pp. 233–237, June, 1956. (Reports a study of how various types of unpleasant voice quality interfere with communication.)

Eisenson, J., and M. Ogilvie: *Speech Correction in the Schools,* The Macmillan Company, New York, 1963, chap. 12. (Explains the various types of voice disorders and suggests procedures for improvement.)

Eldred, S. H., and D. B. Price: "A Linguistic Evaluation of Feeling States in Psychotherapy," *Psychiatry,* vol. XXI, pp. 115–121, June, 1958. (Gives the results of a study which show what changes in voice and rate are associated with different feeling states.)

Evertts, E. L.: *Dimensions of Dialect,* National Council of Teachers of English, Champaign, Ill. 1967. (Contains a series of articles about social dialects.)

Fónagy, I.: "Electrophysiological and Acoustical Correlates of Stress and Stress Perception," *Journal of Speech and Hearing Research,* vol. IX, pp. 226–230, June, 1966. (Explores technical aspects of the stress factor.)

Gleason, H. A., Jr.: *An Introduction to Descriptive Linguistics,* Holt, Rinehart, and Winston, Inc., New York, 1961.

Greene, M. C. L.: *The Voice and Its Disorders,* J. B. Lippincott Company, Philadelphia, 1964. (Deals with vocal pathology and treatment of vocal disorders.)

Hollien, H.: "Some Laryngeal Correlates of Vocal Pitch," *Journal of Speech and Hearing Disorders,* vol. XXV, pp. 52–58, March, 1960. (Investigates relationship between pitch and size of larynx.)

————: "Vocal Pitch Variation Related to Changes in Vocal Fold Length," *Journal of Speech and Hearing Disorders,* vol XXV, pp. 150–156, March, 1960. (Investigates relationship between pitch and length of vocal folds during phonation and at rest.)

Johnson, W., F. L. Darley, and D. C. Spriestersbach: *Diagnostic Methods in Speech Pathology,* Harper & Row, Publishers, Incorporated, New York, 1963, chap. 6. (Suggests procedures for finding optimum pitch.)

Joos, M.: "The Five Clocks," *International Journal of American Linguistics,* vol. XXVIII, no. 2, part V, 1962. (Discusses a wide variety of speech styles, from the most intimate to the most formal.)

Kaplan, H. M.: *Anatomy and Physiology of Speech,* McGraw-Hill Book Company, New York, 1960, chaps. 5–11. (Describes the structure and function of the mechanisms for producing voice and articulation.)

Kenyon, J. S., and T. A. Knott: *A Pronouncing Dictionary of American English,* 2d ed., G. & C. Merriam Company, Springfield, Mass., 1949. (Provides an excellent source for the pronunciation of American English words.)

Laver, J. D. M.: "Voice Quality and Indexical Information," *British Journal of Disorders of Communication,* vol. III, pp. 43–54, April, 1968.

Lefevre, C. A.: *Linguistics and the Teaching of Reading,* McGraw-Hill Book Company, New York, 1964, chap. 4. (Deals with pitch, stress, and juncture as aspects of intonation in the spoken language.)

Lloyd, D. J., and H. R. Warfel: *American English in Its Cultural Setting,* Alfred A. Knopf, Inc., New York, 1965, chap. 18. (Discusses the phonemes of pitch, stress, and juncture.)

Loban, W.: "Teaching Children Who Speak Social Class Dialects," *Elementary English,* vol. XLV, pp. 592–599, May, 1968. (Describes standard and nonstandard English and explains the need for children to perfect or acquire the prestige dialect.)

McDavid, R. I., Jr.: "The Dialects of American English," in W. N. Francis, *The Structure of American English,* The Ronald Press Company, New York, 1950, chap. 9.

————: "Variations in Standard American English," *Elementary English,* vol. XLV, pp. 561–564, May, 1968.

McGee, V.: "Semantic Components of the Quality of Processed Speech," *Journal of Speech and Hearing Research,* vol. VII, pp. 310–323, December, 1964. (Investigates some of the relationships between subjective impressions of vocal quality and physical measurements of voice distortions.)

Miller, G. A.: *Language and Communication,* McGraw-Hill Book Company, New York, 1951 chap. 3. (Discusses how various aspects of speech production are perceived.)

Rubin, H. J., and I. Lehrhoff: "Pathenogenesis and Treatment of Vocal Nodules," *Journal of Speech and Hearing Disorders,* vol. XXVII, pp. 156–158, May, 1962. (Discusses pathological considerations and procedures for vocal rehabilitation of cases with nodules of the vocal bands.)

Starkweather, J. A.: "Vocal Communication of Personality and Human Feelings," *Journal of Communication,* vol. XI, pp. 63–72, June, 1961. (Reports research dealing with voice as one facet of nonverbal communication.)

Stevens, S. S. (ed.): *Handbook of Experimental Psychology,* John Wiley & Sons, Inc., New York, 1951, chap. 26. (Deals with characteristics of speech and how they are perceived by listeners.)

Thomas, C. K.: *An Introduction to the Phonetics of American English,* 2d ed., The Ronald Press Company, New York, 1958. (Chapter 22 describes speech areas. Chapter 23 discusses standards of pronunciation.)

Thurman, W. L.: "Frequency-Intensity Relationships and Optimum Pitch Level," *Journal of Speech and Hearing Research,* vol. I, pp. 117–123, June, 1958. (Examines a popular procedure for determining optimum pitch.)

Trager, G. L., and H. L. Smith: *An Outline of English Structure,* Battenburg Press, Norman, Okla., pp. 11–52, 1951. (Discusses onflowing speech. Gives an explanation of juncture.)

Van Riper, C., and J. V. Irwin: *Voice and Articulation,* Prentice-Hall, Inc., Englewood Cliffs, N.J., 1958. (Chapter 8 discusses the causes and treatment of functional voice disorders. Chapter 9 gives detailed procedures in treatment of voice disorders. Chapter 13 describes the mechanism for phonation.)

Weaver, C. H.: "Don't Look It Up—Listen!" *The Speech Teacher,* vol. VI, pp. 240–246, September, 1957. (Points out the constant shift in the pronunciation of words. Discusses the use of the term *cultured speech.* Indicates that the dictionary is a guide not a refuge in matters of pronunciation.)

DESK DICTIONARIES FOR THE COLLEGE STUDENT

The American College Dictionary, Random House, Inc., New York.

New College Standard Dictionary, Funk & Wagnalls Company, New York.

Thorndike-Barnhart Comprehensive Desk Dictionary, rev, ed., Funk & Wagnalls Company, New York.

Webster's New Collegiate Dictionary, G. & C. Merriam Company, Springfield, Mass.

Webster's New World Dictionary of the American Language, college ed., The World Publishing Company, Cleveland.

The Winston Dictionary, Holt, Rinehart and Winston, Inc., New York.

OTHER RECOMMENDED DICTIONARIES

Gove, P. (ed.): *Webster's Third New International Dictionary of the English Language, Unabridged,* G. & C. Merriam Company, Springfield, Mass., 1961.

Kenyon, J. S., and T. A. Knott: *A Pronouncing Dictionary of American English,* 2d ed., G. & C. Merriam Company, Springfield, Mass., 1949. (Includes pronunciation of most words. Uses the International Phonetic Alphabet.)

Murray, J. H., H. Bradley, W. A. Craigie, and C. T. Onions: *The Oxford English Dictionary,* Oxford University Press, Fair Lawn, N.J., 1933. (Gives the history of each word, with changes in meaning, spelling, and pronunciation for the past 800 years. An extensive work.)

Stein, J. (ed.): *Random House Dictionary of the English Language,* Random House, Inc., New York, 1966.

INDEX

INDEX

Addition of sounds, 238–239
Affricates, 121, 159–169
  definition of, 159
  drill material for, 159–161
Aggertt, O. J., 90
Allophone, 118
Alternate pronunciations, 106–107
Articulatory agents and consonants, 118–122
Articulatory mechanism:
  figure, 119
  for vowels, 122–123
Assimilation, 108–111, 114
  definition of, 109
  listening for, 114
  types of: progressive, 110
    reciprocal, 110
    regressive, 109–110
Attitudes toward change, 114

Back vowels, 213–223
  definition of, 213
  /u/, 213
    practice material for, 214–215
  /ʊ/, 214–215
    practice material for, 215
  /o/, 215–216
    practice material for, 217
  /ɔ/, 217
    practice material for, 217
  /ɒ/, 217
    practice material for, 218–220
Bloomfield, L., 44
Bowen, E. R., 90
Breathiness, 33–34, 56, 76–79
  and hoarseness, 80
  reducing, 77–79

Breathing, 32–37
  abdominal, 34–37
  exhalation in, 33
  inhalation in, 32–33
  mechanism for, 32–33
  problems of, 33–34
Bronstein, A. J., 95, 159, 216

Centering diphthongal glides, 234
Central vowels, 207–212
  definition of, 207
  /ɝ/ or /ɜ/, 208
    practice material for, 209
  /ɚ/ or /ə/, 209–210
    practice material for, 210–211
  /ʌ/, 211
    practice material for, 211–212
  tongue positions for, figure, 208
Communication:
  integrating voice and pronunciation in, 243–261
  nonlinguistic, 4–12
    and concept of self, 5–7
    and cultural group, 8–9
    and emotion, 7
    and formality, 11–12
    and intelligibility, 5
    and region, 9–11
Consonants:
  of American English, chart, 122
  definition of, 117
  involvement of articulatory agents, 120–121
  manner of production, 120–121
    affricates, 121
    continuants, 121
    stops, 120

Consonants:
production of, 117–122
chart of, 120
voice in, presence or absence of, 120
(See also Affricates; Fricatives; Glides;
Lateral; Nasals; Stops)
Continuants, 121

Decibel, 26–27
Denasality, 73–76
and hypernasality, 74
reducing, 74–76
Denes, P. B., 95
Dentalization:
/n/, 165
/t/ and /d/, 133
Diaphragm, 32, 33, 35
Diphthongs, 124–125, 224–233
definition of, 117, 124
nonphonemic, 124
phonemic, 124
/aɪ/, 224
practice material for, 225–228
/aʊ/, 228
practice material for, 228–231
/ɔɪ/, 231–232
practice material for, 232–234
/oʊ/, 215
/eɪ/, 198
/iɪ/, 193
Dissimilation, 110

Eisenson, J., 43
Elasticity:
and vibration, 20
of vocal bands, 42
Emotion and voice, 7
Excrescent sounds, 129

Fairbanks, G., 47, 90

Feedback, 31, 61, 127–128
Fónagy, I., 248
Formants, 28–29
Frequency, 22–25, 41, 66
Fricatives, 140–162
definition of, 140
/f/ and /v/, 140–141
practice material for, 141–143
/θ/ and /ð/, 142–143
practice material for, 143–146
/h/, 146–147
/s/ and /z/, 148–149
practice material for, 149–158
/ʃ/ and /ʒ/, 158
practice material for, 158–159
/ʍ/, 161–162
practice material for, 162
Front vowels, 193–206
definition of, 194
tongue positions for, figure, 194
/i/, 193–194
practice material for, 194–196
/ɪ/, 196
practice material for, 196–198
/e/, 198
practice material for, 198–199
/ɛ/, 199–200
practice material for, 200
/æ/, 200–201
practice material for, 201–205
/a/, 206
practice material for, 206

Glides, 180–192
/r/, 180–181
intrusive, 181
linking, 181
practice material for, 181–188
/j/, 188–189
practice material for, 189–190
/w/, 190
practice material for, 191–192

Glottal stop, 138–139
Goodman, K. S., 9, 224

Habitual pitch, 42–44, 47
Hanley, T. D., 43
Harmonics, 27
Harshness, 83
Hoarseness, 56, 80–83
    and breathiness, 80
    organic causes of, 80
    reducing, 80–83
Huskiness, 83

Improvement program, 13–15
    for pronunciation, 126–129
Inertia, 20
Intelligibility, 5
Intensity, 26–27, 66
International Phonetic Alphabet, 117
Intonation, 244

Johnson, Samuel, 107
Joos, M., 111
Juncture, 250–251
    internal open, 250
    and pitch contour, 251
    terminal, 250
        falling, 250
        level, 250
        rising, 250
    using, 256–259

Kelly, J. C., 90
Kenyon, J. S., 107, 117, 218, 241
Knott, T. A., 107, 117, 218, 241

Labov, W., 10, 11

Language:
    attitudes toward, 114
    changes in, 107–108
Lardner, J., 10
Larynx, 32, 35, 42
Lateral /l/, 174–175
    practice material for, 175–180
Lip rounding of vowels, 123
Lloyd, D. J., 244
Loban, W., 9, 113
Loudness, 55–65
    and articulation, 56
    and breathing, 34
    cultural determinants of, 59
    evaluating, 61
    increasing, 63–65
    and intensity, 26–27
    and meaning, 55, 58–59
    mechanism for, 56
    perception of, 56–57
    problems of, 59 60
    reducing excessive, 61–62
    and stress, 55, 58
Lungs, 32, 33, 35

McDavid, R. I., Jr., 11
Monotony, 50
Morpheme, 244
Mouth, as resonator, 67–68
Muscle tension in vowels, 124

Nasal passages, as resonator, 67–68
Nasality, 69–73
    reducing excessive, 70–73
Nasals, 163–174
    definition of, 163
    /m/, 163–164
        practice material for, 164
    /n/, 165–166
        practice material for, 165–167

Nasals:
/ŋ/, 167–168
practice material for, 168–174

Ogilvie, M., 43
Omission of sounds, 239–241
Optimum pitch, 42–43, 47–50, 56

Packard, V., 8
Paralinguistic factors, 244
Pharynx, 31, 34
as resonator, 67, 68
Philhour, W., 43
Phoneme:
definition of, 118
segmental, 108, 244
suprasegmental, 108, 244
Phonetic symbols, 108
Phrasing, 95
achieving meaningful, 96–98
variety in, 98–101
Pinson, E. N., 95
Pitch, 41–54
contours, 256–259
and emotion, 44
and frequency, 22–25
habitual, 42–44, 47
judgments of, 46
levels of, 246
and meaning, 44
mechanism for, 41–42
of men's voices, 43
monotonous, 50
optimum, 42–43, 47–50, 56
phonemes of (see Suprasegmental
phonemes)
problems of, 45–46
ranges in speaking and singing, 43–44, 50
and self-concept, 45–46
shifts in, 51–52
using effective, 46–48

Pitch:
using for meaning, 252–256
of women's voices, 43
Plosives (see Stops)
Priestley, J. B., 10
Production of consonants, 120–121
*Pronouncing Dictionary of American
English, A,* 107, 117, 218, 241
Pronunciation:
and spelling, 116
of words, 252–254
Pronunciation errors:
addition of sounds, 238–239
omission of sounds, 239–241
spelling pronunciation, 241
transposition of sounds, 241
Purposes of speaking, influence on speech
patterns, 110–111

Quality of voice, 28, 66–87
and breathing, 34
improving, 68–87
mechanism for, 66–68

Range of pitch, 43–44, 50
Rate, 88–101
acceptable, 90–91
achieving appropriate, 91–94
evaluation of, 90–91
rapid, 89–90
for reading, 91
and rhythm, 29, 88–101
Regional dialect, 9–11
Regional differences in speech, 111–113
areas representing, 112
listening for, 114
map, 112
Resistance to change, 12
Resonance, 28, 56, 67–68
Rhythm, 94–101
duration of speech sounds and, 95
problems of, 96

Schneiderman, N., 46
Segmental phonemes, 244
Self-concept, 5–7
Snidecor, J. C., 43
Sound, 19–29
  complex tones, 23, 27
  definition of, 19
  duration of, 28–29
  onset of, 20
  pure tone, 23
  sound wave, 22, 23, 66
  transmission of, 20, 21
Sounds (see Consonants; Diphthongs;
  Vowels)
Speaker, the, and the listener, 3–15
Spelling and pronunciation, 107–108, 116
Standard English, definition of, 106
Standard speech, definition of, 106
Standards of speech, 105–115
Starkweather, J. A., 7
Steer, M. D., 90
Stops, 120, 129–139
  characteristics of, 129–130
  definition of, 129
  /p/ and /b/, 130
    practice material for, 130–131
  /k/ and /g/, 131–132
    practice material for, 132
  /t/ and /d/, 133–134
    practice material for, 134–139
Strained voice, 85
Stress, 248–250
  heavy, 248
  light, 248
  and meaning, 249
  medium, 248
  using, 252–256
  in vowels, 124
  weak, 248
Stridency, 83
Strong forms, 249
  using, 254
Substandard usage, definition of, 106

Suprasegmental phonemes, 244–261
  integrating with segmental phonemes,
    259–261
  of juncture, 250–251
  of pitch, 246–247
  of stress, 248–250

Thin voice, 84
Thomas, C. K., 107–109, 163, 194, 217,
  220
Thorax, 32–33
Tongue height and vowels:
  high, 123
  low, 123
  mid, 123
Trachea, 32, 35, 36

Variant pronunciations, listening for, 115
Velum, 67
Vibration, 20, 21
  energy for, 20
  medium for, 21
  of vocal bands, 42, 56
Vocal bands, 32, 37, 41–42, 45, 56
Vocal qualifiers, 244
Voice:
  analysis of, 29–30
  change in adolesence, 42, 50
  initiation of, 37–38
  mechanism for, 31–32
  presence or absence of, in consonants,
    121–122
  production of, 31–40
  and relaxation, 38–40
  and tension, 38–40, 85
Vowels:
  characteristics of, 122–125
    articulation place, 122–123
    degree of stressing, 124

Vowels:
  characteristics of: lip rounding, 123–124
    muscle tension, 124
    tongue height, 123
  definition of, 117
  diagram of, 123
  (*See also* Back vowels; Central vowels;
    Front vowels)

Warfel, H. R., 244
Wavelength, 22, 23
Weak forms:
  definition of, 249
  using, 254
Webster's *Third New International
  Dictionary, Unabridged,* 105–106
Wolfe, T., 8–9

GALVESTON COMMUNITY COLLEGE LIBRARY

This book was set in News Gothic by Graphic Services, Inc., and printed on permanent paper and bound by The Maple Press Company. The designer was J. Paul Kirouac; the drawings were done by BMA Associates, Inc. The editors were Robert Fry and Madelaine Eichberg. Stuart Levine supervised the production.